CRACKING
THE CODE
SECOND EDITION

Successful Strategies for Business Writing

Cherilyn Boyer | Cheryl Brodersen | Mikel Chertudi
Caitlin Hills | Michael Mandel | Kim Marchesseault
Marisa Michaels | Diza Sauers

Kendall Hunt
publishing company

Cover image © Shutterstock.com

Kendall Hunt
publishing company

www.kendallhunt.com
Send all inquiries to:
4050 Westmark Drive
Dubuque, IA 52004-1840

Copyright © 2017, 2018 by Cherilyn Boyer, Cheryl Brodersen, Mikel Chertudi, Caitlin Hills,
Michael Mandel, Kim Marchesseault, Marisa Michaels, Diza Sauers

PAK ISBN: 978-1-5249-6223-4
Text Alone ISBN: 978-1-5249-6224-1

Kendall Hunt Publishing Company has the exclusive rights to reproduce this work,
to prepare derivative works from this work, to publicly distribute this work,
to publicly perform this work and to publicly display this work.

All rights reserved. No part of this publication may be reproduced,
stored in a retrieval system, or transmitted, in any form or by any
means, electronic, mechanical, photocopying, recording, or otherwise,
without the prior written permission of the copyright owner.

Published in the United States of America

Table of Contents

Preface   ix

UNIT 1: COMMUNICATION FOUNDATIONS   1

Chapter 1-1: The Standards for Success   3

Skills to Succeed in the Business World 4

Business Communication Standards 4

Critical Thinking   5

Logic and Reasoning   6

Structural Coherence   6

Information Design   7

Error Interference   8

Application in the Workplace 9

Chapter 1-2: Strategic Business Communication   13

Strategy Starts with Your Audience. 14

Reaching Your Audience   14

Establishing the Purpose of Your Communication 15

Determining Your Strategic Approach 16

Unit 1 References 17

UNIT 2: PROFESSIONAL WRITING   19

Chapter 2-1: Planning Your Message   21

Preparing to Write 21

You Are What You Write   21

Employer Expectations   22

Business Writing Is Different   22

How to Begin   24

Analyzing Your Audience. 24

Identifying and Analyzing Your Audience   24

Defining Your Purpose 26

Setting the Right Tone   27

Chapter 2-2: Composing Your Message   31

Correspondence Messages   31

Composing Business Correspondence   32

Thank You Messages   33

Meeting Invitation   33

Report Writing   34

Common Purposes of Business Reports 36

Reporting Findings   36

Drawing Conclusions   37

Making Recommendations   37

Informal & Formal Reports 39

Informal Reports   40

Informal Report Sample Document: Research Summary   41

Informal Report Sample Document: Strategy Summary   44

Transmittal Messages 45

Formal Reports 46

Under Armour Final Communication Plan 49

Unit 2 References 64

UNIT 3: WRITING STRATEGIES   65

Chapter 3-1: Informative Messages   67

Overview 67

Prewriting 69

Structure 69

Common Organizational Patterns for Informative Messages 70

Introductions   71

Conclusions   73

Body   74

Chapter 3-2: Communicating to Persuade   77

Identifying Types of Persuasive Messages 78

Understanding Audience Responses to Persuasive Appeals 79

Receptive Audiences   79

Resistant Audiences   79

Matching Approach to Potential Audience Response   79

Using a Direct Persuasive Approach 79

Direct Persuasive Introduction   80

Direct Persuasive Body   80

Direct Persuasive Conclusions   81

Direct Persuasive Examples 81

Using an Indirect Persuasive Approach 83

Introduction 83

   Alignment and Attention   *83*

Body 84

   Interest and Information   *84*

   Direct Benefits and Deflection   *84*

Conclusion 84

   Action   *84*

Tailoring Your Tone For Persuasive Messages 87

   Avoid Implied Entitlement   *87*

   Respect Readers' Autonomy   *88*

   Maintain an Objective Tone   *89*

   Make the Ask   *89*

Chapter 3-3: Delivering Negative News   91

Conveying an Unwelcome Message 91

   Types of Bad News Messages   *92*

   Understanding Audience Reaction to Bad News   *93*

   Identifying Resistant Audiences   *93*

   The Two Most Common Responses to a Threat are Fight or Flight   *94*

Writing the Bad News Message 94

Direct Approach: Delivering Negative News 94

   Introduction   *95*

   Body   *95*

   Conclusion   *95*

   Sample Direct Bad News Message   *96*

Indirect Approach: Delivering Negative News 96

   Introduction   *97*

   Body   *98*

   Conclusion   *98*

Sample Scenario and Indirect Bad News Message 99

Tone—Indifference or Empathy; What Do Your Words Convey? 103

So, What Do You (the Writer) Have to Gain? 103

Chapter 3-4: Document Design   105

Maximum Effectiveness, Minimum Effort 105

   Margins   *106*

   Paragraphs   *106*

   Words   *107*

   Not Words   *108*

   All Right, Break it Up   *108*

   Section Headings/Subheadings   *108*

   Bullets and Outline Lists   *111*

Unit 3 References 112

UNIT 4: GRAMMAR   113

Chapter 4-1: Understanding Grammar   115

A Word about Consision 116

Grammar 116

The Basics: Nouns and Verbs   116
Principle #1: Use Active Verbs   117
Principle #2: Use Concrete Nouns   120
Principle #3 Avoid There is/There are & It is/It was   121
Principle #4: Avoid Why/How, the reason for, due to the fact that   121
Principle #5: Watch out for Misplaced and Dangling Modifiers   122
Principle #6: Keep Structures Parallel   123

Chapter 4-2: Understanding Punctuation   127

Punctuation 127

Credibility Errors   127

Sentence Structure 127

Four Ways of Combining Sentences   127
Way #1: Use Simple Sentences   128
Way #2: Commas after Introductory Phrases and Clauses   128
Way #3: Use Coordinaating Conjunctions and Commas in Compound Sentences   130
Choosing Compound or Complex Sentence Structures   132
Way #4: Using Semicolons; Comma's Snobby Cousin   133

Colons: The Real Story 139

Putting It All Together 136

Chapter 4-3: Sample Messages   139

Email 139

Letter 142

Memo 144

Industry Report 146

Direct Informational Memos with APA Citations 163

Annotated Bibliography 169

Unit 4 References 175

UNIT 5: CASE STUDIES   177

Chapter 5-1: Chipotle Case Study   179

Fast Casual Chain Sickness Scandal Heats Up 179

Timeline of Outbreaks   179
Legal Woes   180
Chipotle Responds   180
Media Response   180

Practice Assignments Context 182

Practice Assignments   182

Chapter 5-2: Facebook Case Study   185

Emotions Run High 185
Practice Assignments Context. 186
Practice Assignments   187

Chapter 5-3: McDonald's Case Study   191

McDonald's Millennial Angst 191
McDonald's Responds   192

Practice Assignments Context. 193
Practice Assignments   193

Chapter 5-4: For-Profit Colleges Case Study   197

New Life or Burnout? 197
Rising from the Ashes? 198
Practice Assignments Context. 199
Practice Assignments   199

Chapter 5-5: Lyft Case Study   201

Driving Toward Success. 201
Brief History of Uber Incidents. 202
Practice Assignments Context. 203
Practice Assignments   203

Unit 5 Appendix: Sample Practice Messages   205

Chipotle Sample Practice Messages 205
Sample Chipotle Direct Informational Message   205
Sample Chipotle Indirect Persuasive Message   207
Sample Chipotle Bad News Message   208
Sample Chipotle Direct Persuasive Message   209
Sample Chipotle Direct Persuasive Instructional Message   210

Facebook Reactions Sample Practice Messages. 211
Sample Facebook Reactions Direct Informational Report   211
Sample Facebook Reactions Indirect Persuasive Message   213
Sample Facebook Reactions Bad News Message   214
Sample Facebook Reactions Direct Persuasive Message   215
Sample Facebook Reactions Direct Persuasive Instructional Message   216

McDonald's Sample Practice Messages. 217
Sample McDonald's Direct Informational Message   217
Sample McDonald's Indirect Persuasive Message   219
Sample McDonald's Bad News Message   220
Sample McDonald's Direct Persuasive Message   221
Sample McDonald's Direct Persuasive Instructional Message   222

For-Profit Colleges Sample Practice Messages 223
Sample For-Profit Colleges Letter of Intent/Cover Letter   223
Sample For-Profit Colleges Indirect Persuasive Message   224
Sample For-Profit Colleges Direct Persuasive Message   225
Sample For-Profit Colleges Bad News Message   226

Lyft Sample Practice Messages 227

    Sample Lyft Stakeholder Analysis   *227*

    Sample Lyft Indirect Persuasive Message   *230*

    Sample Lyft Bad News Message   *231*

    Sample Lyft Direct Persuasive Message   *232*

Index   233

Preface

Our students are curious, insightful, engaged, and conscientious.

They deserve educational resources that are thorough, useful, efficient, and fun.

As business communication educators, we strive to create a resource uniquely tailored to our Millennial and Gen Z student population as they prepare to enter an increasingly globalized and online workforce. This text aligns closely with our own industry-informed, cohesive , and strategically formulated curriculum.

We continuously seek feedback from our students and the employers who hire them to inform our content, approaches, and learning outcomes. This title is a product of a continuous feedback loop. As authors whose primary responsibilities are teaching, we remain in the classroom year-round. As a team, we annually instruct more than 2,000 undergraduates in writing, presentation, interpersonal, and intrapersonal communication skills.

We spend significant time both inside and outside the classroom, teaching, mentoring, and coaching our students to become "workplace ready." We believe in helping our students develop practical skills they can immediately apply. Over the years, we found that not all business communication educational resources shared this depth or sense of urgency.

As an author team with nearly a century of combined teaching experience, we have used our share of textbooks to help us help our students develop these workplace-ready skills. While many of those textbooks had qualities we each liked, none of them fully met our students' needs. After years of working with textbooks we liked but didn't love, we decided the time had come to write our own.

There is no better way to grow as a team than to co-author a book (we could write a whole volume just on this experience!). The textbook you now hold in your hands/are reading on a screen is the result of years of discussions, sharing our content matter expertise, observing each other's teaching, collaborating with employers, arguing with each other, burying the hatchet with each other, and genuinely collaborating every step of the way.

Our students successfully use this title in our own undergraduate courses; we hope you will have similar positive experiences when you use it in yours.

Cracking the Code: Successful Strategies for Business Writing is designed to walk students through the process of determining the right strategy and approach for any given written communication situation. Rather than providing specific formulas or structures for the infinitely diverse situations business communication professionals may encounter during their daily activities, this title empowers students to use their innate critical thinking skills.

As students read through each unit of *Cracking the Code,* they will discover meaningful concepts that will help them become more credible business writers. The sample writing exercises will help them develop the critical business skill of agility in the workplace. On a more mechanical level, this textbook also offers best practices for document design and an entire chapter on grammar, complete with practice exercises. Students gain a comprehensive understanding of business writing that covers form, function, and strategy.

Cracking the Code concludes with an entire unit of case studies, complete with writing prompts and student sample responses to those prompts. Rather than hunting for level-appropriate case studies or writing their own, business communication instructors will save time and effort by using these cases in their courses. Even if instructors choose not to assign any of these cases, students have extra opportunities to further explore their business writing skills.

From cover to cover, *Cracking the Code* empowers students to increase their professional credibility. This textbook inspires students to build the skillset that is often the first way they will communicate with potential employers, colleagues, or customers: their writing.

We designed this text to be engaging for undergraduate students, with helpful tips for even the most advanced business writers. We know our students have many competing demands for their time, so we have created this textbook that they actually enjoy reading.

This textbook is dedicated to students; may it help you move forward on your paths to success.

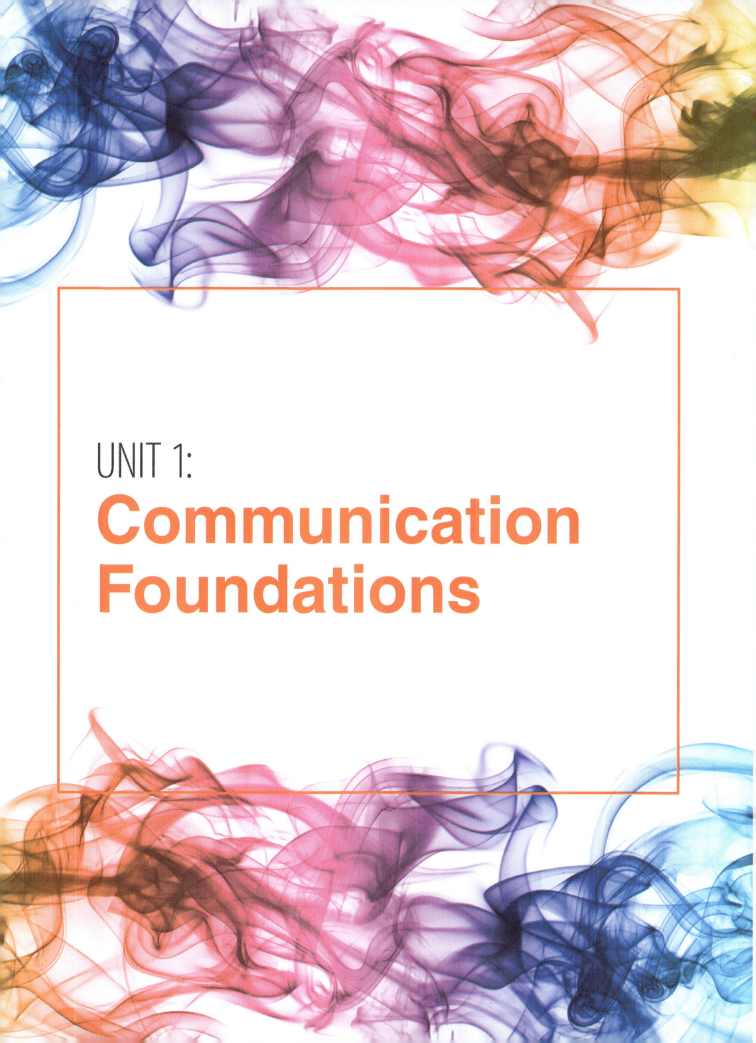

UNIT 1:
Communication Foundations

The Standards for Success

As a faculty, we have spent the past decade speaking with recruiters and teaching business communication to more than 10,000 students—undergraduate business students, MBA candidates, and executives. We have worked with hundreds of recruiters, alumni who have flourished in their various industries, and other colleagues who teach business communication across the world. After studying thousands of business documents, presentations, and scholarly research on the field of business communication, our team documented trends, refined coaching techniques and teaching strategies, and arrived at some best practices and guidelines for coaching leaders as they hone their communication skills.

It probably comes as no surprise to you that distinguishing yourself from the competition stems from your ability to skillfully communicate your knowledge and experiences. For the past decade, communication skills have been in the top five skills most valued by recruiters (NACE, 2014). Whether you are communicating in meetings, presentations, video conferencing, or writing on screens, your ability to manage your message largely reflects on you and "your brand." Effective training in business communication is essential to your development as a business professional.

What have we come to understand about standards and best communication practices through years of training thousands of business professionals? The answer is simple: the practice of effective communication is what weaves an entire organization together. Without communication, an enterprise cannot serve its mission, its customers cannot be served, and its management cannot be effective. While each division of a business is essential to the entire enterprise, the basic principles of communication are what keep the whole organization running. Without communication best practices, cross-functional coordination would not be possible.

When you couple the importance of communication with the recent explosion of technologies, the ravaging effects of globalization, and the acceleration of disruptive industries, suddenly the importance of communication becomes clear. Even if you can find footing in such turbulence, recent data confirms that declining literacy rates and gutted educational systems have had a direct impact on the development and mastery of basic communication skills. Even if your communication skills are well developed, the same may not be said for your colleagues. Learning to work with people at all communication skill levels will help position your organization for success.

Skills to Succeed in the Business World

Positioning for success requires professional standards. For this book to assist you in your own development, you'll need to understand the pieces—the individual components of the standards—in order to understand how the pieces make up the whole. Each standard represents a key component to successful messaging. This book is designed to help you master the various workplace communication scenarios and tasks you will encounter in the work world. Since every individual has natural strengths and weaknesses, understanding the standards will help you identify what areas you need to improve. As with any set of standards, these are a reflection of common industry practices that will provide you with the ability to move forward and succeed in your chosen field of business. It sounds so simple, and yet it is one of the areas leaders at all levels return to again and again to shore up their training, refine their skill set, and continue to build upon in their own evolution as successful professionals.

In 2008, Tony Wagner published his landmark book, *The Global Achievement Gap.* He caused a furor and sparked a national debate in curricular redesign for American schools to catch up to the needs of the rapidly emerging global "knowledge-based" economy. His book highlighted several key areas that are required for any worker in the 21st century:

- Critical Thinking/Problem Solving
- Collaboration Across Networks/Leading by Influence
- Agility/Adaptability
- Initiative and Entrepreneurial Nature
- Effective Oral and Written Communication Skills
- Accessing and Analyzing Information
- Curiosity and Imagination

Not surprisingly, educators, trainers, and leaders across the country took notice of Wagner's alarming claims. While the rallying cry continues to reinvent the education system, more commonly embraced is the concept that education must align itself with business trends. Our program recognizes and adapts these trends into our programmatic standards so every working professional we partner with will be better equipped to participate in the new global knowledge economy.

Business Communication Standards

Our standards provide you with the language to name and identify the skills and strategy needed to construct an effective message. When we evaluate written work, presentations, or even group communication efforts (meetings, feedback sessions, video conferencing), we look at the components of critical thinking, logic and reasoning (data), structural coherence, visual strategy, and error interference. Individually, each one of these categories gives you a set of strategies to use to make your messaging stronger; collectively, they pack a wallop.

CRITICAL THINKING	LOGIC AND REASONING	STRUCTURAL COHERENCE	INFORMATION DESIGN	ERROR INTERFERENCE
Audience	Logical units of discourse	Coherent "whole"	Format and channel	Disruptive errors
Purpose	Claim or assertion	Internal logic	Visual design	Credibility errors
Context	Idea unity and integrity	Section unity and integrity	Readability/Skim	Etiquette errors
Frame	Supporting evidence	Transitions	Professionalism	Accent errors
Strategic approach		Language use		

Critical Thinking

Why have employers across the world pushed to recognize critical thinking ability as a key indicator and predictor of employee success? Karen Bruett of Dell Corporation's Strategic Business Development Department sums it up best when she states: "Corporations have changed dramatically in the last 20 years in terms of the way work is organized. Now lots of networks of cross-functional teams work together on specific projects. Work is no longer defined by your specialty; it is defined by the task or problem you and your team are trying to solve. Teams have to figure out the best way to get there—the solution is not prescribed" (Wagner, 2008).

"The biggest challenge for front-line employees is having the critical thinking and problem solving they need to be effective because nobody is there telling them exactly what to do..They have to figure it out" (Wagner, 2008).

Working on teams, sometimes across departments or even physical locations around the globe, requires top-notch communication skills and strategies, and these, in turn, require keen critical thinking skills.

Your success rests in your ability to recognize trends, problems, patterns, and root issues. Rarely does the working world offer a clear, black-and-white set of problems.

Perhaps in some of your academic coursework you have been asked to solve concrete problems. In many instances, these are set up for you to easily understand how to construct or apply a particular formula to arrive at a conclusion. This is seldom the case in the working world.

To clearly articulate a problem statement, you must have a clear understanding of many different (often conflicting) data sets. Only after you have identified these deeper structural issues can you address the real (not perceived) problem at hand. This implies critical thinking skills are measured through the ability to:

- Raise vital questions and problems
- Gather and assess relevant information and effectively interpret it
- Come to well-reasoned conclusions and solutions
- Think within alternative systems of thought
- Recognize assumptions, implications, and practical consequences
- Communicate effectively with others in identifying solutions to complex problems (Paul, 2002)

As you progress through the chapters in this book, we will both revisit and apply how critical thinking is fundamental to every aspect of successful communication.

If you truly consider it, you already use your critical thinking skills without really being aware of them. When you apply for a job and you put the most relevant information that meets the employer's needs in your cover letter, you are thinking critically. When you build a "frame" for your message so that it is easily understood by your particular audience, you are using critical thinking skills. As you determine the true root cause of an issue to then determine recommendations or summarize key conclusions, you are using your critical thinking skills. As you identify the most relevant strategic approach to formulate your message, you are thinking critically.

To write well and to speak eloquently is to witness critical thinking in its most visceral and powerful form. This is why our programmatic standards evaluate our students' critical thinking skills so rigorously: to help them adapt and be agile in their communications.

Logic and Reasoning

As Tony Wagner identifies, "analyzing and accessing information" is clearly a 21st century skill. Mike Summers, Global Talent Management agent at Cisco, agrees. He states, "There is so much information available that it is almost too much, and if people aren't prepared to process the information effectively it almost freezes them in their steps" (Wagner, 2008). Quite often, when we join the working world, we need to build our own reputation and credibility. We start with a blank slate; you might have come highly recommended, but you haven't proven yourself in your new workplace. One way to build your credibility, and one key indicator of an employee's ability to solve problems, is to demonstrate a solid sense of logic and reasoning in how you present data.

© ImageFlow/Shutterstock.com

Figure 1   *"Don't be the Data Dump Guy!"*

When we build credible messages, we need to include data and information that is both relevant and timely. A message that builds credibility includes relevant information that has been analyzed. Effective communication takes into consideration communicator credibility by always "treating" the data, not merely reporting it.

One of the most common feedback loops we hear about, particularly from recruiters, is the clear preference for applicants who can distinguish themselves by not merely presenting data, but by having a clear understanding of what to *do* with the data.

Increasingly, with the overwhelming amount of information available at our fingertips, it is not enough to present a cascading stream of information. This is known as a "data dump." Recruiters look for applicants who can determine what data to include and what to discard.

ANALYSIS

Take a problem or data set and break it down. Examine the pieces, and see how they relate to one another and to the bigger picture (i.e. your bottom line).

SYNTHESIS

Look at your analysis. Are there ways to put the pieces back together to create something new, insightful, and original? This is your opportunity to teach your audience something new.

The ability to analyze data also predetermines the ability to find patterns, underlying causes, and root cause issues that might shed new light on the information. Putting the information back together to reveal new patterns is called *synthesis*, and it is a key aspect of your ability to apply logic and reasoning to your message. Being able to group information, present similar units (not compare apples to oranges), and to tease out the key pieces of data most relevant to a specific audience is key to success. Generating a well-crafted message requires that you understand what information to include and, most importantly, what the information signifies to varying audience members.

This is a key component in building and sustaining any message of validity, and it is one critical step in solidifying your success (and reputation) as a savvy professional. It is only through a trustworthy and reliable reputation that you can begin to collaborate across networks, exercise influence, and persuade. Your own professional capital is only as powerful as your ability to build and sustain your credibility.

Structural Coherence

Have you ever wondered why your eyes glaze over during the middle of a long lecture? Have you ever found yourself using "TL;DR" (Too Long; Didn't Read) as you try to wade through a policy handbook, online diatribe, or posting? Conversely, have you ever hung on a speaker's every word and felt your point of view changing? In the world of work, there are many practices or "secret handshakes" that are used to keep our messages clear, focused, and effective. In a fast-paced world, understanding how to generate a coherent message can make the difference between sealing the deal or losing a job.

Understanding strategic organizational structures is so important that we devote the entire next chapter to mastering the various forms. Strategic organization helps you finesse a resistant audience member or determine the best way to present information to someone who is anticipating or expecting your information. Keeping the Bottom Line on Top (BLOT) is a key standby, and when you understand this is what business professionals are looking for from you as a potential partner, it will become a rule you live by, too. Whether you memorize SBAR (Situation, Background, Analysis, Recommendations) for your next report, or you learn the wily ways of an indirect bad news message, strategically knowing how to organize your message not only helps you finesse a business exchange, but also builds your credibility in the process.

We signal professionalism through the logical coherence of our messages. Structural coherence can be examined on a sentence-by-sentence level, or applied to the construction of an entire message. Much like a Jenga™ tower, each building block needs to be placed precisely and with care to keep the tower—the overall message—standing. Whether you are speaking or writing, the coherence of your message is determined by your capability to shape and match your message according to accepted organizational strategies. Further, a sense of coherence to any message has to do with your ability to bend language to your will. A gifted communicator uses not one word more than is needed per sentence, not one line more than is needed per paragraph, and not one more paragraph than is necessary. Less is more.

Information Design

One clear outcome of the technological revolution has been to accelerate a communal understanding of visual literacy. We fundamentally understand the concept of "brand," as we are savvy consumers. In fact, social media has made all of us frontline marketing experts, selling products, services, and ideas to our personal networks. We are told to "manage our brand" and to have a savvy sense of "brand awareness." While this is certainly vital to your success as a business professional, you want to heighten your understanding of the basics in visual design and its impact on every aspect of messaging. Not surprisingly, one critical aspect of our standards has to do with understanding the impact of visual strategy. Whether you are improving the "skim" factor and readability of a document or selling your own image in a presentation by how you are dressed and positioned, you are using visual appeal to help convey your message.

Figure 2

© Ozerina Anna/Shutterstock.com

While there are many books written on the topic of information design, our units on professional writing (Units 2 and 3) and grammar (Unit 4) will provide you with practical working approaches for making your work more polished and professional. While visual literacy is rooted in aesthetics, there are some best practices for document design and formatting.

As a business practice, the field of design has been integrated into most business communication channels. The Hichert Partner's International Business Communication Standards (IBCS) includes a comprehensive argument for the necessity of visual design to increase transparency and facilitate better decision making. Their research led them to conclude that strong design and clear communication improve business outcomes through:

i. **Improved quality:** The quality of the deliverables in every process stage will increase. This means more readily understood dashboards, clearer messages in more comprehensible reports, and—ultimately—better decisions.

ii. **Reduced reaction time:** The speed of the overall decision-making process will increase. The delivery time of new dashboards will be shorter, business analysts can answer the questions more quickly, and executives can make sound decisions faster.

iii. **Reduced costs:** Saving time in the delivery of dashboards, in the analysis of data, and in the creation of reports and presentations will reduce costs. But reducing the time executives spend on trying to understand the reports will be the biggest advantage. (Hicher, 2014)

Apparently, a picture is worth a thousand words, but a well-designed business graphic can be translated into bottom line dollars. As we explore and apply these standards in other chapters of this book, we will return to the discussion of how design impacts far more of our credibility, reputation, and reception of our messages than you might think.

Error Interference

Most of us are afraid of making mistakes: they are embarrassing or can be costly. We lose face and feel as if our credibility has been eroded in some way when we make a mistake. And, to a certain extent, this can actually be the case. Certain types of errors can diminish your credibility with your audience. Knowing how to avoid landmines can go a long way toward saving you some embarrassing moments in the workplace. There is a difference between making a mistake and "failure," but we can train you to be aware of common errors so you can avoid them growing into failures.

In our standards for both written and spoken channels, we distinguish between the types of errors. These errors can manifest anywhere along the communication continuum, and we will conclude each chapter with fatal errors that are easy to avoid in your messaging and communication.

Disruptive Errors

Disruptive errors are errors that are so egregious that the meaning of your message is completely lost. When you make these disruptive errors, the reader or listener is no longer engaged. Basically, your message gets dumped. In an accelerated and fast-paced business world, errors can be annoying. But a disruptive error is fatal. We have all heard the story about the applicant who misspelled the name of the employer. We've all heard recruiters talk about "reading for an error" so they can reject the application (mostly because there are so many qualified applicants). Or worse, the classic example of a disruptive error, the widely circulated story of the Cisco Fatty. In 2009, a competitive candidate landed a coveted job at Cisco, and on the ride home tweeted a snarky "Cisco just offered me a job! Now I have to weigh the utility of a fatty paycheck against the daily commute to San Jose and hating the work" (Wong, 2009). By the time the candidate got home, the offer had been rescinded. In these instances, a fatal error can cause your cover letter to sit unread, your presentation to be tossed, or your promotion denied.

Disruptive errors can be recognized in unintelligible sentences, omitted words/phrases, unclear pronoun references, wrong words and visuals, inappropriate actions, miscues, erratic behavior, and non-verbal delivery. This type of error tends to make the audience's task more difficult, even intruding on the listening or viewing process. Disruptive errors may cause even deeper problems that interfere with your audience's very understanding of what you are trying to say.

Credibility Errors

Credibility errors can be recognized in lack of poise and professional confidence in verbal and non-verbal delivery (including appearance and vocal quality). While these do not usually disrupt communication, they tend to reflect negatively on the presenter's credibility, reducing the audience's confidence in not only what you have to say, but also in your ability to say it. These types of errors can be as simple as reading your corporate culture incorrectly (shuffling into a more formal corporate event wearing your favorite jeans and t-shirt), or they can be more serious, like not taking the time to adhere to company-provided templates. Your range of language and ability to adhere to agreed-upon corporate norms can manifest as credibility errors. This type of error can become serious if they cause the audience to judge your character by how frequently they occur or go uncorrected.

©txking/Shutterstock.com

Figure 3   *Your Image Sends Signals*

Etiquette Errors

Some audiences (but not all) hardly notice etiquette errors, especially if they happen quickly and are passed over uncorrected in the moment. Etiquette errors arise from misjudgment of cultural and contextual expectations, such as levels of formality and familiarity. Etiquette errors can reduce the presenter's credibility, especially with audiences who are concerned about professional image or those who believe that critical thinking is reflected in the observance of protocol and social rules. In written language, these sometimes manifest in the use of emoticons or acronyms (TTFN, OMG, LOL etc.) when the intended audience either wants more formality or has other workplace expectations. The use of slang or vernacular when speaking can initially be considered an etiquette error, but can rapidly escalate into a disruptive error if not corrected.

Accent Errors

Accent errors rarely interfere with communication, and they usually do not seriously damage your credibility. In writing, these include missing or incorrect articles (a, an, the), wrong prepositions (at, for, by, around, etc.), or incorrect use of idioms. In oral communication these errors are often found in the speech of non-native speakers and are nearly impossible for non-native speakers to correct in the short term. These are often overlooked and ignored by the audience. Accent errors are not to be confused with language usage errors. If language-based issues are grievous enough to eclipse the message, then they are considered disruptive errors regardless of the speaker's native language.

Application in the Workplace

Once you start to master the standards, you'll notice you can apply them in any number of circumstances to improve communication in the workplace, in relationships, and in online formats. You will start to notice that more people listen when you speak, more of your ideas get bought into, and soon you'll be building a reputation as a skilled communicator. Or as Bill Gates so succinctly says, "I'm a great believer that any tool that enhances communication has profound effects in terms of how people can learn from each other, and how they can achieve the kind of freedoms that they're interested in." In the spirit of making the world a better place, one skillful communicator at a time, we welcome you on your journey to becoming a skillful and strategic communication master.

PROFESSIONAL WRITING STANDARDS
ELLER COLLEGE OF MANAGEMENT, BUSINESS COMMUNICATION PROGRAM

CRITERIA	CRITICAL THINKING	LOGIC AND REASONING	STRUCTURAL COHERENCE	INFORMATION DESIGN	ERROR INTERFERENCE
	• Audience • Purpose • Context • Frame • Strategic approach	• Logical units of discourse • Claim or assertion • Idea unity and integrity • Supporting evidence	• Coherent "whole" • Internal logic • Transitions • Section unity & integrity • Language use	• Format and channel • Visual design • Readability/accessibility • Professionalism	• Disruptive errors • Credibility errors • Etiquette errors • Accent errors
EXCEEDS EXPECTATIONS	• Demonstrates **sophisticated** understanding of audience, purpose, and context through framing and strategic approach, including, not limited to: 1. **purpose** statement that is articulate, coherent, over-reaching, encompassing higher view; 2. **forecasting** that provides structural cohesion and unity and acknowledges and informs audience of guiding structure; 3. **professionalism** that acknowledges relational value and confirms audience status and knowledge base.	• Demonstrates **exceptional** logic and reasoning through 1. **claims/assertions** that are logically sound, clear, cred-ible, valid, and substantiated; 2. **unity, integrity,** and **thoroughness** of ideas and reasoning provided to support claims and assertions; 3. **supporting evidence, information, and data** that are accurate, concrete, explicit, relevant, well explained, varied, and engaging.	• Demonstrates **integrity** of structural coherence through 1. the development of a **mean-ingful "whole"**; 2. **well-structured, logical flow** of ideas; 3. **cohesive development** within sections (sections can "stand alone"); 4. **seamless** transitions; 5. **precise, concise,** and **accurate** language patterns.	• Demonstrates **mastery** of information design through 1. **optimal** format and channel choice; 2. **sophisticated** visual design strategy; 3. compression of complex infor-mation into **clear visual patterns** for rapid intake and high skim value; 4. **enhanced** reader compre-hension of complex material through clear, concise, visual and verbal elements.	• **No etiquette or credibility errors.** Although minimal disruptive or accent errors may be present, no error interference. Document is client-ready and professional.

(Continued)

MEETS EXPECTATIONS	• Demonstrates **clear** understanding of audience, purpose, and context through framing and strategic approach, including, not limited to: 1. **purpose** statement that is clear and coherent; 2. **forecasting** that provides basic structural unity (often as a list); 3. **professionalism** that employs established protocol for specific audience and context.	• Demonstrates **clear** logic and reasoning through 1. **claims/assertions** that are explicitly stated, logical and credible; 2. **evident ideas and reasoning** provided to support claims and assertions; 3. **supporting evidence, information, and data** that are relevant and varied.	• Demonstrates **clarity** of structural coherence through 1. an overall **sense of meaning** evident in the text; 2. **general flow** of ideas; 3. **clear** section development; 4. **effective** transitions; 5. **clear** language.	• Demonstrates **effective** information design through 1. **appropriate** format and channel choice; 2. **professional** visual design strategy; 3. use of common strategies (bullets, headings, graphics) to promote **clarity** and **readability**; 4. **improved** reader comprehension of complex material through clear, concise, visual and verbal elements.	• **Minimal etiquette or credibility errors.** Although occasional disruptive errors and frequent accent errors may be present, there is no serious error interference. Document needs minimal revision before submission to client.
DOES NOT MEET EXPECTATIONS	• Demonstrates **rudimentary** understanding of audience, purpose, and context through framing and strategic approach, including, not limited to: 1. **purpose** statement that is awkward or absent; 2. **forecasting** that is absent or irrelevant to the message; 3. **lack** of professionalism that results in erratic and inappropriate statements or language use.	• Demonstrates **poor** logic and reasoning through 1. **claims/assertions** that are vague, inadequate, unsubstantiated or incomplete; 2. **underdeveloped or absent ideas and reasoning** provided to support claims and assertions; 3. **insufficient, irrelevant, vague,** or **absent evidence,** information, and data provided to back claims.	• Demonstrates **lack** of structural coherence through 1. **lack of coherence, unity** and **cohesion** in the text; 2. **inconsistent flow** of ideas; 3. **erratic** section development; 4. design strategies (i.e. lists, visuals) used as **compensation** for lack of cohesion, logic, and meaning; 5. **poor** transitions; 6. **imprecise, unclear language.**	• Demonstrates **ineffective** information design through 1. **inappropriate** format and channel choice; 2. **unpolished** visual design strategy; 3. interference or absence of **clarity** and **readability** through use of common strategies (bullets, headings, graphics); 4. **reader comprehension** of complex material is **impaired** by visual and verbal elements of the text.	• **Errors damage message comprehension and writer credibility.** Document needs substantial revision before submission to client.

Error Interference Definition

Disruptive Errors: Disruptive errors can be recognized in unintelligible sentences, omitted words/phrases, unclear pronoun references, incorrect verb forms, run-on sentences, or wrong words. This type of error tends to make the reader's task more difficult, even intruding on the reading process. Disruptive errors may also interfere with communication, preventing the reader from comprehending what the writer means.

Credibility Errors: Credibility errors can be recognized in faulty subject/verb agreements, some punctuation errors, or spelling errors. While these do not usually disrupt communication, they tend to reflect negatively on the writer's credibility, reducing the readers' confidence in what a writer has to say. Credibility errors become serious if they cause the reader to judge a writer's character or management ability by the frequency of the mere presence of certain violations of Standard English.

Etiquette Errors: Many readers (but not all) hardly notice etiquette errors, especially if reading quickly for the moment. Etiquette errors include substituting "I" for "me" after prepositions; misplacing apostrophes (team's /teams'); confusing it's and its; or excessive use of passive voice. However, etiquette errors can reduce the writer's credibility, especially with those readers who are concerned about professional image or those who believe that critical thinking is reflected in the observance of grammar rules.

Accent Errors: Commonly found in the writing of non-native speakers – (which are nearly impossible for non-native speakers to correct in the short term) – these are often overlooked and ignored by readers, particularly if they are cognizant of the non-native-speaker status of the writer. Accent errors rarely interfere with communication, and they usually do not seriously damage the writer's credibility. Accent errors include missing or incorrect articles, wrong prepositions, or incorrect use of idioms.

Strategic Business Communication

Ever wish you could crack the code that would let you win at work? Ever wondered how one salesperson can be so annoying, yet another anticipates exactly what you want or need even if you don't know? Would you know how to send a letter to someone rejecting their candidacy? Denying their claim? Would you draw a complete blank if your boss asked you to write an informational report compiling the data from three different news sites, each one with a slightly different perspective? Wouldn't it be great if you knew the "secret code" to allow you to finesse any of these circumstances?

A large part of skillful communication involves audience analysis: understanding the right approach to reach a particular audience, in a specific circumstance, at a given time. While experience is always the best teacher, it is not always the most forgiving. Undoubtedly, life will provide you with many learning moments, but you'll be better equipped to navigate a variety of audiences by learning a variety of strategic approaches. Think of it as learning the secret handshake, a shortcut into your audience's good graces. Our intention is to make you as workplace-ready as possible, and to equip you with the basic knowledge to navigate any scenario that might require a special approach.

If you've ever played sports, then you know that there are certain "plays" that get made—both teams know the play when they see it, and they know how to react and respond. These are rules of engagement. Similarly, if you are a musician, you recognize notation in music that not only tells you how to play, but if you are playing with others (in a quartet, or in a symphony), it also helps you anticipate and know the other players' parts before they are played. You not only know how to respond, but also how to collaborate so you create meaning (music). Understanding when and how to play—the game or melody—is very similar to selecting the right strategy for any workplace messaging you might be asked to create. And, in the same way an athlete or musician learns the proper approach and commits it to muscle memory, you can also learn what organizational strategies are most commonly used and for what specific types of circumstance.

Strategy Starts with Your Audience

As with most messaging, we start with the audience. Understanding your audience, their positions, values, and circumstances, remains a critical component of successful engagement. A message, no matter how eloquent, must be crafted with a particular audience in mind. Therefore, an effective communication strategy requires forethought and careful planning. Part of this process involves identifying the audiences with whom you wish to communicate and tailoring your messages to meet the needs of each particular group. In business, we call these different groups *stakeholders*. Think of them as various players on a team; each one of them has a particular function or relationship to the central mission. If you needed to explain a botched play, you wouldn't speak the same way to an angry coach as you would to a vivacious cheerleader—the messages, the approach, and probably the content would be very different. Still, they are stakeholders because they are invested in the outcome of the game, and your message still needs to be delivered. Accordingly, you would need to adapt your strategy to accommodate each one of their sets of needs.

©Fotoluminate LLC/Shutterstock.com

Figure 1   *Know your stakeholders*

In the business world, your stakeholders are the people or groups affected by your organization's performance. Generally, they have something to lose or gain by your company's activities, and often, stakeholders can influence the success or failure of your projects, ventures, or events. From an organizational perspective, tailored communication is not only wise, but vital to your survival.

A need for strategic messaging usually arises from exigency; that is, a situation or event that calls for audience engagement. These situations are innumerable and range from circumstances like new product launches, to corporate mergers, or changes in leadership or policy. It's important to remember that you have both internal and external audiences: the stakeholders within your organization, and those who don't work for the company, but have some kind of monetary, emotional, or practical interest in the situation at hand. As you develop a stakeholder or audience analysis for purposes of communication, you may consider factors like stakeholders' levels of influence, or the timing and channels in which messages should be sent. These elements will help you further refine your message once you've chosen a strategic approach. In order to select the appropriate strategy, first determine the correct channel for your message.

Reaching Your Audience

In an omni-channel world, knowing the right channel to reach your audience can sometimes determine if your message is received at all. Knowing how your audience prefers to receive information is critical to the success of your message. Your boss might not want you to text her at all hours. Your co-worker might insist you post your collaborations on Google Docs. Your mother might not want to hear from you on Facebook. A co-worker needing a new job might want you to ping them on LinkedIn. And sometimes, people even pick up the phone and talk to one another. You'll want to be sure you select the right channel for your message.

Choosing the optimal channel and format for your communication demonstrates that you understand whom you're talking to. The channel refers to the medium by which the message is transmitted. Are you making a phone call, collaborating via Google Docs, presenting to a large crowd in a hotel banquet hall, or sitting down across a conference table from someone in a more intimate setting?

The format refers to the type of message or document that you are sending. What format is the most appropriate for the purpose, audience, and occasion? The two tables below can help you make some of these important decisions.

VERBAL MESSAGES	FORMAL	INFORMAL
Internal	Formal presentation or seminar Formal virtual/remote presentation (i.e. conference call or video conference)	Informal presentation Informal virtual/remote presentation (e.g. conference call, Apple FaceTime, Google Hangout, etc.)
External	Formal presentation or seminar Formal virtual/remote presentation	

WRITTEN MESSAGES	FORMAL	INFORMAL
Internal	Formal report Contractual letter	Informal report Memorandum Email Text/Instant Message
External	Formal report Formal letter	Email Hand-written correspondence

Each channel has its benefits and drawbacks. As you select your channel, be sure to consider critical elements such as whether or not you are creating a permanent record.

How rich is the channel? Face-to-face communication is the richest because you can read so many nonverbal cues. How much feedback do you need? Is your client angry? Does your message contain unpleasant information? Is the receiver expecting to hear from you? How much control do you need over your message? All of these variables are taken into consideration as you determine the best way to reach your audience.

Establishing the Purpose of Your Communication

CHANNEL SELECTION CONSIDERATIONS

Richness vs. leanness

Need for interpretation (ambiguity)

Speed of establishing contact

Immediacy of feedback

Cost

Amount of information conveyed

Permanent record

Control over message

If you're presenting information to someone, chances are you're doing one of three things: you're informing them about something, persuading them to do something, or delivering bad news. Keep in mind, these categories are not always mutually exclusive. In fact, you may see some overlap. For instance, a bad news message may contain a persuasive appeal like a special offer or consolation gift. These nuances become more apparent as you gain experience messaging.

Inform (positive or neutral): You wish to convey positive or neutral information to your audience.

Inform (negative): You must deliver bad news or unpleasant information.

Persuade: You want to influence your audience in some way.

Generally, you should be able to identify your message as informative (positive or neutral), informative (negative), or persuasive. Once you have done so, you can build the most appropriate strategy for your purpose.

Determining Your Strategic Approach

Based on your experience as a communicator, you have probably encountered this choice before: is it best to present your core message upfront, or to reveal it later in the conversation or document? Your ability to choose the appropriate approach is a reflection of your communication competence. In 1975, H. Paul Grice identified four conversational maxims: quantity, quality, relation, and manner. Manner, or the way in which you convey a particular message, is intimately linked to your audience's perceptions of you and your message. Therefore, the choice between direct or indirect is more about effectiveness than it is about style. The tables below provide the basic approach for direct and indirect messages.

DIRECT MESSAGE

Bottom Line On Top

INDIRECT MESSAGE

Bottom Line On Bottom

Direct messages place the bottom line on top (BLOT). This means that the most important information is concisely presented early on, and clearly arranged throughout the message. There are many advantages to using the direct approach. It decreases the likelihood of misunderstanding and can save your listeners or readers time. In a culture where time is often equated with money, people grow impatient if they have to hunt for meaningful content. Further, the direct message design, when used in a written correspondence, provides readers with an easy-to-navigate reference document. Despite its utilitarian appeal and intuitive design, a direct approach won't always serve your purposes.

Enter the indirect approach, used when a blunt, front-loaded message simply won't do. The indirect approach places the bottom line on or near the bottom (BLOB) of your message. It's wise to use an indirect approach when you need to provide readers and listeners with some logical or emotional preparation before you present the bottom line. For instance, you may attract more consumers if you first describe your fair and sustainable production process before revealing the higher-than-average price point. By offering a bit of background, your audience may be more receptive to your product.

No two situations are exactly alike, so you will often choose your approach at the intersection of purpose and audience. Though it may appear that some purposes are always best suited for either the direct or indirect approach, it's important to look both ways before making your decision.

Once you identify your purpose and approach, you can craft your message for success. These approaches will be more fully presented in later sections. We will delve deeper into the various purposes and approaches you will encounter in professional business messages and reports. Examples of direct and indirect strategies for neutral or positive informational, negative or bad news informational, and persuasive messages will also be provided. Before that, let's explore a few more foundational concepts to help you be a successful communicator.

Unit 1 References

Gardner, H. (2006). *Changing minds: The art and science of changing our own and other people's minds*. Boston: Harvard Business School Press.

Grice, H. P. (1975). Logic and conversation. In P. Cole & J. Morgan (Eds.), *Syntax and semantics: Speech acts* (Vol. 3) (pp. 45–47). New York, NY: Academic Press.

Hicher, R. (2014, August 30). International Business Communication Standards: http://www.ibcs-a.org/

NACE. (2014, August 3). National Association for Colleges and Employers: http://naceweb.org/s10242012/skills-abilities-qualities-new-hires/

Paul, R. A. (2002). In Elder, *Critical thinking*. Upper Saddle River: Financial Times Prentice Hall Books.

Popkin, H. (2009, March 23). www.msnbc. http://www.nbcnews.com/id/29796962/ns/technology_and_science-tech_and_gadgets/t/twitter-gets-you-fired-characters-or-less/#.VAs78MvjjIU

Tufte, E. (n.d.). Visual Explanations by http://www.amazon.com/gp/reader/0961392126/ref=sib_dp_pt/104-8905861-4503115#reader- link. Retrieved from "Visual Explanations" by Licensed under Fair use of copyrighted material in the context of Edward Tufte via Wikipedia—http://en.wikipedia.org/wiki/File:Visual_Expl

Wagner, T. (2008). *The global achievement gap*. New York: Basic Books.

Walker, R. (2011). *Strategic management for leaders*. Stamford, CT: Cengage.

Wong, W. (2009, March 3). "Twitter gets you fired in 140 characters or less." *Chicago Tribune*. http://www.nbcnews.com/id/29796962/ns/technology_and_science-tech_and_gadgets/t/twitter-gets-you-fired-characters-or-less/#.VAs78MvjjIU

UNIT 2:
Professional Writing

Planning Your Message

"Easy reading is damned hard writing." ~ *Nathaniel Hawthorne*

Preparing to Write

Have you ever wondered why someone reacted the way they did to something you wrote? Did your email cause confusion or your text message elicit anger? Perhaps your boss returned your report to you for further editing, or your résumé, so thoughtfully crafted, landed with a dull "thud."

In today's screen-dependent, virtual world, we communicate in writing more than ever. While it is true that visual and auditory media comprise a larger share of communication (e.g., videos posted on the Internet, Apple FaceTime, Google Hangouts, Skype, VOIP, telephone, etc.), the sheer volume of communication has increased, and the written word remains one of the most powerful tools for expressing an idea. Unfortunately, as we have gotten better at producing visual and auditory media, our writing skills have suffered.

We designed this chapter to help you turn that tide and become a skillful business writer. In our highly connected business environment, you can take advantage of a quick video chat or phone call with anyone in the world. On the other hand, your written communication—be it an email, a memo, a report, or a letter—is the most lasting impression you can leave with someone. Easily forwarded and shared with others, it is an indelible record of your interaction, an encapsulation of your thought process, and a representation of who you are. What should your writing say about you? Take time to plan it, craft it, and polish it so it gets the reaction you intend.

You Are What You Write

Your professional success depends upon how well you write. The first interaction you have with a potential employer, especially early in your career, will probably be through your written cover letter and résumé. Your opportunities for advancement will depend, in part, on how well you express your company's objectives in writing. When you seek new opportunities with other companies, the process will start all over again.

Communications professionals are not the only ones who know this to be true; a large and ever-growing body of evidence supports our claims about the importance of competent writing skills.

ARE YOU READY FOR THE WORKPLACE?

In 2006, a consortium of four organizations, The Conference Board, Partnership for 21st Century Skills, Corporate Voices for Working Families, and the Society for Human Resource Management, released a report on a survey of more than 400 employers, entitled "Are They Really Ready for Work?"[1]

Among other findings, the report found that 27.8% of employers find that four-year college graduates are deficient in written communication skills, even though 89.7% of employers view these skills as "very important," more than any other desired skill for four-year college graduates.

One of those consortium members, Partnership for 21st Century Skills surveyed registered voters a year later and found that 58% of voters ranked written communication as a 9 or 10 on a 10-point scale of importance; only 5% of same voters ranked schools as a 9 or 10 on similar 10-point scale.[2]

In 2012, the American Management Association released the results of a survey it conducted of employers that found that communication skills were the highest priority, most measured, and most assessed during the hiring process.[3]

For as long as the National Association of Colleges and Employers (NACE, http://www.naceweb.org) have been conducting semi-annual surveys of employer needs, the ability to create and/or edit written reports has consistently been listed as a top ten skill.

[1] http://www.p21.org/storage/documents/FINAL_REPORT_PDF09-29-06.pdf
[2] http://www.p21.org/storage/documents/P21_pollreport_singlepg.pdf
[3] http://www.amanet.org/uploaded/2012-Critical-Skills-Survey.pdf

Employer Expectations

Employers generally commit to helping new employees acquire skills needed for their job functions, but they expect you to come into the organization with strong writing skills. While companies want employees with both written and verbal communication skills, it is your writing that will get your foot in their door. The statistics in the inset "Are You Ready for the Workplace?" clearly show the emphasis employers place on written communication skills. After all, a future employee will be representing the company in his or her everyday business correspondence. Your writing is literally a record of your communication competence; poor writing is hard to ignore, and effective writing is nearly impossible to forget.

Effective writing means more than just using correct spelling and proper grammar, though both are crucial. You must strategically construct your messages for maximum effectiveness. This chapter will help you put all of the pieces together.

Business Writing Is Different

You have probably taken several writing courses and written numerous academic papers. You may wonder why you need to read yet another book on the topic of writing. You probably believe the writing you have done so well up to this point has prepared you for writing in the workforce.

That belief is wrong. Your skills in academic writing may be well established, but you will need to develop new skills to be an effective business writer. Business writing is different from other forms of writing in several ways. The following table highlights some of the differences between academic and business writing.

	ACADEMIC WRITING	BUSINESS WRITING
PURPOSES FOR WRITING	To explain knowledge or new ideas To inform (positive or neutral) To demonstrate author's understanding	To inform (positive, neutral, or negative) To persuade
TYPICAL AUDIENCES	Academics or experts in their fields	Specifically targeted, depending on the unique purpose of each communication
COMPLEXITY OF LANGUAGE	Lengthy words and sentences Repetition to emphasize points	Concise and precise, to be easily understood by as many stakeholders as possible
SCOPE	Specifically tailored for academics Usually non-fiction	Specifically tailored to primary audience Uses carefully chosen facts
STRUCTURE	Long paragraphs Paragraphs indented	Short paragraphs Paragraphs not indented
LENGTH	Usually longer	As short as possible
SPECIFICITY	Usually on a specific topic	Specific to meet the needs of primary Audience

The primary difference between business and other forms of writing is that business writing is always tailored to a specific audience, depending on the situational context and purpose of the document. You must customize your business writing approach for your audience and purpose. Regardless of whether you are informing or persuading, consider what your audience already knows about your topic and what you want them to know.

It is common for a business writer to overshoot the "what the audience already knows" target. This overestimation is often due to the author's assumption that their audience has the same information he or she does. This happens so frequently there is a name for it: The Curse of Knowledge.

In their 2007 book, *Made to Stick*, an exploration of how to make your messages memorable, brothers Chip and Dan Heath coined the phrase "The Curse of Knowledge" to describe that sensation of forgetting a time when you did not know something. Perhaps you have sat through a business meeting in which colleagues are throwing around abbreviations and acronyms to describe processes, products, and competitors. As an intern or new employee, you may not know what these abbreviations and acronyms mean, and so you cannot tell a business process from a competitor. Your colleagues are so familiar with these shorthand terms that they do not even think about the fact that these phrases are totally foreign to you. Your colleagues suffer from The Curse of Knowledge.

The Heath brothers offer two ways to avoid The Curse of Knowledge. The first, offered facetiously, is to never learn anything. This, of course, is neither feasible nor practical. The second way and only true hope for overcoming The Curse of Knowledge is to be vigilant about remembering your audience and what they do or do not already know. Business writing is not about you; it should always be crafted with the audience and end purpose in mind.

To help you be effective business communicators, this unit and the next one will help you plan and compose messages using specific strategic approaches that you can tailor for your specific purposes and audiences. For your reference, we have also included a chapter of common workplace documents at the end of Unit 4.

How to Begin

How do you know where to start when you write? How do you determine what is relevant and what is not? How do you make sure you write everything you want to write? How do you know what to keep and what to cut? How-to books on writing will tell you specific ways to create a document. But how do you generate content?

TWO KINDS OF WRITERS

Writers fall somewhere on the continuum between free-writers and outliners.

Free Writers Some people write everything down on paper at once without editing; they simply let their pen flow and produce content. When they think they have all the information on the page, they go back and organize it by fitting the different parts into their structure or outline. This method works well when you are not exactly sure what you want to write because it helps you "think out loud." It also works well when you have very little content and need to allow your mind the open space to just write.

Outliners Other people are more structured in their approach. An outline allows you to start with the structure and generate content systematically into each content area as laid out in the outline. This method serves the logical thinker well since the process is step-by-step. It also works well when you know exactly what it is you want to convey and simply need to drop the content into the correct format or structure.

No matter your personal preference, you may find yourself trying out both methods to see what works best. If you are like most people, your personal style of writing will probably employ elements from both methods. It is not important how other people write; it is important to find what works best for you.

Analyzing Your Audience

Identifying and Analyzing Your Audience

Before writing a business message, you will need to determine who is going to read your message. In most cases, you will need to communicate with key players and decision makers in the situation at hand. For example, if you are proposing a new safety policy for your company, your audience might include the Chief Operations Officer, the Human Resources Director, and the Chief Financial Officer, since each of these parties will be involved in the decision. Once you have determined who your audience is, you can think about how to address their unique concerns so that you can persuade them to implement your proposal. You start by strategically analyzing your audience.

Primary and Secondary Audiences

You will always have a primary audience to whom you are sending the message, but you will want to consider any secondary audiences as well. A secondary audience is anyone who needs to see the message or someone who has requested that you write the message for a third party. Keeping all potential audiences in mind will help to ensure you deliver a message that reaches its target and engenders goodwill. For our purposes we will focus on analyzing our primary audience.

Audience Analysis

There are many aspects of the audience that you will need to consider. You will need to identify such things as your audience's demographics and lifestyle. By understanding your audience's interests and needs you can better determine their motivation for making decisions, which may help you to frame a message specifically for them. You should also consider how much your audience knows about the topic you are presenting so that you do not present unnecessary information or fail to include explanations your audience needs. Beware of The Curse of Knowledge!

The following list of questions can be a good place to begin your audience analysis:

- Who is the audience?
- What is the age, gender, educational background, etc.?
- What is the audience's previous knowledge of the subject?
- Why are they reading your document?
- What is your audience most interested in, and what are their most pressing needs?
- How will the information in your document be useful to your audience?
- What will your audience likely expect to learn from your document?

Establishing Relevance

You now have a handful of questions to ask about your audience to help you understand them better. Understanding who your audience is and what they expect from you is critical to crafting a document that is relevant to them. The concept of relevance threads audience awareness and purpose together. You must convince your audience that what you have to say is relevant to them, meaning that:

1. It should advance their understanding of a topic they care about, and
2. It should provide the information they need to make the decision you want them to make.

The following is an example of an analysis of a specific audience group: new employees of ABC Wealth Management, Inc., welcoming them to the company and preparing them for their new hire orientation.

WHO IS THE AUDIENCE?	New employees, beginning training next week.
WHAT IS THEIR AGE, GENDER, EDUCATIONAL BACKGROUND, ETC.?	Age and gender will vary, but they are highly educated.
WHAT IS THE AUDIENCE'S PREVIOUS KNOWLEDGE OF THE SUBJECT?	They researched the company and positions during the hiring process, but do not have any details about the upcoming orientation.
WHY ARE THEY READING YOUR DOCUMENT?	They are eager to begin work.
WHAT IS YOUR AUDIENCE MOST INTERESTED IN, AND WHAT ARE THEIR MOST PRESSING NEEDS?	They are interested in making a good impression, so they need to know what is expected.
HOW WILL THE INFORMATION IN YOUR DOCUMENT BE USEFUL TO YOUR AUDIENCE?	It will inform them about what they can expect and what is expected of them. The audience should walk away having their initial questions answered and explained. They should learn about a meeting they can attend, which will provide them answers to their questions.
WHAT WILL YOUR AUDIENCE LIKELY EXPECT TO LEARN FROM YOUR DOCUMENT?	They will expect to receive schedules, task descriptions, resources, etc. They will feel more at ease knowing the company plans to address their needs.

<u>INFORM (POSITIVE OR NEUTRAL)</u> You wish to convey positive or neutral information to your audience.

<u>INFORM (NEGATIVE)</u> You must deliver bad news or unpleasant information.

<u>PERSUADE</u> You want to influence your audience in some way.

To determine your purpose, you might begin by considering questions such as the following:

1. Why am I writing this message?

2. What has led up to this message?

3. What is the situation?

4. What is the desired outcome?

Taking the time to analyze your audience positions you to write more compelling and effective messages. The next step is to think about your purpose and how it relates to your reader.

Defining Your Purpose

Clearly defining and stating your purpose is essential to effectively communicating a message in any business context. If you define your purpose thoughtfully, you will connect with your audience and give yourself an anchor for the rest of your document.

Articulating your purpose can be difficult. It may help to look at some examples below. In the first example, the writer aligns with the reader and establishes relevance by stating the purpose and explaining how the information will help him.

Dear Mr. Voss,

We appreciate your desire for excellent customer service and increased profitability. Our corporate goal is to build and maintain customer satisfaction at all of our properties. With enhanced customer satisfaction, our company is able to thrive and increase profits. I am glad to inform you of new changes to our sustainability initiative, GREEN. These changes will increase our customer satisfaction and fuel your property's profitability.

In the next example, the author presents a common goal and gives the reader a reason to keep reading:

Dear Mr. Kline,

On behalf of the Organization X, we would like to congratulate you for being elected Mayor of Tucson. We appreciate your dedication to the growth, safety, infrastructure, and people of Tucson. Organization X also cares about the enrichment of Tucson.

We are excited to provide accessibility and exposure to the arts to all Tucson residents. I am writing to introduce you to our new membership program catered to lower-income patrons.

Once you determine the purpose of the message, you can plan the rest of your document accordingly. Every piece of information and analysis in your document should relate directly to your purpose. This will help you focus on the information you need to include, and discard that which you do not need.

For example, if you are the IT manager informing employees of a new system upgrade, you might first establish the need for the upgrade. Then, you might provide a comparison between the upgraded system and the current system being used. You will want to list the features and benefits of the new system for the specific work being performed. If there will be system downtime while you perform the upgrade, your audience would surely appreciate knowing about that. Finally, you will need to provide instructions for using the system, along with information on available support.

Setting the Right Tone

Even if you have analyzed your audience and established a clear sense of purpose, it is possible to alienate your reader by using the wrong tone. Tone is critically important because your audience cannot physically see you or hear your voice; therefore, they do not have the benefit of your nonverbal cues to understand how you intend your message to be read. You may have limited experience in business writing, and you may not know how your writing comes across to another person. This section will help you put your best foot forward.

Your attitude toward your subject matter and your audience comes across in your tone. Your tone, for example, can be formal or informal, depending on the purpose of your message and its intended audience. If you sent an email to a friend and co-worker asking them to go to lunch, your tone would be more casual than if you were asking a supervisor. Your tone is also conveyed in your choice of words. You can sound angry, arrogant, or apologetic, depending on your vocabulary. You may describe someone as bossy rather than assertive, or you may ask for something immediately as opposed to at your earliest convenience; these choices add up to create the tone of your writing. Pro tip: read your writing out loud and put yourself in your reader's shoes. How would someone take this? Does it sound too pushy or impatient? Does it sound respectful without coming across as too passive? Did you exaggerate or say something over the top?

The "You" Attitude

Setting the right tone involves putting your audience at the center of your document. To successfully get your message across to a specific audience, all information must be relevant to his or her situation, interests, and needs. The term "You Attitude" conveys the practical application of audience analysis. Several practical techniques will assist you in developing the appropriate tone, but the most important is to convey genuine empathy for the person or group to whom you are sending the message (Kamalani Hurley, 2007).

Pronoun Consideration

When corresponding with a customer or client, you can use the second person pronoun ("you," "your," and "yours") to connect with and to put the focus on the reader rather than on you as the author or your company. In the examples below, you can see two different approaches to saying the same thing.

Instead of "We have looked over your request for material on our services, and we will do our best to send out the material needed as soon as we can."

Write "Thank you for your interest in our services. You will receive the material you requested within the week."

Read the two examples and consider which response makes you feel like the company values you.

There are times when the "you" pronoun is not preferable. On occasion, the second person pronoun can be offensive rather than inclusive. For example, if you need to tell a customer that he has made a mistake, it is best to avoid an accusatory tone in your language. In the following examples, fewer second person pronouns is the better choice for gaining the cooperation of the reader.

Instead of "You failed to submit your correct mailing information, so we cannot send the product you requested."

Write "Once we receive your complete mailing address, we will send you the product you requested."

Consider which of these statements would elicit a more positive response, and which would make the customer rethink ordering from this company again. Nobody likes to be called a failure.

While using the second person pronoun "you" will help you connect with your readers and make them feel valued, in some cases, you may want to convey a more collaborative tone. For example, when writing to employees, consider using "we" to make them feel like they are part of the discussion, rather than like they are being spoken to or, even worse, about.

Instead of "You should read and follow all the safety rules imposed and posted by the company so that nobody gets hurt."

Write "In order to avoid accidents, we must all follow the safety rules posted in our break rooms and on our employee website."

By paying attention to the use of pronouns, you can successfully communicate with your audience and ensure a more positive response. While your readers may not even notice this technique, they will have a sense that they are being considered in every message.

Another practical technique to generate a "You Attitude" is to interpret information for the reader; that is, you must translate features into benefits. The following table demonstrates the evolution of moving the reader from "that's nice" to "that's for me."

FEATURES (THAT'S NICE.)	BENEFITS (THAT'S FOR ME!)
We have the largest selection of coats in the city.	You can find the perfect coat for any situation or weather condition.
Our organization helps the homeless.	Your donation will help find a home for a homeless individual or family.
We can quickly print and bind reports.	Each of your 30-page reports can be professionally bound in 90 seconds.

By showing how the features of a business are relevant to your audience, you can move them more quickly toward a decision. Of course, it is essential that your company's goals be aligned with the best interests of your audience, both for ethical and practical reasons.

Finally, the "You Attitude" conveys a positive and confident tone. As you work to achieve this, eliminate unnecessary fillers that weaken your delivery. As you read the two options below, ask yourself, "Which one would instill a greater level of confidence?"

Instead of "I will try my best to solve your problem with the resources I have."

Write "I will use every resource available to find a solution to your problem."

Your writing should be strong and confident. You do not want to sound wishy-washy, or worse, like you are making excuses. Keep these elements in mind as you plan your messages. The more careful thinking you do prior to composing, the better your message will be when you finally begin to write.

Composing Your Message

This chapter offers strategies for composing common workplace documents. Whether you find yourself writing a report, emailing an update, or crafting a proposal, this chapter provides the framework for effective content development and organizational strategies that enable you to deliver a final written product that is effective, concise, and clear.

Before we begin, it is important to make a distinction between reports and correspondence messages. Correspondence messages are often used to convey or request information. They may sometimes contain report-like elements including some data and/or analysis, but in general, they provide a means of routine information exchange. Depending on the formality of your work environment, you might find some overlap in these approaches. For instance, if your manager sends you an email request for a summary of a news article, it may be perfectly appropriate to provide the summary in the body of your email response. However, some organizational cultures might encourage a more traditional report format for these types of exchanges. While correspondence messages tend to use more first and second person, reports favor the use of third person as it promotes a more objective and professional tone.

Correspondence Messages

From emails to letters, correspondence in the workplace is the most common form of writing that takes place. Essentially, correspondence is any written or digital information that is exchanged between two or more parties. These exchanges could come in the form of postcards, notes, emails, or letters.

The content of these messages can vary greatly, and the examples below are but a few possibilities:

- making simple announcements
- describing protocol
- congratulating someone on a promotion or new job
- requesting something

- thanking someone
- letting a customer know that their order has shipped
- confirming an appointment or meeting time
- giving information that was requested

Obviously, some of these can be very short—one or two sentences—and others can be more lengthy. In general, business correspondence is predominantly under one page, as people are busy and want information quickly.

Composing Business Correspondence

If you have experienced writer's block, you know how paralyzing it can be. The good news about business writing is that if you are clear in your purpose, you need never be stuck for what to say next. Ask yourself what the reader will need to know to enable them to take your desired action. In a business message, establish your purpose and audience. Then, make a list of all the necessary information and categorize it into sections that you can develop into paragraphs in the rest of the document. Consider the following scenario:

You are the marketing director for a local credit union. You and your six-person team are responsible for developing all of the credit union's advertisements. At a recent meeting with the company's top executives, you agreed to launch a new service. The credit union will start offering a series of three workshops to its current customers in January. You have been asked to coordinate a marketing campaign that will begin in November. To get started, you send an email to your team to arrange a meeting.

Here is your introduction:

To: marketingteam@creditunion.com
From: ghaussmann@creditunion.com
Date: September 8, 20XX
Re: Marketing Team Meeting, September 12th

Hello Team,

The company will be offering an exciting new service beginning next year, and our team has been tasked with creating the marketing campaign to be launched in November. We'll need to get started right away, so I'd like for us to meet this Friday, September 12th. Please look over the brief description of the service below and come with your most innovative ideas for this campaign.

Your purpose is clear and the audience has been established. So, what information should you include to ensure a productive first meeting? Put yourself into your readers' place and anticipate their questions. Some of these questions might include:

DESCRIPTION OF SERVICE	MEETING LOGISTICS	TEAM RESPONSIBILITIES
What is the new service?	Who will be in attendance?	What level of preparation is required?
Who is the target market?	What is the format (discussion, etc)?	Are visual aids expected?
How will the target market benefit?	What time and how long will it be?	How much time will each individual have to present ideas?

Once you have these questions written down, you should have no problem completing your message. You may need to do some legwork, such as arranging a meeting room or drafting an agenda, but you can use these questions as a checklist to ensure that your readers will arrive at the meeting fully prepared.

Thank You Messages

Though most short correspondence does not need a full introductory paragraph as was described earlier, some semblance of the same structure should be present: beginning, middle, end. Some of these, like thank-you letters, have their own formulaic structure. Here is an example of a typical thank-you message:

Hello Mr. Cliff,

Thank you for taking the time to speak with me Friday about the internship opportunities at Colby and Whitlam.

It was nice to finally meet you after our phone calls and emails. I enjoyed learning about the roles that interns play in your company. I was heartened after our conversation as I realize that I have the qualifications and skills that this position requires. I am confident that my skills and abilities make me a great candidate for an internship.

I am excited by possibility of becoming a summer intern and would appreciate a follow-up as you comb through the candidates and get closer to making a decision. I am happy to provide any additional information you may need. I can be reached at (520) 555-1212 or at happyintern@bigjob.com

Thanks again, and I look forward to hearing from you soon.

Best regards,
Nicole Taylor

> Note the positive professional tone. Since this is a thank you letter, the BLOT is clear in the opening sentence.

> Note the body is only a few sentences, but it goes into more specific details.

> The polite close includes a summative purpose sentence, invites inquiry, and gives contact info.

Meeting Invitation

Another common workplace message is a meeting invitation. Leaving out important pieces of information can lead to back and forth emails between multiple parties as the invitees try to get all of the facts that they need.

A surefire checklist for meeting invitations is below:

1. Succinct subject line with most important details: Team Meeting 3.14 @5:30 Rm 117
2. Meeting date start and end times
3. Location of the meeting
4. Purpose of the meeting
5. Expectations from attendees
6. Items attendees should bring
7. Agenda (if necessary)

Here is an example of a routine meeting invitation:

This is to inform you that our monthly "Planning & Review" Meeting will be on Monday, March 10th at Conference Room #2 from 9-11 a.m.

The following will be discussed during the meeting:

- Staff review/requirements

- Audit procedures

- Sales review

- Production review/requirements

Please make sure that all team leaders are prepared to give updates regarding the status of ongoing projects. If you are unable to attend the meeting, please make sure that your assistant can deliver your report for you.

Please feel free to add to this agenda by notifying us in advance prior to the day of the meeting.

This strategy can be used in composing email messages, memoranda, or business letters. It will also be useful when writing informal business reports; however, longer documents will require additional content development.

Report Writing

Sharing information in a professional setting can come in different forms for different purposes. While the routine messages discussed above are the most common, you will also be required to compose longer and more formal messages throughout your career.

Sometime in the course of your career, you may be asked to write a report. It could be as simple as a one-page industry overview for a busy boss who wants to understand the lay of the land in an industry with which s/he is unfamiliar. Or, it could be a longer report on a crisis in an industry or within a particular company, i.e. Volkswagen, Nike, or Chipotle. Regardless of the length of the report, the general structure remains fixed: Introduction, Body, Conclusion.

That said, the only sections that change are the body, which could be forty or fifty pages long, and the inclusion of front (cover page, table of contents, and executive summary) and back matter (appendices).

The variations and degree to which you go in-depth in a report can be accommodated by proper formatting—everything from font size and style to placement and spacing of headings determines the organization of your information. Thus, writing a report is simply an expanded version of a short report that you may have to produce for a class. If you follow the rules governing headings, subheadings, etc., you will produce polished deliverables that underscore your competence and professionalism.

How to Write a Report

As with any message—of any length—you will need to systematically work through the three-step writing process: planning, writing, revising. This three-part structure is tried and true, and taking short-cuts is not advised. Remember, your professional reputation is on the line whenever you write for an audience.

Planning

It bears repeating that the key difference between business writing and academic writing is that business messages have a purpose and a specific audience. In academic writing, you are often writing to no one in particular, but you know that your instructor will be grading it, so you often skew your message to that audience of one.

In business writing, you must ask yourself a few key questions:

1. To whom am I writing?
2. Why am I writing it? (persuade, inform, deliver bad news)
3. What do they already know?
4. What do they need to know?
5. What is the proper tone I should use in this instance?
6. What do I ultimately want from them?

Next, you will need to *gather the information* you need to flesh out your message. If that includes research, then you will need to gather the facts and data that will support your claims and aims. Choose reputable publications from common business databases or peer-reviewed sources. Keep track of the citations for later referencing and to use in in-text citations and on the reference page.

Once you have the information you need, you need to take some time to organize your message. You will want to identify your main point/points, cluster supporting data around these points, choose your strategy (direct or indirect), determine the appropriate level of formality, and create an outline ordering the information in a logical construct.

Writing

If you have successfully worked the planning process, the actual writing should take less time: You know what you want to say, you have done your research, and you know the structure and approach your message will follow.

Your introductory paragraph should have the standard information: Frame/Context, Purpose, WIIFY, and Forecast. Next, you will fill in the paragraphs under the headings that succinctly identify the main point of the paragraph/s. Each paragraph will follow the Claim, Evidence, Reasoning construction, and you will wrap it up with a standard conclusion that offers a brief, high-level summary (repeat the forecast), a WIIFY, an invitation for inquiry, and your contact information.

Remember to use strong verbs to drive the sentences and hold the readers' interest. As to tone, aim to sound even more formal than you might be inclined; it is better to error on the side of professionalism than to come off too casual.

Revising

Your work is not quite over! Revise your document carefully, checking for spelling and grammatical errors and making sure that it flows easily. Use transition words to maintain flow and clarify the relationship between sentences and between paragraphs and sections.

Once you are finished, you will have a professional business document that showcases your ability to plan, write, and polish a workplace message.

Common Purposes of Business Reports

The type of content development outlined in the previous section is common for everyday workplace scenarios. However, more formal and comprehensive business reports will require more extensive research. You will also need to apply rigorous thought processes to extract meaning from the data you gather. You may do this by classifying information, analyzing data, and synthesizing data from more than one source.

You will also need to determine the type of reporting your audience is requesting from you to properly present the information you have gathered and analyzed. The three levels of reporting you will likely be asked to do are 1) reporting findings, 2) drawing conclusions, and 3) making recommendations. When researching information for a business report, you will always be asked to present your findings; however, often you will also be expected to show relevance and possibly make recommendations based on your findings. The next three sections will walk you through the three levels of reporting information for business purposes. Keep in mind that the purpose for all business research and reporting is to prompt and enable a company and/or its stakeholders to take action.

Reporting Findings

When you are asked to report findings, you should present information completely and objectively. You may classify or summarize data using charts, graphs, or tables when appropriate to help your reader access information at a glance. As you discuss the graphics, you will need to interpret the data for the situation; that is, make the information meaningful and useful to the reader. You may even go as far as to offer factual explanations for the findings. You do not want to draw conclusions prematurely or offer opinions or recommendations if you have not been requested to do so.

Let's look at an example of reporting findings, using a survey conducted by Fresh-mart grocery store. Here are the results of a section of the survey in which customers were asked to rate the importance of service items. The chart is followed by a brief email message to the Fresh-mart CEO, Jeff Curtis, reporting and interpreting the results.

FRESH-MART SURVEY: CUSTOMER SERVICE PROGRAMS

SERVICE	AVERAGE RATING (OUT OF 5)
2% discount on purchases of $20 or more	4.50
5% senior discount on Wednesday	4.10
Free delivery of orders within a 10-mile radius of the store	1.75
Frequent shopper discount card	3.97

Dear Mr. Curtis,

Average ratings of the section of the survey on customer service programs indicate strong customer interest in new services that enable them to save money.

Discounts on all purchases of $20 or more, a senior discount on Wednesday, and frequent shopper discount cards all received ratings above 3.95 out of 5.00, indicating that Fresh-mart customers consider those services to be important or very important. By contrast, removing fees from seldom-used services, such as free delivery, appears to be of little importance to Fresh-mart customers.

Let me know how I can help with Fresh-mart's decision on how we can use this data moving forward.

Best Regards,
Ted Neal

Notice that the explanation does not offer suggestions based on the data; it simply reports what was found and makes it relevant to the situation.

Drawing Conclusions

When you are expected to take the report to the next level, you will need to draw a conclusion that suggests how the reader might respond to the findings. In this case, you do more than merely restate the findings, but you still remain objective. Your conclusion should flow naturally from the findings themselves and your clear analysis of them, and it should be justified by your findings. This demands that you consider the needs of your reader more thoroughly than you did when simply reporting the information. The following would be an appropriate conclusion to the previous email message, based on the Fresh-mart survey item.

Conclusion:

Since Fresh-mart customers are more interested in ways to save money on their grocery purchases than in saving money on peripheral services, we can increase customer satisfaction by offering a variety of discounts.

Making Recommendations

A recommendation is a confident statement of a proposed action based on your findings and the conclusion you have drawn. As with your conclusion, a recommendation must flow from specific data and your analysis of it. In many cases, you will make more than one recommendation. In that case, you will need to organize your recommendations by some form of metric.

There are several criteria for organizing recommendations. These can include the following:

- **Time** How urgent is the problem? Should the recommendation be implemented in phases?
- **Priority** Which recommendations are the most critical? Organize your recommendations in descending order of priority.
- **Costs** How much will it cost to implement your recommendation(s)? What type of investment will be necessary?
- **Stakeholders** Who will your recommendations affect? What groups are critical to target first?

Be sure to state your metric (or metrics) clearly so your audience understands your logic and how to implement your recommendations. If your report includes an executive summary, echo this logic in the executive summary.

When making a recommendation, use imperative sentences and action verbs. State the recommendation specifically, including a plan for implementation. Ask yourself if this is an actionable recommendation. Could you implement it tomorrow if necessary?

By applying these strategies to your business writing, you can ensure the content of your documents is logical and is based on sound reasoning. You also ensure you are providing the reader with the precise, yet comprehensive, information required to act on your recommendations.

The following is an outline of what an initial recommendation might include in the Fresh-mart case. Note that the metric of organization is priority. Items are presented in order of importance to customers based on the rankings found on the previous survey. The following report presents an outline of your recommendation for the CEO of Fresh-mart.

Recommendations for Increasing Customer Satisfaction

After analyzing the results of our recent customer satisfaction survey, it is clear that Fresh-mart shoppers want greater savings on groceries. To increase customer satisfaction and loyalty, Fresh-mart should initiate two new cost-saving services immediately. The outline below offers preliminary recommendations, listed in order of importance based on our customer-satisfaction survey. We should also conduct further research to determine the feasibility of a third service in the near future.

Customer Savings Programs

The following recommendations will ensure our current customers stay loyal and will increase our customer base as we market these new services. Specifically, Fresh-mart should:

1. **Provide a 2% discount on orders totaling $20 or more.** We can implement this by:

   - Programming point-of-sale registers to compute a 2% discount on orders over $20

   - Training check-out associates to highlight savings on receipts and point them out to customers

   - Advertising this new service in store and on existing TV commercials

2. **Give an additional 3% discount to seniors on Wednesday.** We can do this by:

   - Programming point-of-sale registers with a key to compute a 3% discount

   - Training check-out associates on how to recognize customers who appear to be 60 years old or older and how to enter the discount code for such customers

   - Designing and publishing an attractive newspaper advertisement announcing the new policy

3. **Investigate the feasibility of issuing a "Frequent Shopper" discount card.** We should focus on determining the following:

   - Criteria to identify frequent shoppers

   - Type of discount card that we can offer

   - Costs of implementation, such as providing the card and maintaining records

Conclusion and Next Steps

The cost for implementing the first two services is minimal. It will consist primarily of training current employees and will include the cost of advertising. However, by implementing these two new services, Fresh-mart will show its loyal customers that we are listening, and attract new customers who find these services appealing.

The IT department has received a copy of these findings and is prepared to program registers to compute discounts. Upon approval, Ms. Applegate's team will begin organizing a training program for our checkout associates. I welcome the opportunity to discuss these cost-saving, customer-requested services and to begin researching the feasibility of a Frequent Shopper card.

As you advance in your career, you will be called upon to deliver your research and analysis at each of the levels we have just discussed. At times, you will be expected to report research findings (just the facts). At other times, you will be asked to draw conclusions based on those findings. Eventually, you will be asked to provide recommendations to solve a problem or take advantage of an opportunity your organization is facing. In longer, more formal written reports, in which you are attempting to persuade your audience to take action, the organization may well be as important as the content itself. In order to hold your audience's interest and keep them reading, you'll need to tell a story that engages them from start to finish.

Informal & Formal Reports

Reports come in many forms, and they vary in their levels of formality. Sometimes, report content is integrated into a correspondence message. For instance, a few pages ago, you read sample email used to report findings. In that example, the document, in this case, an email, contained many features of general business correspondence. Elements like salutations and the use of first and second person may appear in some informal reporting; it really depends on your purpose, your audience, and the situation at hand. Think of formality as existing on a spectrum. The figure below illustrates where certain documents might fall on the continuum.

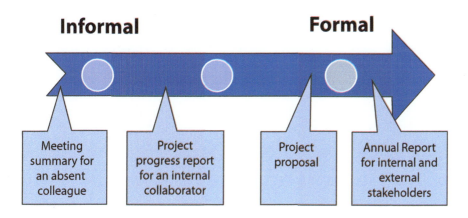

When selecting a report format, first, consider the audience. Are you reporting out to one or more readers? Then, determine how much information is needed to accomplish your objective. Generally, longer and more detailed the content lends itself to a more formal approach. As indicated by the continuum above, reports can be informal, formal, or somewhere in between. Depending on your readers' needs, you may find yourself integrating some formal elements into a relatively informal report. For instance, you might find it appropriate to include a bibliography if you use sources or an appendix if you have supporting figures or information. In the following sections, we will explore the characteristics and applications of formal and informal reports.

Informal Reports

Informal reports serve a variety of purposes and may be used to accomplish informative or persuasive purposes, and they are often designed as memos, letters, or modifications of these formats. Some common informal report types are listed below. Though, as a delivery system for relatively brief and modestly-scoped content, the informal report can serve many purposes.

	COMMON INFORMAL REPORT TYPES
Progress Report	Provides a project update to internal or external stakeholders
Periodic Report	Provides information or updates to supervisors on a regular basis
Trip or Meeting Report	Provides a detailed account of findings/outcomes following work travel or a meeting
Test Report	Describes findings from product experiments
Recommendation Report	Communicates support or opposition of a particular action or proposal
Summary Report	Details and distills information on a given topic

The following memo was drafted by an intern, in response to her supervisor's request for a summary of three, shoe industry-related articles.

Informal Report Sample Document: Research Summary

INTEROFFICE MEMORANDUM

to:	Zack Wilson
from:	student
subject:	Footwear Industry Research Summary
date:	March 22, 2019
cc:	N/A

As you requested, I have evaluated three articles pertaining to athletic footwear products and produced relevant summaries for your use. This document will give you the information to adequately procure an appealing line of athletic footwear in university bookstores. To guide your focus, I have separated the analysis into three distinct topics: superior footwear brands, footwear ecommerce trends, and economic factors.

Author uses a memo format

Frames for a particular recipient, & uses first and second person, a less formal approach

Superior Footwear Brands

One of the foundations to maintaining revenue streams in retail is the proper brand selection. Low's (2016) article compares Under Armour and Nike as they compete for top market share in footwear. Nike's top lines are based off of basketball stars Michael Jordan and Lebron James. Under Armour has created its most recent shoe line based on current basketball prodigy, Stephen Curry. While the two companies leverage athletes as their primary foundation for footwear design the factor important to our business is overall sales trends. According to Low (2016), "a Slice Intelligence report that examined sales of the top four NBA-player shoes, Curry kicks are in vogue, but Nike is still king of the cash register" (p. 1). The information in the article shows that in regard to longevity and consistency of sales, Nike is the primary brand we should offer in broad capacity at our bookstores.

Footwear E-Commerce Trends

University of Arizona bookstores currently offer online shoe retail, however, many challenges still remain in ensuring that our e-commerce sales portals are in adherence with modern retail trends. In her industry report on online shoe sales, Madeline Hurley demonstrates the growth of shoe retailers online and industry trends. According to Hurley (2016), online footwear retail has increased from 7.0% in 2011 to 14.2% in 2016. The reason for the growth of the industry online lies in consumer information trends. Over the past five years, online shopping has become increasingly consumer friendly. With a growing number of online operators, consumers can increasingly compare prices, read product reviews and browse merchandise with virtual ease (p. 6). Overall, the offering of consumer options and comparable product reviews increases online traffic.

Headings are used to clearly signal document sections

Economic Factors

Economic factors that contribute to cyclical sales trends and retailer insolvency are crucial data points that our bookstores need to take into account. A Forbes article highlights data for the upcoming quarter in the shoe retail industry. He stated, "With 10 percent of the sporting goods retail space closing by Labor Day, the remaining market will be stronger and healthier" (Powell, 2016, p. 2). In our division, we can use this data to procure athletic shoes after Labor Day to minimize costs and stand out from the degrading competition in the retail space.

Conclusion summarizes and invites inquiry. First and second person use corresponds to language in introduction

This summary analyzed three articles and their relevance in enhancing our footwear procurement division: superior footwear brands, footwear e-commerce trends, and economic factors. The outcomes of my analysis demonstrate that with a culmination of proper brand selection, e-commerce consumer accommodation, and seasonal sales focus our athletic shoe revenues can reach new highs. Thank you for letting me analyze these documents and formulate conclusions that can improve our footwear division. Feel free to contact me at student@gmail.com if you have questions.

References

Hurley, M. (2016, September). IBIS world industry report OD5093. Retrieved March 19, 2017, from http://clients1.ibisworld.com/reports/us/industry/default.aspx?entid=5093

Low, E. (2016, June 02). Under Armour's golden boy vs. Nike's lifetime king: Whose shoes sell? *Investors Business Daily.* Retrieved March 19, 2017, from http://www.investors.com/news/under-armours-golden-boy-vs-nikes-lifetime-king-whose-shoes-sell/

Powell, M. (2016, June 06). Sneakernomics: What's really happening in the U.S. sneaker business? *Forbes.* Retrieved March 19, 2017, from https://www.forbes.com/sites/mattpowell/2016/06/06/sneakernomics-whats-really-happening-in-the-u-s-sneaker-business/#40a57f311dc3

References are listed at the end of the document

Informal Report Sample Document: Strategy Summary

To: Marketing Team
From: Ben Marchos, Intern
Date: March 31, 2018
Subject: ZonaZoo's Marketing Strategies

The ZonaZoo is an award-winning student section and student-ticketing program for University of Arizona Athletics. This document provides a summary of the ZonaZoo's marketing strategies which center around member benefits and special events, both of which contribute to their success in student engagement.

This introduction is framed for a large audience and was not composed in response to a request. Therefore, it does not use first or second person.

Member Benefits
Attendance
The Zoo markets itself to students by communicating the benefits enjoyed by members. Lower cost admittance is a very popular feature, so it is clearly highlighted on their website. Further, since many games sell out, they promise the first 9000 student members who swipe their CatCards a seat at each event (ZonaZoo, 2018). By having a large group of ZonaZoo members at each game, the club achieves its goal of supporting UA teams and benefits from a high-visibility factor, which has the potential to attract more students, media, and community members. Additionally, this kind of notoriety further enhances the club's reputation.

T-Shirts
Every ZonaZoo member receives a free branded t-shirt. This helps the club gain attention on game days and provides additional signage when worn by students. With over 9000 members, these shirts provide free advertising for the club and ensure name-recognition among fans and nonmembers.

Newsletter
The ZonaZoo markets to attract new members and retain those already in the club. All club members receive the ZonaZoo Gazette, an online newsletter that provides Zoo-related content to users, highlights club and member successes, and commemorates special game day moments. By maintaining a high level of member excitement and commitment, the club garners attention from others.

Special Events
The ZonaZoo hosts many pre-game events that invite community members to join in the game day excitement (ZonaZoo, 2018). All are invited to attend and enjoy learning UA cheers, hearing guest speakers from UA's athletic community, and sharing in a strong sense wildcat fever. Partnerships with local shops and restaurants add to the events, and these parties, rallies, and tailgating days attract attention from media outlets that broadcast footage of ZonaZoo and further promote the club on a state and countrywide level.

Conclusion quickly summarizes content and offers a closing thought.

The ZonaZoo employs several key marketing initiatives. However, by communicating member benefits and hosting media-friendly special events, they continue to attract attention from sports enthusiasts on campus and all over the country.

Transmittal Messages

When delivering a formal report, it may be appropriate to include a transmittal message. The transmittal message will serve as a cover letter or brief introduction to the business document. It provides context for the report and serves the purpose of a traditional introduction that offers context, a "what's in it for you?" (WIIFY), and purpose statements, and it provides a general overview of the report content. Many times, this type of targeted message is included in informal reports, but formal reports are often written for a wider audience, and they do not include the use of first or second person phrasing. So, the transmittal message alerts your contact or point person that the document is ready for them and their team. Depending on your receiver's channel preference, transmittal messages may be formatted as a letter or memo. If you send the report electronically, you may choose to write the transmittal in an email. The transmittal is essentially your introduction to a formal report. The message below illustrates the nature of a transmittal:

To: marin.a@company.com
From: liu.m@company.com
Date: March May 17, 2018
Subject: Under Armour Communication Plan

Hello Charles,

As planned, our team completed and attached the Under Armour communication strategy to assist the expansion team in their initiative to grow UA's reach in untapped markets. This plan explores our potential move into the Brazilian market and provides communications recommendations for the expansion. Through analyses of the current situation, past expansions, and opportunities in the Brazilian market, the enclosed document identifies critical stakeholders and details targeted messaging for each group. Executive management, manufacturers, retailers, and consumers emerged as most influential to the expansion's success. It is our hope that this plan will aid your team in bringing UA's quality products to new consumer audience. Please contact me with questions or requests for further information.

Regards,
Ava Marin

Formal Reports

Formal reports are generally used to convey information on major findings, proposals, or extended research. Like informal reports, they are used for many purposes. Unlike informal reports, they often contain a great deal of content. So, the formal report format allows for effective, logical integration of content and supporting documents like figures and references. In addition, features like the table of contents make for easy navigation of materials.

This section will describe the parts of a formal report the contents and organizational structure that create an effective final product. As the word implies, a formal report is written at a higher professional level than an informal report. Formal reports often include an external audience, thus the need for elevated language and clarity of purpose. Informal reports are often targeted at an internal audience and may use humor, idiomatic language, and other more casual elements. This is not true of a formal report. The writer might also consider that a formal report could be shared in a business environment outside of the United States. With differences in language and culture, a more formal and less idiomatic language style must be used to increase the probability that the document's message will not be lost on the audience.

Major projects such as the feasibility of a new service or product, a year-end review of an organization, or research into a specific field would all be appropriate topics for formal reports. Formal reports are often comprehensive and must address diverse and disparate audiences. The need for a clear organizational structure and relevant signposts is never stronger than when writing these documents. Depending on the topic covered, a formal report can be a few pages long to hundreds of pages. Again, these longer reports necessitate an organizational clarity that is easy to grasp from skimming the table of contents.

That said, reports are divided into three main parts: front matter, body, and back matter. Brief descriptions of each are as follows:

Front Matter

This section includes all of the elements that come before the actual body of the report. This important section lets the reader know the purpose and topic of the report as well as the structure and organization of what is to follow. It is here where the reader can determine whether the information they seek will be contained within this report. Save the audience time by clearly showing them what the report will include in detail.

Title page: Note that title pages may vary from organization to organization, but in all the title itself should reflect the purpose and scope of the report. The title should be neither too long or too short, nor too vague or too specific. Accurately capturing the high-level view of the content in the title itself is critical.

Table of contents: This offers an overview and a roadmap of the report itself. It should include a list of all the front and back matter with exception to the title page. All the headings in the report will be listed in the order in which they appear in the document. A busy reader might look here to skim and find the section and the page number in which they are interested. The table of contents provides a useful way for readers to quickly find exactly what they are looking for. The table of contents also provides a clear progression for those writing or contributing to the report and helps keep the content on track.

List of figures: Immediately following the table of contents, a writer will include a list of figures if there are five or more included in the body of the report. This section will be separate from the table of contents beginning on its own page and will list them by title and will include their page number. Throughout the report itself, figures should be numbered consecutively throughout with Arabic numbers.

List of tables, abbreviations, and symbols: When these elements are numerous, they should be called out separately in their own section so that the audience can more readily comprehend the content of the report. This is especially true for technical reports and any content that might include many abbreviations and symbols.

Body

The information that you have gathered during your research or investigation will be presented, analyzed, and synthesized in the body section of the report. If the document is persuasive, then a recommendations section must be included and the suggestions offered should clearly and logically follow from the careful analysis. The body of a formal report will include the executive summary, an introduction, the text itself and any conclusions or recommendations.

Executive summary: This is a vital part of a formal report and is a high level view of the entire report condensed to approximately one page of text. This will often be read by high-level executives who want to understand the gist of the report without getting into granular detail. Thus, this section is aptly named executive summary. This portion should clearly describe the purpose and scope of the project and provide conclusions that detail any recommendations made.

The executive summary is often written after the entire report so that key and relevant material is included and nothing critical is forgotten. Keep in mind the executive summary is meant as a stand-alone document and should not contain confusing jargon, acronyms, or symbols left unexplained. This document should be comprehensible and complete without any accompanying material yet should still allow the reader to understand the findings, conclusions, and recommendations—minus the detailed descriptions that generated said findings.

Introduction: As it has already been described in previous sections of this textbook, the introduction should let the reader know why the report was written (purpose/opportunity/problem), what the report contains (scope), and what specifically will follow, and in what order. Essentially, it is here that the report is framed and forecast for the audience. This is another way of ensuring that the BLOT—Bottom Line on Top—has been successfully delivered.

Body Content and Strategies: The organization of this section will be determined by the purpose of the report, and generally this part will comprise the bulk of the report. A common organizational structure is SBAR.—Situation Background, Analysis and Results for an informative report and Recommendations for a persuasive document. But, again, a decision will have to be made as to the best way to structure the report for easy readability and the high skim factor. Headings and subheadings will be utilized to separate relevant sections. Be sure to use varying formatting conventions to designate differences between headings, subheadings, and sub-subheadings. The goal is always to make it easy on the reader to follow a logical and clear structure.

Tables, charts, and infographics can be used within the body to explain concepts, present data, or otherwise show complex material in a visual form. These visuals can also help to break up large bodies of text and provide much-needed white space for the eye.

Whatever organizational structure is chosen, the information should be clearly presented, analyzed, and synthesized with supporting reasons offered for the recommendations or conclusions. Again, if a recommendation is required, it should clearly be drawn from the analysis and the synthesis. Connections between the most important information should be concise and accurate and all results should be drawn from cogent analysis.

Conclusion/Recommendations: Depending on the purpose of this report, this final section will summarize the key takeaways and main points of the message. If the report utilizes a direct approach and an informative strategy, this section will reiterate conclusions that were asserted in the introduction and proved in the body. The key points should be wrapped up here in the same order as they were presented in the body. Remember that no new evidence or facts will be presented in the conclusion; the careful groundwork will all have been completed in the body of the report. Keep in mind this is your last chance in the document to drive home the purpose of the report in a compelling and complete manner.

However, if the indirect approach is used then the body, evidence and reasoning will lead to conclusions presented here in this section. If the strategy used is persuasive, the same goes for recommendations and suggestions: If the approach is direct, the conclusion will restate the recommendations from the introduction; if the approach is indirect, the conclusion will culminate in the recommendations for which a strong case has been built in the body. Finally, this is the place to direct the reader to take action and should clearly delineate next steps.

Back Matter

Following the main body of the formal report are the references (or bibliography) and appendices. Each of these should begin on their own page.

References: In alphabetical order and using proper formatting (i.e. APA, MLA) cite all sources used to create the report. Keep in mind that you should also list sources that were consulted but not directly cited in the report. This also gives the reader more resources from which to do their own research.

Appendices: An appendix is an additional section where documents, tables, questionnaires, and/or any other supplementary material is saved. Housing the extra material here ensures that the flow of the report is not disturbed and concision is observed. Items in the appendix are organized as Appendix A, Appendix B, Appendix C, etc. Each appendix should be begun on a new page and appropriately labeled at the top.

The following sample document demonstrates how many of the above elements were integrated into a formal report. As you will see, the authors elected not to list figures and abbreviations separately.

© Casimiro PT/Shutterstock.com

UNDER ARMOUR
FINAL COMMUNICATION PLAN
Team 18

Table of Contents

Under Armour, Inc.

Executive Summary 2

    Situation 2

    Background 2

    Analysis 2

    Recommendation & Response 2

Communication Plan 3

    Assessing the Past 3

    Evaluating Opportunities 3

    Moving Forward 4

    Communicating Effectively 5

        Executive Management 5

        Manufacturers 6

        Retailers 6

        Consumers 7

    Creating the Future 7

        Budget 7

        Timeline 8

References 10

Appendix 11

Executive Summary

Under Armour, Inc.

Situation

While Under Armour, Inc. (UA) is extremely successful in North America, the brand has had difficulty increasing market share on a global scale. This communication plan addressess potential opportunities for UA to alleviate this issue.

Below is an assessment of expanding UA further into the Brazilian market. The UA brand is synonymous with innovation and quality, and that already-established perception will allow the company to flourish as it takes the first steps into global expansion.

Background

Through extensive research of both the North American and Brazilian athletic apparel markets, the team has determined several key factors that will determine the success of this expansion initiative. Several crucial highlights are listed below:

- Brazil is the 7th largest rapidly-growing economy in the world
- 14% of manufacturing is locally sourced in Latin America
- Sport-centric culture creates a high demand for athletic apparel and footwear
- Competitors Nike and Adidas already have established presence in Brazil

With the positive forecasts for Brazilian market growth and the demand for athletic products high, our team has labeled Brazil as the top market for UA to consider while moving forward globally.

Analysis

Ultimately, the Brazilian market is a low-risk, high-potential opportunity for companies looking to operate in foreign countries, making it the ideal option for UA's imminent expansion. To determine the success of the communication plan, the team leads must assess the achievement of two goals:

- 200% increase in UA's share of the Brazilian Apparel and Footwear market
- doubled number of retailers committed to selling the brand

While the Olympics will provide an initial platform to judge our success, UA's Brazilian campaign will continue indefinitely as the brand gains momentum in the market.

Recommendation & Response

Research suggests the Brazilian market is an ideal place for UA's expansion, and the time to take advantage of this opportunity is now. The outline of the recommendations is as follows:

- Appropriate a budget of approximately $100 million
- Notify key stakeholders: Executive Management, Manufacturers, Retailers, Consumers
- Identify brand voice to unify UA across all markets, tailoring messages to stakeholders
- Assess plan success following 2016 Olympics before moving forward

Understanding Brazilian culture is crucial to the effectiveness of UA's communication plan. The UA Team is innovating, empowering, and rapidly expanding, and Brazil is the next step toward the company's further success.

Communication Plan

Under Armour, Inc.

The communications team compiled a series of recommendations based upon UA's mission to expand Under Armour (UA)'s presence in Brazil. This report includes an audit of the company's current issues, lack of global market presence, and concludes that the Brazilian market is a key step in creating a stronger brand presence worldwide.

The following recommendations will provide UA with the opportunity to understand our mission and determine the effectiveness of our research. The communication plan below reviews UA's past situation, current opportunities, and future potential, and explains internal and external stakeholders' needs for targeted messaging and effective channels. A budget and timeline are provided for each element of the communication plan.

Assessing the Past

In 1995, University of Maryland football player Kevin Plank began his mission to find the perfect blend of materials for athletic wear that would not become quickly soaked through with sweat during his workouts. Plank engineered his first prototypes after touring New York's Garment District and proceeded to give them away to his former teammates, many of whom held current contracts with NFL teams (Under Armour, 2015). He only had one request of those who received his garments: "If you love it, call me." (Under Armour, 2015).

Utilizing the feedback from his former teammates, Plank refined his prototype, quickly emerging with a T-shirt built from microfibers that wicked moisture and kept athletes cool, dry, and light. Plank charged the limit on all of his credit cards and was working out of his grandmother's basement for twelve months before he made his first sale: outfitting all of Georgia Tech's athletes in the Under Armour brand.

Since that breakthrough, UA has grown exponentially in both profit and market share, launching it to the second-largest athletic apparel brand in the United States (Mirabella, 2014). UA's top competitors are Nike and Adidas, with approximately 30% and 6% of the North American market share respectively (Mirabella, 2014). While UA surpassed Adidas in both revenue and American market share in 2014, the brand's general lack of recognition in foreign markets where its competitors dominate is a major issue.

Evaluating Opportunities

While UA's humble beginnings and the tale of CEO Kevin Plank's journey to success resonate well with North American consumers, the success story has yet to create a substantial impact on foreign markets (Gondo, 2015). However, our team recognizes an emerging market that caters to a variety of consumers with a similar appreciation for rags-to-riches stories: Brazil.

With an expanding middle class that accounts for 54% of the population, new brands looking to penetrate the market like UA will have no problem finding a consumer base (Gomes, 2015). Brazil is also ranked as the 7th largest economy in the world. Additionally, UA outsources 70% of its overall production, and 14% of the manufacturers can be found in Latin America (Sainte Croix, 2012).

One potential issue with the Brazilian market that may have scared UA off in the past is the country's high taxation on material goods. The Brazilian government charges a 35% tax on clothing sales, and payroll taxes consume approximately 42% of every employee's salary (Euromonitor, 2014). These levels of higher taxation will lead to increased price point on all UA products sold in Brazil. However, despite the 30–40% markup on merchandise, American companies such as The Gap have successfully maintained profitability while expanding into the Brazilian market (Euromonitor, 2014). Brazil's taxes may be high, but the economy is growing in comparison to growth around the rest of the world.

The Latin American Apparel and Footwear market grew 11% in 2013, while the market in the United States only grew 1.7% (Euromonitor, 2014). The country of Brazil is the largest apparel market in Latin America, accounting for 17.5% of total sales in the region (Euromonitor, 2014). Out of all Latin countries, Brazil places second in compound annual growth rate for sales at 4.3%, behind Chile at 8.7% (Euromonitor, 2014).

UA has already looked to China to expand. According to Forbes, the company has introduced an "experience store" into Shanghai (Forbes, 2014). This store is unique in that it allows the customers to see UA's story through videos. Plank wants to immerse the consumer in the story before they are marketed for the product. They currently have five stores with three more to come in China, although the overall market share remains relatively inconsequential.

As of now, UA has done little to publicize the possibility of expanding further on a global scale. Plank briefly discussed the immense potential in foreign markets and was quoted as saying, "Wherever we go around the globe, we will lead first with our story and bring the people into the best Under Armour experience possible" (Newswire, 2013). Despite this proclamation, UA's triumphant story is still unfolding, and Plank has yet to unveil plans for a foreign campaign. The communication team is prepared to provide UA with the next steps toward making the global "Under Armour experience" a reality, starting in Brazil.

Moving Forward

Now that UA's presence has spread throughout North America, it is time for the company to prioritize international sales as a primary objective. Since 2008, North America has been UA's primary business, as the market is responsible for generating approximately 96% of the brand's total earnings (Passport, 2015).

Since 2013, UA has developed a moderate amount of market share in the Asia Pacific region, primarily in China. However, as reported by Passport's graph of UA's Share in 2013 (See Fig. 1), Brazil did not accumulate any shares (Passport, 2015). While the country has a smaller number of net retail sales than China, our team has chosen to focus expansion in Brazil due to the fact that it has a lower risk for operation and is therefore an ideal environment for further growth (Cunha, 2015) (See Fig. 2).

UA can remedy the current state of market myopia by focusing on expanding the brand's presence in Brazil as opposed to remaining in solely North America and, minimally, China. Should expansion prove to be successful, UA expects to collect at least $6 million from Brazil in 2018 (Passport, 2015). This value would add to the company's overall revenue dramatically, as the Chinese market is less volatile and there would be lower profits with a less-diverse market range.

According to the Economist, Brazil is forecasted to have a five-year high in demand for apparel with a staggering $25.2 billion in 2017. Footwear is also seeing an increase in demand reaching $19.7 billion in 2015 with forecasts projecting a demand come 2017 (See Fig. 3). If we were to ignore the bourgeoning opportunity of expanding into Brazil, our company would overlook the chance to dramatically grow our global market share and revenue. Expansion would also increase UA's competitive edge, as competitors such as Nike and Adidas have already gone global and are flourishing.

An effective communication plan will help to align us with future stakeholders in Brazil. Cultivating those relationships will allow us to run a more efficient and profitable business in Brazil, and therefore increase our overall market share while building the framework for further global expansion.

In order for UA to succeed internationally, especially within Brazil, the company needs to understand Brazil's traditions and culture. There are differences between all five cultural dimensions, but the largest difference is the individualism versus collectivism dimension (See Fig. 4). Brazil scored low on individualism, and is hence considered a collectivistic country. Therefore, doing business in Brazil means that is important to build up trustworthiness and to create long-lasting relationships with consumers and other businesses. Compared to the individualism of the United States, Under Armour will need to learn how to gain Brazil's trust in order to succeed.

Communicating Effectively

Compared to its competitors, UA is a relative newcomer to the North American athletic apparel market. However, in the past decade, the company's market share has increased dramatically to 14%, which established it as the second-largest athletic apparel brand in the United States (Mirabella, 2014). This rapid growth has solidified UA as a household name domestically, but the opportunity to expand globally creates the need for a better understanding of other cultures in order to communicate successfully.

The key to communicating across cultures while maintaining a unified brand is to identify and implement a consistent brand voice. UA's most prevalent association in the North American market is that of the underdog: humble, innovative, and empowering. The company's mission is "to make all athletes better through passion, design, and the relentless pursuit of innovation," which is a goal that needs to be established in Brazil during expansion (Under Armour, 2015).

Each stakeholder requires a different pragmatic approach regarding these recommendations, the team intends on cultivating a universal brand voice and regulating message channels in order to promote the culture of unity for which UA is known. Below are descriptions of the four most crucial stakeholders for UA's expansion into Brazil and the tailored messages each will require as UA moves forward in this initiative.

Executive Management

The first step in this expansion plan is to notify UA's executive management at company headquarters in Baltimore. UA upper management consists of eight presidents, executive vice presidents, and officers who act as both the representatives and the decision-makers of the company (Under Armour, 2015).

In order to communicate with these executives most effectively, the communication team will schedule a formal announcement to be delivered by CEO Kevin Plank. The announcement will be in-house, but there will be a Skype link implemented should any of the executives be unable to attend.

The purpose of this meeting will be to maintain a feeling of common stake and ensure that each manager understands the next steps so as to better direct employees as the company moves forward. Additionally, by speaking in a more intimate environment, Plank will be able to continue cultivating the team-spirit mentality for which UA is known (Under Armour, 2015).

The message will focus on what is in it for the executives: specifically, how increasing the market share globally will positively impact UA's profits with minimal additional workload to the North American force, due to the implementation of a Brazilian communications team.

Manufacturers

The majority of UA's merchandise are developed by nonaffiliated third-party manufacturers, whose fabrics and finished products are inspected by UA to gain approval. UA manufactures primarily overseas, utilizing short-term contracts with fabric mills and factories to produce approximately 70% of all branded apparel (Morgan, 2015). As of 2014, UA's products were primarily manufactured in Asia, Central and South America and Mexico.

Currently, UA's Chief Supply Chain Officer and his team meet with each of these manufacturers on a monthly basis to review market performance, projected sales, and adherence to the company's standards of quality and ethics (Morgan, 2015). These manufacturers are crucial to UA's success in expansion, as the movement toward a global initiative and increased market share will require a much higher volume of product to be manufactured.

To inform manufacturers that an increased supply will be required with the renewal of their contracts, UA will send memorandums to the contacts with whom monthly meetings are held (See Appendix B). Our team has determined that sending memorandums as opposed to formal letters will acknowledge the current relationships that UA has with their manufacturers, and therefore encourage a positive reception of the request.

The approach to take with manufacturers will be to focus on what the increase in volume will mean for workers: primarily, the opportunity for more jobs and larger profits. The manufacturers who choose to renew contracts under the new workload will be able to continue working as a part of the UA team, and will enjoy the benefits that UA provides for its affiliates (Under Armour, 2015). Our team is adamant that this approach will encourage manufacturers to continue producing with UA and strengthen their commitments to producing quality product for the expansion into Brazil.

Retailers

In order to secure the potential sales of the UA brand to Brazilian consumers, we must first communicate our brand's value to several major retailers in Brazil. Without their full support, UA will be virtually unable to make strides in this new market. The three main retailers of interest are WalMart Brazil, Carrefour, and Casino Guichard, or, as it is known in Brazil, the "Extra Store."

The communication team will first send out a formal offer to all retailers in Brazil via letters to their corporate office (See Appendix C). After this initial step, the team will follow up with the most important companies by sending personalized representatives to engage protential partners.

The strategy throughout this contact with retailers will be to highlight what UA does better than competitors in ways specific to the Brazilian market. First, UA will communicate our lower price points in comparison to competitors such as Nike. This lower price point will appeal to retailers because the primary consumers of large department stores in Brazil earn between $687.69 and $1719.22 monthly yet have significantly growing purchasing power (Gomes, 2015).

To appeal to the retailers' internal business, we will reinforce the importance of our close-proximity manufacturing. Having factories within the area will make logistics easier and ensure full inventory of products, without the necessity of adding additional markups to compensate for tariffs. With this strategy, UA can grow the number of committed Brazilian retailers from 70 to 140 stores by the end of 2016.

Consumers

Because of their influence regarding UA's revenue in this new market, Brazilian consumers need to be aware of new products available to them before they can make purchases. As a company, UA must ensure that the brand is well-represented and have reached every potential consumer in each target markets. Additionally, it is crucial that UA remains unified in vision and voice across all markets, so as to remain true to the integrity of the brand.

In reaching out to consumers, it is critical to establish a friendly connection between the North American and Brazilian markets in order to unify the brand and generate a positive image in our new venture. To establish the connection, UA will expand current spokesperson Gisele Bundchen's job description to act as a foreign liaison between both countries.

UA will also expand our social media platforms to connect most effectively with new consumers. Brazil is currently one of the largest users of social media in the world, with approximately 98% of the country using Facebook as of this year (Chao, 2015). Using a variety of platforms and reaching out through a respected figurehead, will initiate strong relationships with Brazilian consumers that will benefit UA in the future.

Creating the Future

In order to successfully implement each approach to the stakeholders outlined above, UA must allocate a reasonable budget and abide by a strict timeline in order to make measures of success more accessible in the future.

Budget

UA has allocated roughly $100 million for our expansion into the Brazilian market (See Fig. 5). This money will be divided into four main parts: the Brazilian Communication Director, the Marketing Team, the Communication Plan, and the Ad Campaign. The communication director's salary will be $2 million with an additional $500,000 in benefits that will include health care, wellness and preventative, and life insurance.

The marketing team will be comprised of twenty people who will be paid $200,000 apiece in salary, totaling to $4 million. We also have provided our team with an additional million dollars to cover any materials needed in their research and development of our plan. For the Communication Plan, we have put aside $7 million to pay for any materials we will need for the plan and transportation needed to travel to and from Brazil.

The most expensive component for our expansion into Brazil is our ad campaign, which totals approximately $83 million. Projected cost for commercials in Brazil to be $50 million, which is the most expensive part of the ad campaign. Another facet of the campaign is the sponsorships of athletes in Brazil, currently costing us $30 million. Finally, $3 million will cover social media and billboards.

Timeline

As UA's presence gradually grows in Brazil, the 2016 Olympic Games in Rio de Janiero will give the company another opportunity to expand their brand presence both in Brazil and around the world. To achieve a successful outcome, our team has created an initial one-year plan called the Road to Rio (See Fig. 6). While we will assess the plan's effectiveness following the Olympics, UA will continue implementing communicative measures and advertising in Brazil indefinitely.

Milestones along the Road to Rio include our initial announcement, the start of the Olympics, and the end of the Olympics, followed by the assessment of the plan's success to date. We will begin implementing the plan on August 5, 2015, a year from the 2016 Olympics.

On August 5, Plank will address executive management in a formal meeting, while the communication team will send out memorandums to all current manufacturers. The subsequent meetings, press conferences, and technical development with both groups will last until September 5, 2015.

Beginning September 6, 2015, the team will send formal letters to potential retailers in Brazil and will work with logistics and transitioning the UA brand into each desired store. This transition will require approximately three months, during which time UA sales representatives will be acting as liaisons for any future assistance to the new retailers.

After informing each key stakeholder, we will deploy our exploration team to research Brazil's culture and market to the country. This will last from September 6, 2015 until May 13, 2016, which is about 8 months. Guided by research, design for the Brazilian advertisement campaign will take about 3 months. It will be finialized and revealed to the public at the Olympics and through the use of primarily television and social media platforms.

Finally, for assessment, the team will evaluate the campaign's success following the end of the Olympics. For instance, the analysis will determine if and how much UA's revenues and market share have increased. To consider this initiative successful, UA should realize a 200% increase in market share from an estimated .5% to 1.5% total Apparel and Footwear market share (Euromonitor, 2015). As of now, UA has such a small market share of the Apparel and Footwear market that it is not even listed among the companies currently operating in Brazil.

This communication plan is tailored to the needs of UA as the company seeks to increase profits and recognition on a global scale. Through research of the Brazilian market, this report identified the most effective methods for reaching out to both current and potential stakeholders and maintaining a consistent brand voice and image while immersing the brand in one of the world's fastest-growing economies.

References

Beekun, R., Stedham, Y., & Yamamura, J. (2003). Business ethics in Brazil and the US: A comparative investigation. *Journal of Business Ethics,* (42), 267–279. Retrieved March 2, 2018

Brazil In The Path Of A Sustainable Future. (2014). *Brazil in the Path of a Sustainable Future // Doing Business in Rio // 1.* Retrieved March 1, 2018, from http://www.ey.com/Publication/vwLUAssets/Estudo_Doing_Business_In_Rio_2014_EY_Brasil/$FILE/LR_doing_business_in_rio.pdf

Chao, L. (2018, February 4). Brazil: The Social Media Capital of the Universe. *The Wall Street Journal.* Retrieved March 3, 2018

Cunha, B., & Rodrigo, D. (n.d.). *Regulatory governance in Brazil: Inconsistent coordination, institutional fragmentation and halfway reforms.* Retrieved February 26, 2018, from http://regulation.upf.edu/exeter-12-papers/Paper.pdf

Export.gov—Welcome to Brazil! (n.d.). Retrieved from http://www.export.gov/brazil/index.asp Gomes, L. (2012, May 16). Brazil's business labyrinth of bureaucracy. Retrieved February 26, 2018, from http://www.bbc.com/news/business-18020623

Sainte Croix, S. (2012). *Middle Class Growth in Brazil.* The Rio Times: English. Retrieved March 2, 2018

Mirabella, L. (2014). Under Armour Launches Brand in Brazil. *The Baltimore Sun.* Retrieved March 2, 2018

Appendix A: Figures

Under Armour, Inc.

Fig. 1
Source: Passport

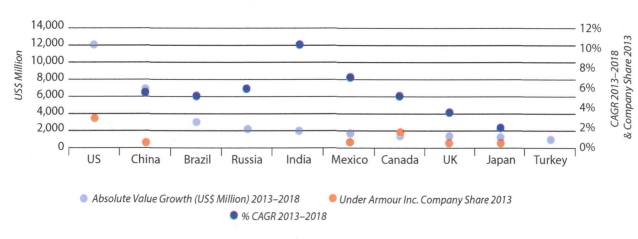

Under Armour Inc. in Global Sportswear:
Company Share in 10 Largest Markets and Forecast Growth 2013–2018

- Absolute Value Growth (US$ Million) 2013–2018
- Under Armour Inc. Company Share 2013
- % CAGR 2013–2018

© Kendall Hunt Publishing Company

Fig. 2
Source: Planet Retail

Fig. 3
Source: The Economist

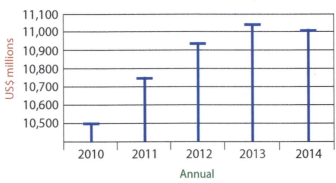

**Brazil—Footwear: Market Demand
(US$ at 2005 constant prices)**

**Brazil—Clothing: Market Demand
(US$ at 2005 constant prices)**

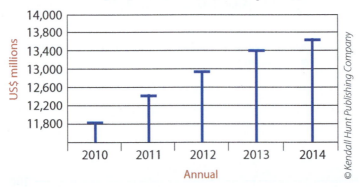

© Kendall Hunt Publishing Company

Fig. 4
Source: Beekun

Cultural Dimensions

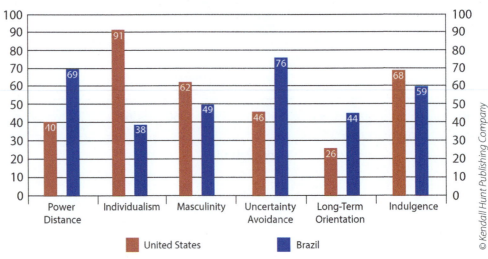

© Kendall Hunt Publishing Company

Fig. 5

Brazilian Com. Director
Salary	2M
Benefits	500,000

Marketing Team (20)
Salary	4M
Other Resources	1M

Communication Plan
Materials	5M
Transportation	2M

Ad Campaign
Commercials	50M
Billboards	1M
Social Media	2M
Sponsorships	30M
	97.5M

Fig. 6

Appendix B: Memo to Manufacturers

MEMORANDUM

Date: August 4, 2018
Subject: Development Expansion
To: Under Armour Manufacturers
CC: Under Armour Executives
From: Under Armour, Inc.

In our ongoing pursuit to expand into new markets, we are happy to announce our plans to enter Brazil, the 7th largest market in the world. With our increased commitment to this plan, your manufacturing operation will have the opportunity to maximize production and increase profits. In the following, you will find the key components to our proposal to introduce Under Armour into Brazil. We have identified them as increased labor efforts, production capacity, and ability to secure raw materials.

Labor

Our company requires that you seek out additional employees to keep up with this expansion. This could include temporary help, but employees who are dedicated in the long term are ideal. Ultimately, we would like to see you develop a strong labor force that will cut down costs in the long run. We see this expansion have a positive impact on your businesses. With increased demand for the products you provide, you will be able to employ others and improve the local economy.

Production

Our quality assurance managers will need to be assured that you are able to keep up production with the levels that we are predicting. We will assess your capabilities during next month's manufacturing meeting and would like to see you have an increase in productivity by 20–30%. This may involve more than one manufacturer simultaneously producing the same product(s). These expansions in production will allow your manufacturing plants to grow and become a thriving business.

Raw Materials

Along with labor and production, we will be looking at your relationships with your raw materials supplier. We would like to see the same effort as the previous challenges go into maintaining a strong relationship with the suppliers, thus allowing a steady stream of materials to the factory. We feel this is crucial to uphold the current demand as well as handling the influx of future orders.

Under Armour is excited to take on this new opportunity and are happy to have you with us. We will be staying in close contact with you over the next few weeks and make our final assessment on our next monthly meeting. Our company will continue to expect the same quality and service that it has received in the past. We see a lucrative future for everyone involved in this process, and we feel this is the beginning of an even brighter future for our collaborative efforts.

Appendix C: Letter to Retailers

Communication Director Under Armour
123 Plank Ave.
Baltimore, Maryland 82001

September 5, 2015

Nathalie Lafont
Casino Guichard
1, Esplanade de France
Saint-Étienne, Rhône-Alpes 42008

Dear Nathalie,

Under Armour, an established American athletic apparel company, has recently decided to expand brand efforts into Latin America, primarily Brazil. Knowing that Casino Guichard is one of the most successful names in Brazilian retail, it is important for us to extend an offer to you first.

We believe that our products can be a great addition to what is offered in your Extra brand storefronts. Having a relatively new and exciting brand to Brazil will prove advantageous for Casino in an extremely competitive apparel retail market. The team at Under Armour has identified three advantages that will prove us to be an invaluable partnership:

- A lower price point than competitors
- Proximity of manufacturing
- A committed support staff

Considering the lower income and tax regulations of Brazil, we understand the need for a lower-priced product. Under Armour offers many products that are of a much lower price point than competitors such as Nike. For example, a pair of Under Armour Men's HIIT Woven Shorts sells for $39.99, while comparable woven training shorts from Nike cost at least $65 on the brand's web store.

One reason we can ensure such low prices is because of our close manufacturing. 40% of our manufacturing is completed in Latin America. With such close proximity to your stores in Brazil, we will be able to cut logistic costs and in turn lower our price points. This will also make it easier for the Extra stores to have the correct product on hand.

It is the employees themselves that set our brand apart. After recently installing a Director of Communication for Latin America, as well as a full marketing team, we are ready to meet the needs of the market and your company. The Director and their staff's sole purpose is to tend to the needs of our Brazilian partners and will be able to help during the transition.

The Under Armour team would like to thank you for your time and consideration. We hope to work with you soon. To reach us, you can contact the Latin America marketing team desk at any time by calling (520) 990-3188.

Sincerely,

Communication Director

This concludes the unit on planning and composing your message. Research, planning, organizing, and writing are key elements to producing a professional document. As with any writing, proofreading and polishing are the final steps to ensure that the finished product is distribution ready and professional. Document design, accurate information, and readily accessible infographics contribute to a high-quality final product tailored to your specific audience.

Unit 2 References

Conciseness: Reducing wordiness in your writing. (February 2013). Purdue OWL—Online Writing Lab.

Purdue University. Retrieved from https://owl.english.purdue.edu/owl/resource/572/01/

Heath, C., & Heath, D. (2008). *Made to stick: Why some ideas survive and others die.* New York, NY: Random House.

Kamalani Hurley, P. (2007). *The you attitude and reader-centered writing.* Leeward Community College, University of Hawaii. Retrieved from: http://emedia.leeward.hawaii.edu/hurley/modules/mod2/2_docs/you_attitude.pdf

Oliu, W. E., Brusaw, C. T., & Alread, G. J. (2013). Writing that works: Communicating effectively on the job. Boston, MA: Bedford/St. Martin's.

UNIT 3:
Writing Strategies

Informative Messages

Much business writing falls under the category of direct messages. Later sections will explain persuasive and bad news messages, but this section will cover standard informative messaging in correspondence (email or letters) and in report writing.

It is important to note that informative messages do not make recommendations, suggestions, or otherwise offer the opinion of the writer. This is difficult for the novice writer, and some believe impossible for students. Notable grammarian and educator Jeffrey K. Pullum quipped, "No force on earth can prevent undergraduates from injecting opinion," (2009). That said, resist you must!

Overview

Informative messaging means just that: the message is meant to convey information. Common workplace informative messages range from reminding co-workers of a meeting to announcing a new addition to the building, detailing the plans for a merger, and so on.

ADVANTAGES OF WRITTEN COMMUNICATION	
Accountability	Mass dissemination
Goodwill and image building	Permanent record
Legal document	Suitable for long messages

© Kendall Hunt Publishing Company

Everyday emails are often informative. Most business professionals deal with email all day—both reading and writing them. These emails are often structurally similar. When a structure is understood, reading and writing becomes more effective. Letters have a standard salutation and closing; emails have a subject line and a greeting.

© svastika/Shutterstock.com

Figure 1

Written communication in business is vitally important. Think of the number of emails exchanged between co-workers, from management to staff, and from the C-Suite to the entire company. A company could not function without written communication. This is even truer in this technological age when virtual employees do not even go to a brick-and-mortar building. Face-to-face communication is not always possible, and written messages serve as efficient vehicles for coordinating, organizing, and disseminating information.

Some mistakenly operate on the principle that written messages are the same as verbal messages—only written down. The truth is that written language, often called "book language" is not the same as spoken language. People learn to speak before they learn to write, and this is true in every country and culture.

It takes many years for people to learn to write, and then another decade to learn complex grammatical and punctuation rules. In some countries, like Japan, approximately 2000 kanji (Chinese characters) need to be memorized in order to read a newspaper. Students in Japan have to learn 1000 kanji by sixth grade, so literacy is a much more daunting task in Japanese than it is in the English language.

Written speech differs from spoken language in many ways. One of the most important aspects of the written word is that it is permanent and serves as a record, a way to document exchanges. As such, these can be used in court or used during a performance review in the workplace. Since written messages can be retained forever, what and how you write can help you—or hurt you.

Spoken language is full of incomplete thoughts, repetition, and interrupters. When writing, the language used is naturally more formal and correct. When speaking to someone, there are more contextual clues to help navigate the import of the message. You receive clues from tone and body language, and any ambiguity can be cleared up in real time. Not so with the written word. When composing, you have to carefully consider this lack of context and strive for clarity and lack of ambiguity.

Clearly, writing requires a lot of effort and thought, and that is why it is essential to learn the fundamentals of good business writing.

Prewriting

First, the writer must ask him/herself questions:

1. Who is the audience?
2. What do they **already know** about what I'm writing?
3. What do they **not know**?
4. What do they **need to know**?
5. Would background information help the comprehension of my message?
6. Are next steps necessary to include?

Once you know to whom you are writing, why you are writing, and what the reader needs to know for your message to be fully understood, you need to determine the correct tone to use. Tone is often what identifies an inexperienced business writer: they either write too formally or casually. Determining the proper tone requires that you ask yourself some critical questions:

1. Am I writing up or down the chain of command?
2. Am I writing to peers?
3. Is my message going to upset people?
4. Am I on good terms with the person to whom I am writing?

Answering these questions honestly helps to determine the tone of your message; this is a critical step that should not be overlooked. In the workplace, a poorly worded message can damage your credibility and harm your chances for a promotion.

Structure

Once you have concluded the prewriting critical thinking described above, it is time to draft your message. Written business messages have standard formats. First, all business writing is single spaced, left justified, and paragraphs are demarcated with a space between paragraphs, not by indenting. This is also called standard block format. Paragraphs should be kept to fewer than eight lines—this means lines of text, not sentences. Longer messages will use headings and sub-headings, but more on that later in the section.

© VTT Studio/Shutterstock.com

Figure 2   *The internal structure of a written message is key to cohesion and flow.*

The introduction and conclusion paragraphs of direct informative messages are fairly formulaic. When communicating across companies, states, countries, and cultures, adhering to a standard allows readers to know what to expect and where to expect it. Standardization doesn't evidence a lack of creativity; rather, it increases the probability that your message will be efficient and effective.

By sticking to the structure, you reduce cognitive dissonance in your reader and increase the readability. How does this work? Stories, myths, and even jokes have three parts: a beginning, middle and end. Famous quotes often have three parts:

- *"Life, liberty, and the pursuit of happiness"*
- *"Government of the people, by the people, for the people"*
- *"Friends, Romans, Countrymen"*
- *"Blood, sweat, and tears"*
- *"Location, location, location"*
- *"Father, Son, and Holy Spirit"*
- *"Faith, hope, and charity"*
- *"Mind, body, spirit"*
- *"Stop, look, and listen"*
- *"Sex, lies, and videotape"*
- *"I came, I saw, I conquered"*

The human brain likes threes. Why? Neuroscientists studying Broca's region of the brain, the area responsible for language, have hypothesized that the area is responsible for language, action, and music as they share common syntactic-like structure (Fadiga, Craighero, & D'Ausilio, 2009).

In an article from *Psychology Today*, Dr. Norman Holland explains, "Broca's area may . . . organize putting one action in the middle of two others. Open the door; turn on the light; close the door. Broca's area may be what allows you to organize those three steps to go into a room."

When you write in concise sentences, short paragraphs, and use active verbs and direct, simple language, you are working with the brain's functioning and reducing the cognitive load. Since it recognizes patterns and the simplest pattern is three, business writing—at its simplest structure—is organized into three: introduction, body, and conclusion. Another way to describe it is by the old maxim: Tell me what you are going to tell me. Tell me. Then tell me what you told me.

Common Organizational Patterns for Informative Messages

There are many ways to effectively structure an informative message. Some of the most common are in the following chart.

CHRONOLOGICAL	SEQUENCE	COMPARISON	GEOGRAPHY/CATEGORY
Main points are sequenced in order of events to show the progression from start to finish of a series of events.	Main points are organized in the steps or sequence of a procedure or process.	Shows the advantages or disadvantages between two topics highlighting the similarities and/or differences.	Organized by grouping regions, states or countries or by topical categories like investments, sales, or profits.

Introductions

The introductory paragraph in a direct informative message tells the reader the point of the message. This is summarized by the acronym BLOT: Bottom Line On Top. This is achieved by incorporating four main points as described in the chart below.

The following is just one way to build an introduction with four simple sentences. Take it as a point of departure or, better yet, use it to break the dreaded "writer's block" by building your introduction one sentence at a time.

1. **CONTEXT/FRAME (FIRST SENTENCE)** Frame your document by describing the situation as best you can in one sentence. What led up to the writing of this document? What background information does the audience need to understand what you're about to discuss? How does the situation relate to the audience? Why should he or she care?

2. **PURPOSE/RELEVANCE (SECOND SENTENCE)** Now drop in your purpose statement. Why are you writing this document, and why are you sending it to this particular audience (rather than to someone else)? What is the most important thing you want your audience to know? This is a broad statement overviewing the content of the document.

3. **WIIFY (THIRD SENTENCE)** "What's In It For You," meaning the reader. Why should they read this? How is this going to help them? How can they use the information that you are giving them? Deliver the goods. Answer the question you raise in your purpose statement. What is the most important thing you want your audience to know? This can be the key takeaway from your research, a summary of your analysis, or it can be a recommendation.

4. **FORECAST (FOURTH SENTENCE)** Provide a road map. Specifically detail the topics that will be covered and in what order they will be presented. In a longer document, these topics can be used as section headings. The clearer the forecast, the easier to organize your document—and the easier it will be for the reader to find what s/he needs.

The goal of this paragraph is to tell the reader *about the document*, not to begin giving details from the body.

Think of it as a sticky note that you slap on a document, say a report, to let the recipient know what this particular document is. It answers these reader questions:

1. *Why is this on my desk/in my inbox? Remind me. Did I ask for it? (Frame/Context)*
2. *What is this about? (Purpose)*
3. *Why should I read this? How is it going to help me? (WIIFY)*
4. *What specifically is in this document? (Forecast)*

© PhotoMelon/Shutterstock.com

Figure 3

Practice: Introductions

Here is an example of a good introduction that includes all four necessary elements:

As we discussed in last week's meeting, our team will be producing a financial overview to assist in the introduction of our new fitness technology. This memo is primarily valuable for analyzing the financial impact that this technology could have on Under Armour by examining previous ventures into new markets. This document will provide financial information, highlight recent trends, and make predictions about new technologies.

Take a look at the following introductions and identify which of the four elements are missing:

A. *I am glad that we all made the decision to choose Tesla Motors Inc. for our BCOM group project preferred company. Please take time to review the information below, as doing so will be crucial to the success of our team at this year's Case Competition. Specifically, this document will analyze Tesla Motors Inc. management by first looking at its history, recent changes in strategy, and trends in Tesla management that will influence the future of the corporation.*

B. *This document contains information regarding the recent health scare that Chipotle has experienced, and it will explain the severity and condition of the situation. Staying informed will dictate Chipotle's action in the coming months, actions that will impact stakeholders and profits. Included in this report will be a summary of Chipotle's health awareness, the E. Coli situation, and Chipotle's permanent and useful solutions moving forward.*

C. *As you requested, our team finished this report about analytical people. Analytics fit well on a team with Amiables because they look for specifics and details that the Amiable often miss. In general, this report will reduce turnover rate and create a better work environment by explaining how best to work with an Analytic. You will find a lot of important information on this report about Analytics.*

D. *At our last meeting, you asked for an introduction of one of the styles in the People Styles book. After you read this introduction, you will understand how to work with the Amiable style of people in your company. Then, this document will illustrate summary of Amiable style, two keys to understand analytical style, and how the Amiables deal with other styles.*

Thus you can see the importance of a well-organized, to the point, clearly structured introduction. It sets up everything that is to follow, helps keep you on track as you write, and lets the reader know what to expect.

Conclusions

Because the structure of conclusions is so tightly tied to introductions, they are explained here before the body of the message.

The conclusion, like the introduction, should offer no new facts, data, or information on the topic covered in the body. It should summarize the highlights of the content. A conclusion also has a standard structure:

1. **RESTATE THE FORECAST (FIRST SENTENCE)** Take the last line—the forecast—from the introduction and repeat it here to remind the reader of the main topics that were just covered.

2. **REPEAT THE BLOT (SECOND SENTENCE)** Remind the reader of the gist of the content. Repeat the key takeaway. Keep this short and to the point. This is a broad statement highlighting the most salient information from the document.

3. **INVITE INQUIRY (THIRD SENTENCE)** It is always polite to let the reader know they can and should contact you if they have any questions or need anything further from you. You could also take the opportunity to remind them of next steps if that is relevant.

4. **PROVIDE CONTACT INFO (FOURTH SENTENCE)** Provide your contact information. Even if the reader already has this, it is considerate to include so that it is easy for them to either call or email without having to look up anything.

Here is an example of a well-constructed, concise conclusion that followed the example of the introductory paragraph in the previous section:

This document provided UA's financial information and detailed recent industry trends. It also provided predictions for the impact that new fitness technology could have. Please email me at teamalpha@email.arizona.edu or call me at (520) 555-1212 if you have any questions or concerns.

Practice: Conclusions

Read the following conclusion paragraphs and identify the missing and/or unnecessary elements:

A. *I hope that the previous sections provided a thorough overview of Chipotle's competitive environment in the food and service industry. Feel free to ask me any questions regarding my research, and share any other trends or opportunities for Chipotle that you have discovered.*

B. *Mattel is one of the strongest toy companies in the world, and have supplied fun for many generations. Though they may have had a down turn in Barbie revenue does not mean that were just going to stand by and let her get neglected. Mattel realized that the competitors were starting to develop an edge on them and if they wanted to get back in the game they were going to have to do some remodeling. After the renovation people have all different types of Barbie's to choose from. Will Barbie always be around? I would say at least for another 100 years. The reason for this is because Mattel's loyalty to their products. I believe this to be true because though there are fluctuations within the toy industry Barbie is a staple for Mattel and will continue to be.*

E. *Tesla's financial goal is to achieve long-term, sustained profitability. It is my opinion that Tesla Motors and its CEO Elon Musk have set themselves up to achieve these goals in the near future, and while their financial statistics are not promising in the short run, they show confidence in their company and promise of large amounts of growth in the long run. Feel free to contact me with any further inquiries you might have at teamtesla@email.arizona.edu.*

F. *Costco has seen tremendous success in Taiwan where it has little competition, a solid reputation, and solid profit numbers. Costco's success in Taiwan bodes well for expanding its operation into similar emerging markets like Brazil. I can be reached at goodemployee@costco.com or on my cell phone.*

Body

Whether you are writing a short memo or composing a long report, the introduction and conclusion can be written before the body. When you break writing down into the three sections, it is much easier to stay organized. Organizing according to this simple structure makes writing less of an exercise in creativity because you know what you will be writing about and in what order.

Body paragraphs contain the following elements: Claims, Evidence, and Reasoning, or CER. The opening sentence should make a claim of some sort. You can think of it as an umbrella covering everything that comes underneath. Next, you support your claim with evidence that offers proof of its validity. This is where you use information and data from research. Finally, you may bolster your claim by giving specific examples. The last sentence should quickly sum the gist of the paragraph by reasoning your way through it. You must make sense of the information so that your readers can follow your logic without having to sort it out for themselves.

You can skip this final summative/reasoning sentence if the next paragraph is going to continue on the same topic. If that is the case, you will want to begin the next paragraph with a transitional word or phrase to signal the reader that the same topic is being continued.

Here is a simple paragraph that clearly illustrates the structure:

Many factors contribute to a lowering of the water tables in city aquifers. (*claim*) *The removal of rock from mining operations, oil and gas extraction, and drainage of marshlands all lead to a problem called subsidence—the gradual sinking in of land. In Tucson, the fast removal of groundwater causes the water lower in the aquifer to be extracted. This lower level of water has a higher salinity, tastes worse, and costs more to extract. (evidence) Overall, subsidence is caused by a complex combination of factors and adversely affect water tables across the United States. (reasoning).*

Practice: Proving It

With each of the topic sentences below, list three pieces of evidence that provide proof of the claim.

A. *Many factors contribute to maintaining a healthy weight.*
B. *Artificial Intelligence is used in many common technologies.*
C. *Military transport and the power grid are hardened against the threat of an Electro-magnetic Pulse, or EMP.*

After a topic sentence, choose a support sentence, then explain it with more detail, and then give an example. Essentially, these get more granular, as is shown in the example below

Penguins come in many shapes and sizes.

   The Fairy penguin is the smallest on earth.

      Measuring only 16 inches tall, it lives in Australia.

         It comes out of the water at sunset to return to its burrow on Phillips Island outside of Melbourne.

Once you have crafted the introduction, body, and conclusion of your message, and you have edited and proofread it, go through the checklist below to make sure you have all the elements.

1. Framing statement
2. Purpose statement
3. WIIFY sentence
4. Detailed forecasting information
5. Claims at paragraph beginning
6. Information-filled paragraphs
7. Sufficient evidence, data, and examples in the paragraphs
8. Reasoning last sentence or transition to the next paragraph
9. Conclusion begins with a restatement of the forecast
10. Conclusion highlights the key takeaway
11. Message ends by inviting inquiry and giving contact information

Now that you are familiar with the structure of messages, it is time to describe some common types of workplace messages you might be asked to write.

Communicating to Persuade

The art of persuasion is an ancient one. Dating back to Aristotle, the line of argument, or the act of persuasion, is familiar to most of us. Any time you take a position to convince someone to change their beliefs, feelings, or actions, you are engaging in the art of persuasion. Unlike the informational approach, where your primary objective is to shape and present data, when you enter into a persuasive strategy, you are actively trying to drive or advocate a particular outcome. This is where things start to get a little complicated and a lot more strategic in design. Perhaps this is why persuasion is often considered more art than science.

Logos, *Pathos*, and *Ethos* were Aristotle's words for identifying persuasive appeals. In contemporary business contexts, these are still readily used, just under different names. Ethos refers to credibility, which depends on the degree to which your audience deems you trustworthy and competent. To influence others, you must impress them as someone who has a reasonable level of expertise or experience on the topic and has the audience members' best interests in mind. It is critical that both characteristics are present; having only one or the other does not work well in most situations. Imagine yourself as a salesperson when delivering a persuasive message.

CLASSIC PERSUASIVE APPEALS

Ethos (credibility): Appeals to author's competence and character

Pathos (emotion): Appeal to values and beliefs through emotional connection

Logos (logic/facts): Appeal to reason through proven facts and logic

Most customers do not want to buy from those they perceive as lacking a sense of honesty and character, no matter how well informed that seller may appear. If a seller seems like a very good person, but demonstrates clear deficiencies in content mastery, this, too, proves problematic for the buyer. The most influential communicators are solid in subject matter and sincere in their motives. This is second nature to some people, but for others, it may entail self-reflection, ethical discernment, skill development in self-presentation strategies, social cognition (awareness of others), or a combination of some or all of the above. Be strategic in your self-presentation; the quality and tone of your written communication directly affects others' perceptions.

To build a convincing message, you'll need to leverage a credible set of evidence relevant to the audience and the case you are making. Your ability to use logic (Logos) and reasoning is critical to creating a persuasive case. Howard Gardner (2006) describes seven "levers" or logical elements used in effective persuasive appeals. Why pull your sled uphill when you can start at the top and zoom down? When you select data, think of the levers as available tactics to persuade your audience. Logical arguments usually feature a well-balanced integration of claims, evidence and reasoning. The claim presents the assertion or proposition, and the evidence offers examples or cases from which the assertion was generated. Reasoning ties the two together by explaining how or why that evidence soundly supports the claim.

LEVERS

Gardner (2006) identifies seven factors or levers that influence and persuade.

1. **Real world events**—similar "real life" examples

2. **Reason**—logical discourse

3. **Research**—fact-based evidence gathered from credible sources

4. **Resonance**—value or belief-based framing and evidence

5. **Re-description**—multiple and varied representations of similar evidence

6. **Resources/rewards**—audience benefit

7. **Resistance**—reframed rebuttal

With data in place and a sense of credibility, you're ready to appeal to your audience's emotions and values. As a savvy consumer, you are probably highly aware when a marketing campaign appeals to your emotions. How does Apple produce all those "feels" around a product? Simple. They appeal to a consumer's emotions—loyalty, excitement, competition, etc. When you have a strong emotional attachment that drives you to purchase a product, you are succumbing to an emotional appeal. Emotions are a central feature of our existence, and they are influential in our decision-making processes. As a communicator, you must identify relevant emotional appeals and apply them in a balanced, ethical manner. Though powerful, emotional appeals are not adequate substitutes for credibility or logic.

When you put all the appeals together, you'll find that you have a substantial and powerful platform to convince an audience of your position. Your logical structure (another form of Logos) will support your ability to build and sustain your claims. In this instance, a strategic structural approach helps you to build a persuasive message. You can do this using a direct or indirect approach as illustrated in the sections below.

Identifying Types of Persuasive Messages

Persuasive messages are ever-present in your personal and professional communications, and you most likely receive and send them every day. Aside from the ever-pervasive advertisements encountered through web, mobile, and print media, persuasive appeals play a key role in daily decision making. They may range anywhere from asking to borrow a colleague's pen to pitching a multi-million-dollar deliverable to a potential client. Some common applications are listed below:

- Application for employment or promotion
- Proposal for a project or service
- Request for a meeting
- Request for information, support, or special consideration
- Letter of recommendation
- Consumer-targeted sales or copy messaging
- Critique or evaluation
- Recommendations to address a particular challenge

This above list is a small sampling of the types of business messages you may employ as a working professional. It is important to note that communication needs are dynamic and nuanced. Your skill in persuasion is a critical competency that will aid you in crafting appropriate, effective business correspondence and composing formal or informal reports and proposals.

Understanding Audience Responses to Persuasive Appeals

Based on your persuasive purpose, you will temper your message with politeness cues to demonstrate regard for your audience and, in turn, increase the likelihood of your desired outcome. Some requests, like one in which you ask to borrow a colleague's pen, do not call for high levels of persuasive finesse. Low-stakes requests—those that require little or no physical, mental, or emotional efforts from your audience—require little more than a brief and respectful line of text. However, the more complex and labor-intensive your ask, the greater care you must take in framing the message. Add to that factors such as whether the message is solicited or unexpected, consistent or inconsistent with audience values or preferences, and aligned with or contrary to your audience members' opinions, and you have a number of variables for which to account as you craft a correspondence or report.

Receptive Audiences

Receptive audiences are generally supportive of your purpose or interests. From the outset, you can expect little resistance or reservation when delivering your message; however, you should not take anything for granted or come across as entitled or assumptive. Such missteps are often avoided through skillful use of tone, which we will address later in this section. Receptive audiences are more likely to grant your request or adopt recommended actions.

Resistant Audiences

If your requested recommendations prove inconvenient or unimportant to your audience, your first challenge resides in motivating your recipients to first read your message. Unlike receptive audiences, resistant ones are less likely to take interest in your purpose. However, unlike receptive readers, resistant audiences are more likely to question your credibility.

Matching Approach to Potential Audience Response

Should you be direct, and come right out and say what you want in the first paragraph? Or, should you be indirect, and build your case before making your request? The difference between the two is where you place your bottom line. In a persuasive document, the bottom line is your request or your recommendation (also called your "ask"). What are you asking your audience to consider or do? If you expect little resistance, you can come right out and make your request in the first paragraph. But if you expect more resistance, you need to move your bottom line down and make your case first.

Using a Direct Persuasive Approach

Direct persuasive messages are most effective when addressing a receptive audience. You may also choose this approach if receivers are time-deprived or if you know they prefer direct communication.

Frame and Forecast in the Introduction

- Frame for your audience to provide context
- State your purpose—present the request
- Forecast information

Position and Present Rationale (Body)

- Provide evidence and reasoning for claims in well-tailored, logical sequence
- Anticipate reader's potential points of resistance and counter with credible facts that matter to them

Restate Request and Call Audience to Action (Conclusion)

- Make action or response convenient and immediate for reader with needed contact information and next steps

Direct Persuasive Introduction

The introduction of a direct persuasive message should follow the same basic "bottom line on top" structure discussed earlier in this chapter. First, provide some context to frame the document. State your purpose (present your request) in the first few sentences of your introduction, and then, forecast the key points of your message. Simple, right? In many ways, yes. However, the tone in your delivery plays an important role in whether even receptive audiences respond—more on that in a bit.

Direct Persuasive Body

The body of a direct persuasive message should explain or support your request. In the body, offer the audience supporting information, facts, details, or additional explanations to clarify your request or directive. This may include the reasons for your request or recommendation. Regardless of audience members' attitudes, you can create interest by highlighting how your proposed action will yield direct and indirect benefits for your audience. Additionally, you might counter potential points of resistance by emphasizing relevant facts to clarify key features of your proposal.

You will craft a great number of business messages throughout your career, and your ability to assess your audience and tailor your message accordingly is essential to building strong professional relationships and advancing your initiatives. Be strategic in the way you structure the body content. Like any other direct message, it should reflect a clear, logical, and accessible design; however, you must choose the appropriate sequence of information, level of detail, degree of formality, and integration of levers for each situation and audience. The table below notes some common organizational patterns associated with persuasive messages. These patterns may be adjusted or combined based on situational needs.

Common Organizational Patterns for Direct Persuasive Messages

There are many ways to effectively structure a persuasive message. Some of the most common are in the following chart.

PROBLEM/SOLUTION	SBAR	COMPARATIVE ADVANTAGES	TOPICAL
Main points are sequenced to first illustrate a problem or need, then offer a proposed solution to address expressed needs.	Main points are sequenced to present Situation, Background, Analysis, and Recommendations.	Main points demonstrate value of proposed action by comparing and eliminating alternative options.	Main points each address a key persuasive argument and are sequenced by author to highlight strongest claims.

Direct Persuasive Conclusions

The conclusion of a direct persuasive message should call your audience to action. You should begin by restating your request and you may briefly reiterate key benefits to your audience. To ensure you obtain the desired results, make the action convenient and immediate for your audience, with needed contact information or next steps. Depending on the urgency of your message and relationship with the recipient, you may provide a deadline by which he or she should respond.

Direct Persuasive Examples

The following examples illustrate how some of these strategies are applied in correspondence and informal reports.

Direct Persuasive Example 1: Response to Interdepartmental request for vendor recommendation.

To: Operations Management Team
From: Communication Strategy Team
Subject: Shipping Partner Recommendation
Date: February 3, 2018

Thank you for inviting the Strategic Communications team's recommendation regarding Fistbump's preferred shipping partner. In light of their shipping failures during last year's holiday season, we propose management discontinue service with Company X and have all orders fulfilled through a different logistics company. We share in your interest in providing customers with efficient, dependable service, and we are confident this transition will help us avoid future issues and improve the Fistbump experience for our customers.

Introduction frames the message, states the ask, and forecasts the problem/solution sequence

Highlights senders' and audience's shared values.

Last holiday season, Company X failed to meet delivery deadlines for over one third of all orders placed in December and January. Our credibility suffered as retailers resorted to using their own funds to issue shipping discounts, and many disappointed customers expressed their frustration through popular social media platforms. Unfortunate events like the holiday shipping breakdown require a quick recovery, and by taking active steps to prevent future incidents, we communicate our dedication to total customer satisfaction.

Explains problem, demonstrates need

Selecting a new shipping partner will

- Reduce costs associated with shipping refunds and product returns

- Demonstrate Fistbump's commitment to convenience and consistency

- Improve Fistbump's reputation on social media and company review sites

- Maintain Fistbump's loyal customer and retail partner bases

Presents solution and related benefits

Applies bulleted list design to draw attention to benefits

These benefits are meaningful and they may outweigh some or all of the costs related to securing a new shipping contract.

In the interest of our continued growth, the Communication Strategy team advises management to designate a new preferred shipping partner to underscore Fistbump's credibility and commitment to customer satisfaction. Please contact us at stratcomm@fistbump.com with questions or concerns, and keep our team informed of your decision.

Restates the ask and appropriately calls audience to action

To: Have Mina
From: Intern
Subject: WebStore's Holacratic Shift
Date: February 3, 2018

Thank you for providing me with the readings on Holacracy and for requesting my perspective on Web-Store's choice to adopt this unconventional organizational style. This analysis is intended to assist you in communicating this concept to clients. Though WebStore's move to Holacratic management caused some confusion, it was ultimately a good choice for the company. The new management style fits the WebStore.com vision, aligns with most of their already successful practices, and serves to create a more cohesive employee base.

Holacracy Fits the WebStore Culture

WebStore is known for its corporate counter-culture. According to the *Atlantic*, the company has a reputation for unconventional work practices. For instance, they offer each new hire four thousand dollars to reject the job offer. This is one of many quirky yet strategic moves designed to hire and retain dedicated, like-minded employees and create buy-in from its members. Given WebStore's already unique approach to business, it may be the perfect environment in which to test new management designs.

Holacracy is Not Radically Different from WebStore's Former Management Policies

According to Steve Denning of *Forbes* magazine, Holacracy is not a dramatic shift in organizational hierarchy; rather, it is simply a new approach to managing those hierarchies. Denning argues that despite role shifts, like the elimination of the word "manager" from job titles, people still operate in managerial capacities. The shift from more inclusive language may serve to encourage a culture of openness and accessibility more than it serves to change leadership roles. The new approach does not radically alter WebStore's business model, but it does introduce a new frame for how work is described.

Holacracy May Increase Employee Commitment

When WebStore's CEO, Carrie Ma, announced the shift to Holacrocy, she asked employees to adopt the practice or take advantage of a three-moth severance and healthcare package to find a job about which they could be passionate. *Business Insider* magazine reported that a large number, thirty percent, opted to leave the company. Though this caused widespread skepticism among investors and analysts, it is too early to assert the exodus was a negative consequence. It is very possible that this process eliminated unen-thused, under-committed, or uninterested employees and maintained a core of high-performing workers better suited to help WebStore grow.

Though controversial, WebStore's decision to adopt Holacracy was a bold choice that will likely benefit the company in the long run. WebStore is a great testing ground for new practices, and the shift is not as profound as it seems. This transition caused some concern, but it helped them retain a solid core of dedicated employees. This case demonstrates that WebStore's shift to Holacracy was the right choice. Thank you for the opportunity to share my thoughts on this interesting case study. Please contact me if I can provide any additional information.

Introduction frames message, states position, and forecasts main points which are arranged topically.

Author integrates a WIIFY (what's in it for you) statement to bolster purpose.

Author uses headings to highlight key claims.

Author attributes information to sources.

Conclusion restates claim, summarizes main points, and includes an appropriate call to action for the nature of the message.

Using an Indirect Persuasive Approach

If any of the following are true, consider using an indirect strategy:

1. Audience has not asked you to prepare this document for them;
2. Your request requires audience members' time, energy, or resources;
3. You are not sure whether they will agree with you;
4. You have reason to believe that they will disagree with you;
5. You want to play it safe and build your case before you make your request.

If your document is unsolicited and you are not sure that your audience will agree with you, then take the indirect approach and build your case before making your request. When in doubt, use the indirect approach. The next two parts of this section will help you organize your document successfully and sequence the information you need to present.

The indirect approach to persuasive messaging requires a bit more skill and finesse. This type of a message usually requires some advance planning to truly align with your audience and position your reader to act. Use an indirect approach in persuasive messages when addressing a potentially resistant audience. This kind of message is often developed using the AIDA strategy.

AIDA (A STRATEGY FOR INDIRECT PERSUASIVE MESSAGES)	
ATTENTION & ALIGNMENT	Build common ground with the audience by referencing common values. Pique interest with an engaging audience-centered appeal.
INTEREST & INFORMATION	Create a sense of interest by offering relevant information and details; set the stage by supporting your impending request.
DEFLECT RESISTANCE & DISCUSS DIRECT BENEFITS	Anticipate points of audience resistance, and counter with information. Identify and express how your request will benefit the audience directly.
ACTION	Make your request for audience action. Provide immediate opportunity for audience response.

Most audiences are very sensitive to a "sales" approach, and your tone can inadvertently cause the audience to resist your message or question your credibility. A flat out "sell" makes most of us suspicious. AIDA strategy helps you present content in a compelling, persuasive manner by sequencing your information strategically.

Introduction

Alignment and Attention

In your first few sentences, get the audience's attention by building common ground. Refer to shared values and interests, mention a commonality, or compliment them on a recent achievement. Be sincere and balanced in your approach. If you seem excessively complimentary or overly familiar, your recipient may interpret your statement as inauthentic. To effectively align with your audience, focus on them and avoid trite, meaningless clichés. Most importantly, do not reveal your request—the indirect approach places the bottom line on bottom, i.e., toward the end of the message. Before you make your "ask," you must build your case by presenting information and direct benefits.

Body

Interest and Information

In this section, present information about your product, service, or situation. Make it relevant for your reader or listener, and highlight details that will likely interest them. Remember, you haven't yet revealed your request; you are presenting data to help your audience understand your product, service, etc. In the next section, you will explain how your product, service, etc., directly benefits your audience members, so provide a basis on which you can make such claims.

Be specific in your description and again, frame the information to the interests of your audience members. Use descriptive language and provide details that may pique the audience's interest. This section should support the next part of your message: direct benefits and resistance deflection.

Direct Benefits and Deflection

Before you present your request, explain how your product or initiative will benefit your audience, and do your best to pre-emptively quell their potential concerns. To do this successfully, describe what readers or listeners will gain by supporting or complying with your yet-to-be-revealed request. Think about it from your audience members' perspectives; explain what is in it for them, not what's in it for you or your company.

Focus on how the information benefits audience members personally. What's in it for them? Indirect benefits like saving the company money rarely inspire action. In addition to discussing direct benefits, use this section to deflect points of resistance.

Once again, think from your audience members' perspectives. Are there potential points of resistance or areas of concern that could cause opposition? If there are points of resistance to anticipate (and deflect), you'll want to be careful not to make over-stated assumptions. Nothing puts off a reader faster than an assumption you make about their thinking, and you can accidentally plant more points of resistance. For example, "You might think the price point is a little high . . ." When in fact the audience wasn't thinking that at all; after receiving your message, however, you can bet they are now. Frame deflection statements in a positive tone, and minimize the inconvenient or undesirable facets of your plan.

Be strategic in your approaches to alignment, information, direct benefits and deflection. These steps lead into the final element of your message: the request for audience action.

Conclusion

Action

Now that you've aligned, informed, deflected resistance and identified direct benefits, you can finally make your request and call your audience to action. The bottom line—your "ask"—should appear for the first time here.

Make the actions as easy to carry out as possible. Think about the strategy of the car dealership that sends out keys to everyone in the community with the message "Come on down on

Saturday. This key starts one of the cars on our lot—if you find it, you'll win the car!" With a key in your hand, you might be more inclined to drive on over and give a car a test drive (which was probably the real intent of the message in the first place). Be thinking about making the next step to "yes" as easy as possible for your audience.

You don't need a fancy giveaway or a fun prop to make your action easy and immediate. Present your request, then tell your audience how and when you'd like a response. It is critical that you make this step clear and provide all the necessary information and resources to facilitate your readers' next steps. Avoid uncertain, vague calls to action.

Indirect Persuasive Example 1: Request for financial support

Tina Van Smith
66 Big Train St
Tucson, AZ 85721

February 2, 2014

Mayor Colin Kline
1 City Hall Square
Tucson, AZ 85701

Dear Mr. Kline,

On behalf of orgnaization X, we congratulate you as the new Mayor of Tucson. We appreciate your dedication to the growth, safety, infrastructure, and people of Tucson. Organization X also cares about the enrichment of Tucson residents. I am writing to introduce you to our new membership program catered to lover-income patrons.

> *Alignment – presents a common goal and gives the reader a reason to keep reading.*

This lower-income patron membership program aims to reduce crime rates in Tucson, but enriching the lives of Tucson residents through exposure to the arts. Research has shown that poverty is directly related to crime. Tucson has a high poverty rate of over 20%; this program is an opportunity to reduce the poverty and crime rates in the city. This initiative will allow lower-income patrons to have the opportunity to be better involved in the Tucson community.

> *Information – provides key information based on the audience's needs and wants.*

Enriching the lives of Tucson residents will also lead to positive publicity for you. In turn, more people will be educated about your initiatives and will want to support you. Your support of these efforts will allow you to become a more proactive figure in Tucson. Most importantly, through this venture, Tucson will become a better city.

> *Direct Benefit – shows reader what they can gain.*

We would like to partner with you on this new program. In order to make this iniative a success, we need funds to subsidize discounted membership rates for lower income patrons. We ask for your assistance to help underwrite this program. Please email me at director@artsong.com for more information. I look forward to hearing from you soon.

> *Call to Action – makes ask and provides next steps.*

Sincerely,

> *This students uses a letter to send an indirect persuasive message to an individua outside the writer's organization.*

Indirect Persuasive Example 2: Wellness program participation encouragement message

28 December 2017

BeWell, Inc. Employees
90 E First Ave
Rahway, New Jersey, 07165
(908) 423-1000

Dear BeWell Team Members,

As a company, we constantly strive for a healthier future. Every day, we take part in improving the health and well-being of people around the world. Just as we enhance our customers' lives, we support your family's healthy lifestyle habits. A healthier body and mind has been proven to create higher levels of happiness and satisfaction in and outside of work. As we aspire to be the best healthcare company in the world, we want to provide you with the healthy work-life balance you deserve.

Every year, more and more people incorporate physical activity into their daily schedules. Since 2013, physical fitness has increased among adults in America. This comes as no surprise; people who live healthier are happier, longer living, and suffer from fewer health-related issues (Hyber, 2017). The Employee Wellness Program (EWP) at BeWell offers you and your family completely free memberships to a select group of fitness centers. Membership to these centers includes access to gym equipment, exercise classes, and nutrition consultations with on-site dieticians.

Not only does BeWell's EWP better your health, it provides a return on your investment. Apex Health, company similar to our own, saved $120 million on healthcare costs in ten years as a result of their EWP. The money we save from our EWP can be allocated to employee reward programs. For instance, savings can be applied to increase base vacation time or enhance other incentive programs. Earning another vacation day is much better than taking a sick day.

More than anything, BeWell cares about the improved well-being of each and every one of our employees. Our Employee Wellness Program benefits your family and our BeWell family as a whole. We want you to be happy with yourself, your health, and your work-life balance. Start the new year out with a free gym membership and commitment to regular exercise. Please visit BeWellemploywellness.com before January 15th to register for the EWP. It's time to start living right—we are all in this together.

Be Well,

Human Resources Department
BeWell & Company, Inc.

Annotations (left margin):

- Builds common ground by expressing shared values
- Demonstrates regard for reader and readers' families
- Recognizes reader's needs and entitlements
- Provides information relevant to upcoming "ask," and highlights points of interests for audience
- Presents direct benefits
- Call to action is clear, easy, and immediate

Tailoring Your Tone for Persuasive Messages

In this text, we often refer to framing as a means of contextualizing your document; however, framing—the perspective from which you tell a story—carries through your entire message and quietly informs your reader about you as an author. It provides key data points for readers as they assess your credibility: your competence and your character. Attend to both what you say and how you say it; consider what your message implies about your intentions and priorities. Frame your message and mind your manners; poorly executed tone will undercut quality content.

Avoid Implied Entitlement

It is very off-putting when communicators make assumptions. In the example below, the author requests, or in the pre-revised message, demands an informational interview with a relative stranger.

Before Revision

Hello Freda,

I asked Jeff to connect us because I am very interested in consulting. I am a second-year MBA student, and I am looking for a position with an established firm. Given your career path, I'm sure you have valuable tips and insights I can use in interviews. I would like to set up a quick, fifteen-minute call so I can ask you some questions about your experience in the field. My first interview is in a week, so I need to talk before next Thursday. Thanks so much. I look forward to hearing from you soon.

Warm Regards

- Lacks "you" attitude
- Self-centered perspective
- Ineffective attempt to lessen inconvenience as sender already assumes reader will comply
- Presumes reader will agree
- Insincere
- Undeserved expectation of prompt response

After Revision

Hello Freda,

Thank you for accepting my LinkedIn invitation. I am a friend of Jeff Carol's, and he speaks very highly of you and your work in project management. As a second year MBA student, I am focused on furthering my knowledge of the field and developing an industry-relevant skillset. Having read and enjoyed your white paper on best practices, I am exceedingly interested in your approach. Your system for team reporting exemplifies a shrewd combination of convention and creativity. If you are willing and your schedule permits, I would greatly appreciate an opportunity to learn more about your experience as a successful project manager. Please let me know if you are open to a fifteen-minute phone or Skype meeting in the near or distant future. I realize your time is valuable and imagine it's very limited, so I appreciate your consideration either way.

Warm Regards,

- Intro demonstrates appreciation, builds common ground and rapport
- Sender implies genuine interest and demonstrates author's intellectual curiosity
- Thoughtful recognition of reader's work
- Request is framed as a request, not a demand
- Recognizes importance of reader's time and energy

Respect Readers' Autonomy

Few people enjoy being told how to think, and fewer appreciate having their decision-making power reduced to someone else's orders. Do not lead your audience with a heavy hand. Instead, recognize their agency as free thinkers. Compose a quality argument, and let the reader draw his or her own conclusion. As well, avoid implicit messages that assume your readers' thoughts, preferences, or values.

Before Revision

Arrogantly assumes sender will dictate audience response

Unnecessarily presumptive and self flattering

Reject's readers' right to draw their own conclusions

> This proposal is submitted in response to the Development Team's call for suggestions, and it will convince you to choose a cloud-based service for our data storage. I have conducted ample research to help you decide this is the best choice for our company's needs.

After Revision

Demonstrates due diligence on the author's part

Objective tone boost's author's credibility

Acknowledges recipient's key concerns

> After a survey of relevant materials and consideration of available options, I composed the following recommendation to address our data storage needs. All potential solutions present benefits and drawbacks; however, my research suggests cloud-based storage is our company's best option for logging data, ensuring security, and providing employees a user-friendly interface.

Before Revision

Gross generalization

Unfounded assumption

Another gross generalization and hasty assumption

> We all love smartphones. In fact, you use yours so often you probably can't remember what life was like before you had one. Everyone knows that an investment this important should be protected, and that is why we created Prosurance—the most comprehensive insurance available for smart phone owners.

After Revision

Statement is more reasonable in its reach: It does not speak for all people or readers

Dramatic generalization more acceptable given the attribution to some, not all people

Invites audience to identify with this group and may spark interest in info to follow

> Some people love their smartphones so much that they don't want to think about living in a world where phone, camera, game, email, text, video, and web browsing capabilities require access to more than one device. We created Prosurance for those people. It's the most comprehensive insurance available for mobile device owners, and it assures users they'll never go a day without their smartphone.

Maintain an Objective Tone

Your message is only as effective as your audiences' perceptions of your credibility. Even when addressing a receptive audience, it's important to maintain an objective tone. Readers may question an author's authenticity, trustworthiness, and even intelligence if the message lacks a sense of balance or poise.

Before Revision

Clearly, Maya thinks she shouldn't have to do her fair share of the work. She prefers to skate by on her likable personality and let her teammates pick up the slack. Our organization should not reward this kind of thinking, as it contributes to lowered morale among our high performers.

Presumes to know and proceeds to judge Maya's internal thoughts and motivations

Personal attack based on assumption

Again, claims to understand Maya's thoughts and motivations

After Revision

Based on her peer evaluation results, it appears Maya's teammates enjoy her personality but perceive her contributions to the team as inadequate. Evaluators reported feeling inconvenienced by her lack of follow-through and frustrated by her inconsistency. My analysis indicates Maya is not ready for a leadership role at this time.

Cites data and does not draw conclusions about Maya as a person

Provides basis for claim

Avoids personal attacks and relies on data, not personal opinion, to drive recommendation.

Make the Ask

If you are going to ask for something, make it count. Whether you choose a direct or indirect approach, make sure your audience has a sense of what you'd like them to do. If you are drafting a persuasive message, you've decided to make a request or a recommendation, and you have done so after analyzing your audience and confirming the appropriateness of your appeal. Sometimes, writers strategize a fantastic persuasive message, but let the air out of its effectiveness by closing with a weak or ambiguous request.

Before Revision

Good sentiment and appreciative tone

Thank you for supporting our effort to provide quality educational materials to children in our community. Your contributions ensure every elementary school student has the resources needed to recognize their dreams and build a brighter future for us all. We hope you will make a donation this year.

Vague, ineffective ask

After Revision

Thank you for supporting our effort to provide quality educational materials to children in our community. Your contributions ensure every elementary school student has the resources needed to recognize their dreams and build a brighter future for us all. Please renew your annual gift of $100 today by visiting www.donate.com/donate. With your help, we can meet our fundraising goal of $15,000 before June 11th.

Specific, immediate, convenient ask and call to action

Whether composing routine correspondence or reports, this chapter offered you strategies and organizational schemas for structuring your messages. By choosing the correct approach, your written deliverables will be on the mark and will showcase the professional level of your writing.

Delivering Negative News

Conveying an Unwelcome Message

The world of business is full of ventures, triumphs, and failures. Though we try our best to avoid the latter, delivering negative news is a skill critical to competent professional communication. If it is done poorly, the consequences can be significant, rippling out beyond the original recipient to other stakeholder groups and destroying trust and loyalty. However, if a writer prepares his reader for impact and demonstrates empathy, the business relationship may even be strengthened in spite of the unwelcome news. The old saying "what goes around, comes around" is not something a company can take lightly, so it is important to remember that how news is delivered is often just as important as the news itself.

First and foremost, a company should consider how decisions made will impact everyone involved. Conducting a stakeholder analysis specific to a new policy or corporate decision can help a business anticipate resistance or negative fallout and move forward accordingly. If a company is to operate ethically and maintain credibility, it must ensure it is meeting the needs and expectations of all stakeholders involved.

A stakeholder analysis includes the following aspects: identifying specific individuals and groups who might be affected, understanding how they are affected, anticipating how their reaction may impact the company, making decisions, and determining a communication plan based on this analysis. The following table shows one way to organize this analysis. The list might be limited to one or two groups, or it may include a dozen or more depending on the situation, but a smart business considers ripple effects as well as immediate and obvious responses.

STAKEHOLDER GROUP	IMPACT ON THEM	THEIR IMPACT ON US	COMMUNICATION PLAN
1.			
2.			

Consider the following example of a company that learned this lesson the hard way.

NETFLIX

On September 19, 2011, Reed Hastings, CEO of Netflix, made a decision without considering his stakeholders. In a blog post on the company's website, he announced that the combined DVD and Streaming service the company had been offering would be split into two separate companies. Netflix would provide streaming services and Quickster would provide mail-out DVD service. (Quickster, 2011)

This, of course, meant two separate accounts as well as an increase in cost if a customer wanted to maintain his/her current level of service. While this seemed like natural evolution for the company, it didn't sit well with some previously loyal customers.

The company lost over a million subscribers over the next few days and stocks plummeted.

Three weeks later, on October 10th, the decision was reversed. In fact, the tone with which Mr. Hastings communicated to the public was quite different. He acknowledged his rashness and overconfidence based on previous success, opening with the simple statement, "I messed up . . ." His message went on to basically acknowledge that they had moved too fast and should have listened better to their customers. In an unusually swift reversal, Netflix announced its decision to keep its DVD-by-mail and online streaming services together under one name and one website. "We underestimated the appeal of the single website and a single service," Steve Swasey, a Netflix spokesman, said in an interview, adding: "We greatly underestimated it." (Stetler, 2011)

How could Netflix have handled the situation better? In this unit, we will discuss the importance of analyzing your audience, both primary and secondary, before delivering negative news. We will also look at ways to convey unwanted news in a more appropriate manner. It's all about taking the time to understand the impact on your reader(s) and demonstrate genuine empathy. Delivering bad news does not have to produce poor results.

Let's first identify other situations in business where negative news must be conveyed. As you skim through the list of examples, think about how you might react to each one. In some cases, you might feel mildly agitated at the news, but not necessarily upset. Other situations may elicit stronger reactions of fear and/or anger. We'll talk more about these natural reactions in the next section.

The following list contains types of bad news messages that are common in business. While these are necessary events, it is important to look beyond the decision you have made and to establish what your desired best outcome would be.

Types of Bad News Messages

Negative information can take many forms, including:

- Rescheduling an appointment
- Saying "no" to a request
- Rejecting a proposal or an application
- Demoting or terminating an employee
- Denying a claim
- Announcing a recall
- Declaring a crisis

You can certainly think of situations in the news or in your own experience where a company had to deliver negative news like the examples in the list. In some cases, the audience or recipient of the news may simply make a change to his/her calendar and move on with little hesitation. If this is the case, the one delivering the bad news can simply deliver the news directly. However, if the news is likely to create resistance, or worse, an indirect approach is in order. Here, we'll focus on the second and third columns of our stakeholder analysis. We will also delve into the world of psychology. After all, business is all about people, and the most successful will have a good understanding of human nature. There are two types of reactions that will help determine how a message should be communicated.

Understanding Audience Reaction to Bad News

As discussed in the previous chapter on persuasive messages, there are generally two types of audiences for bad news messages too.

- **Receptive**—news is inconvenient but acceptable
  May feel annoyed and respond disapprovingly, but will likely comply without incident.
- **Resistant**—news is damaging or disruptive
  May experience fear and panic and exhibit either a fight or flight response.

Identifying Resistant Audiences

In this section, you will learn how to identify when an audience may be resistant to what you are writing.

First, it is necessary to understand a little about what people most value and are most afraid of losing. Looking at the triangle depicting Maslow's Hierarchy of Needs (Maslow, 1943), we can see 5 levels of human needs and why each is important to our existence. The most basic needs are those we cannot live without, such as air, water, food, etc. Even these most basic needs can be threatened by employment status or other professional situations.

Employment is specifically mentioned in the second level, along with personal and community well-being. In order to feel "safe," people must have adequate resources for themselves and their families and be in relatively good health. An employer is instrumental in helping individuals achieve these goals. Salary ensures the ability to purchase basic necessities, and company health insurance provides a means for maintaining good health and treating illnesses.

Figure 1

In the fourth level, we see the need for both self-esteem and respect from others. These are closely related to an individual's financial situation. Having gainful employment gives a person a sense of pride, as well as security. What happens when a person feels his or her needs and values are being threatened, and what might that mean in the workplace? What about a customer applying for a loan from his/her bank or someone applying for a job? If the answer they receive is positive, they'll experience a sense of relief or contentment. However, if they receive a negative answer and it is perceived as a threat to their needs and values, their emotions may range from depression to resentment.

The Two Most Common Responses to a Threat are Fight or Flight

If an employee feels his or her safety or self-esteem are being threatened, the first response might be to fight back. This may result in arguments between co-workers and mistreatment of customers. This anxiety will most likely be evident in a significantly reduced job performance and may affect employee morale throughout the workplace. It may also result in lawsuits and negative publicity.

The second type of response to a perceived threat involves "flight" or avoidance. Some people do not like to confront a problem directly; instead they complain to co-workers or argue over unimportant matters, while avoiding the real issue. This response, like the fight response, can cause anxiety in those around the person, resulting in a negative work environment and may lead to a negative corporate image.

In business, there are many situations that can cause people to feel their self-worth or livelihood is being threatened. In most cases, a person is informed of the situation in some type of written message. Since negative news messages may elicit a fight or flight reaction, it is essential to identify how a reader will respond in various situations and adapt our communication regarding the issue.

Writing the Bad News Message

Now that you can more easily identify and understand the responses your readers may demonstrate, we will look at how delivering written news either directly or indirectly can help create messages that will be more easily accepted. First we'll look at delivering this type of news with a direct approach; then, we'll take a close look at communicating negative news with an indirect approach. Of course, the approach you take should match potential audience reaction.

Direct Approach: Delivering Negative News

If your audience will likely be accepting of the news or if the news is urgent and requires an immediate response, follow a direct approach. Sometimes, a situation calls for a direct, immediate message. Imagine a car company needing to inform the public about a critical product recall, or a food chain needing to warn consumers of contaminated ingredients: time is of the essence, and clarity is essential. In this instance, the audience needs the information delivered directly.

Here is the pattern for a direct bad news message:

DIRECT BAD NEWS: DO IT RIGHT!

1. **Establish Rapport and State the Bad News**

   Use the You Attitude!

   Pull off the Band-Aid™!

2. **Explain the Reasons**

   Present relevant causes, etc.

3. **Close with Goodwill**

   Play nice and be sincere!

Introduction

Establish Rapport

Begin your message with a cordial introductory sentence or greeting. Use the "You" Attitude, but keep the lead-in brief, and get down to business. This helps win the audience to your side, even a little, before you drop your bombshell.

Present Negative News

The introduction of a direct negative informational message must present the bad news. This might be seen as pulling off the Band-Aid™, as the goal is to make it as quick and painless as possible. So, state the reason for your communication. In this case, present the bad news.

Body

State the Reasons or Causes

Explain the reasons for the negative news. Offer your audience an account explaining the reason or cause for the negative news. Avoid making disparaging remarks or denying responsibility. It is usually best to be as dispassionate as possible here. Think of the old Dragnet tagline: "Just the facts."

Explain Details

It may be appropriate to explain some details of the negative event or message. If you have information that might benefit the audience, you can share this in the body of your message. Show the audience that you recognize their needs, and appreciate the impact your negative news has on their lives. It is crucial that you do this with sincerity.

Conclusion

Close with Goodwill

Conclude a direct bad news message with a message of goodwill. This should include an invitation for future interaction.

Sample Direct Bad News Message

The following email is a negative response to an invitation to attend a charity golf tournament. The two men are friends and several other golfers are being invited. Thus, the direct approach is appropriate. Notice that direct does not mean blunt or uncaring.

Hi Don,

I appreciate your invitation to attend the charity golf tournament at the Sheraton on March 3rd. As much as I'd like to be there, I won't be able to make it this year.

I am attending a conference that week on the latest trends in home security. Our company is updating products and services, and I'll be making purchasing recommendations based on what I see there. While I'd rather be on the golf course, it's imperative that I attend this conference.

I know your fund-raiser will be a success. I'll send a contribution for the charity even though I can't attend the event, and I'll call you when I get back to see how it went.

Best Regards,
Steve

How would you feel about this bad news if you were Don? As you can see, if handled correctly, bad news can actually enrich the relationship and leave a positive impression on the recipient. Notice that empathy is not just conveyed by empty words. Actions speak louder than words, so put your money where your mouth is when possible.

Now let's turn our attention to the resistant audience or the urgent negative news.

Indirect Approach: Delivering Negative News

When dealing with unfortunate, but non-life-threatening news, communicators may benefit from taking an indirect approach. This eases your audience into the message, preparing them emotionally and logically for the bottom line. Though an audience might expect an immediate and direct notification of danger, indirect messages are often more effective for conveying bad news, especially when that audience may be resistant or hostile.

In the direct approach, remember, the purpose or **Bottom Line** is on top. This is what is meant by the acronym BLOT. You tell your readers exactly why you are writing, and how it relates to them, in the first paragraph. The body paragraphs of the message; then, provide more details on the situation and inform the reader of reasons for and consequences of the decision. Action may be required by the reader, and this will be stated in the final paragraph.

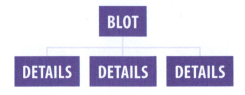

In an indirect message, the structure is reversed. Details are presented first, and the Bottom Line (the bad news and how it affects the reader) is presented near the end of the message.

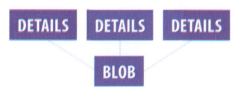

So how is a negative message like this organized? How does it begin and when is the bad news presented? Consider the approach below. Then we'll walk you through each of the four elements and provide a sample document to make it easier to understand.

INDIRECT BAD NEWS

BUFFER

Prepare the reader and soften the blow.

EXPLAIN YOUR REASONS

Help the reader understand what led to the decision.

BLOB

The BLOB is the bad news. You can deemphasize it by placement and wording.

CLOSE WITH GOODWILL

Close your message with a sincere recognition of how the news will affect them and offer an alternative if appropriate

Introduction

Start with a Buffer

Think about the buffer like the airbag of an automobile. In the photo, it is clear that this man is about to experience a negative event. Is he calm about the inevitable crash? No, he's fearful and resistant. If he could change the outcome, he certainly would; however, he cannot. The results may be softened if his automobile is properly equipped with an air bag. The airbag will inflate when the crash occurs and it will protect the man from more serious injuries. In addition, his vehicle may offer online services which will be activated by the crash. These services may include an automatic 911 call and even instructions on what the driver should do.

© Dean Drobot/Shutterstock.com

Figure 2

When delivering negative news, a buffer can soften the blow, and the rest of the message can provide support to the reader.

A buffer is a statement that establishes common ground with your audience and may communicate appreciation, understanding, or praise for your audience. It should be relevant and sincere in nature. Don't become effusive in a buffer; indicate the topic at hand while you align yourself with your reader. For example, if you have to close down a franchise but want your customer base to continue to frequent your other franchises which are further away, you might say, "Like you, we've always been committed to going the extra mile to make sure we get it right at Happy Burger." You've now aligned yourself with your audience and appealed to their sense of "going the distance" to get what they want. With alignment, you are ready to move forward with your message, and your reader is more likely to read on.

Body

Offer Reasons

In an indirect negative news message, present the reasons or causes before you reveal the unpleasant bottom line. If you do this well, your reader sees how this bad news naturally follows the reasoning, and it brings them into your thought process, conveying respect. In effect, priming the reader for the bad news to come can lessen its shock or disappointing effects. In fact, when done effectively, the reader may reach the same conclusion you have and understand the need for the negative outcome. He/she may still not like the outcome, but he/she will accept it more readily.

State the Negative News

Once you have created some common ground and prepared the audience for the unfortunate news, you must reveal the news itself. Be clear, but don't dwell on this news or offer unnecessary details. Consider how you phrase the bad news, and attempt to sandwich it between the reason and the goodwill. If possible, minimize the bad news with a silver lining. For example, you may point out that the inconvenience of a franchise closure means larger dining space at the newer, bigger Happy Burger. Other ways to deemphasize the bad news are presented in the table below.

STRATEGY	INEFFECTIVE	EFFECTIVE
Use passive voice	You did not buy a warranty.	A warranty was not purchased.
Subordinate it	Your credit is bad. We cannot approve your loan.	While we cannot approve your loan at this time, we will gladly consider it once your credit has improved.
Use positive language	Employees must not park in the customer lot.	Employees may park in the designated lot on the east side of the building.
Imply it	You did not get the position.	The position has been awarded to an external candidate.

Conclusion

Close with Goodwill

Once you have prepared your audience and delivered the bad news, close your message with goodwill. You may reference the silver lining, and if you are willing, offer an alternative that meets an immediate need:

"Please accept the attached coupon to use at your nearest Happy Burger. You can easily find a location near you by going to our website: www.happyburger.com/locations."

You may also invite future communication, but not about the negative news itself:

"Thank you for supporting Happy Burger, your family-friendly neighborhood restaurant. We appreciate your understanding and look forward to serving you our award-winning burgers for years to come."

The conclusion is brief, positive, and respectful in tone. The bad news message, especially when indirect, demonstrates a unique challenge for communicators. It requires a sincere understanding of the situation and audience, and the ability to honestly address the matter at hand in way that maintains a positive sender/receiver relationship.

In some cases, well-wishes will suffice. However, remember that actions speak louder than words, and avoid empty words of consolation. If there is something you can do to help readers with a necessary transition, do so, and put them into action to receive your assistance. This will help them to move past the problem and into the solution, winning you favor as someone who cares.

Sample Scenario and Indirect Bad News Message

The following example of a negative news message involves a rejection of a job application. Since the company wants to maintain a good image and might consider this applicant at a later date, it is important that the message helps the reader to accept the message. She may not like it, but she will better understand the reasons behind the decision and will feel valued by the company.

The introduction, or buffer, establishes a connection with the reader. In some cases, the writer may express appreciation or compliment the reader for something he or she has done. Sometimes a buffer simply reviews the facts of a situation so that the reader is more prepared for the upcoming news. In any case, if the writer establishes common ground first, the reader will be less defensive and more open to hearing an explanation. As you read this letter to Ms. Beltran, analyze its effectiveness:

> Dear Ms. Beltran,
>
> Thank you for your interest in the Inventory Management position at Ace Hardware. My staff and I enjoyed meeting with you, and we all agreed that you possessed several of the skills and qualifications we were looking for.

Notice that the writer shows appreciation and compliments the reader on her skills and qualifications. However, to avoid sounding overly positive, a single word provides a neutral "hint" at the rest of the message. That single word is "several" as opposed to "all" skills and qualifications needed. So, while the reader feels respected, she is beginning to think there's more to the upcoming message she needs to understand. So she reads on . . .

The next paragraph presents an explanation for the decision before announcing that Ms. Beltran did not get the job. The writer discusses the requirements and the previous knowledge necessary for someone to fill the position. The reader will see that she does not possess all the qualifications the company requires, and may even come to the same conclusion the writer has on her own.

The Inventory Management position requires an individual with a unique combination of skills and experience. Since we work with various independent and government contractors, we need someone with extensive knowledge of the hardware industry and specific experience in responding to RFPs. Through the interviewing process, we found someone who met all our criteria and have offered the position to her.

When and how does the reader learn that she has not been selected? An indirect bad news message attempts to avoid negative terms, so in this case the news is implied, ". . . we . . . have offered the position to . . ." (someone else). At this point, the reader understands the company's decision.

An indirect bad news message does not stop there, however. To demonstrate to the reader that he or she is valued, the writer offers encouragement and the option of reapplying for another position at a later date.

With your exceptional skills and credentials, you will, no doubt, add value to the retail company fortunate enough to hire you. In the meantime, we would like to keep your resume on file for six months, and if a general store manager position opens up, you will be the first to be considered.

This "goodwill" gesture will ensure that the reader understands and accepts the decision and will help her to focus on what is possible, not what isn't. The indirect approach is useful whenever you anticipate a negative response to the news you are presenting and when you want to maintain a positive relationship with the reader as well as a positive public image.

Sample Scenario and Indirect Bad News Message

In this chapter, we have walked you through the strategy behind delivering bad news. In this section, we will review the approach and look at another example that uses the indirect structure.

In the following situation, Sean Harrison, the Director of HR, must deliver bad news about a sensitive topic. The situation is as follows:

On Friday, a laptop was stolen from a representative in the human resources department of your company. The stolen laptop contained Social Security numbers and contact information for 3,600 current and former employees. You have been asked to draft a letter to be sent by Mr. Sean Harrison, the Director of HR, to each of the employees affected by the computer theft. Mr. Harrison realizes this is a serious matter, which puts each of these employees at a potential risk for identity theft.

Your company is concerned about its employees and also wants to preempt any negative publicity, lawsuits or other claims. Mr. Harrison knows he must show genuine concern for employees' personal and financial safety, while assuring them that the company is doing everything possible to locate the laptop computer and secure this sensitive information.

Mr. Harrison crafts a letter that provides a buffer and explains the situation before delivering the bad news. He closes the letter by focusing on specific next steps that should be taken to reduce any potential risk and by offering to keep the employee updated on any developments. As you read through, ask yourself if you would feel valued by the company.

September 22, 2014
Ms. Rebecca Albright
7390 E. Kimble Avenue
Tucson, Arizona 85710

Dear Ms. Albright,

Buffer establishes rapport and hints at bad news

All of us at Nordstrom value our past employees as much as our current ones, and thank you for your years of service within our company. Our company always has our employees' best interest in mind when dealing with sensitive information. The human resources department, in particular, strives to keep personal employee information private when issuing checks and sending out other important documents.

Explanation leads into bad news and silver lining leads into goodwill

Recent technology advancements have made completing this task much more efficient, but have also challenged the company with additional risks. HR has numerous security checks and safeguards that protect personal employee information from being compromised. However, large companies such as ours can still fall victim to theft. It is for this reason that we are contacting you. A laptop from our human resources department containing Social Security and contact information of several past and present employees, including yourself, was stolen yesterday. We have no proof that this information has been accessed or is being used in a fraudulent manner. Nonetheless, our security department, along with local law enforcement, is working to locate the laptop and retrieve the compromised information as quickly as possible in an attempt to keep all employee information safe.

Goodwill is developed and meets immediate need

In the meantime, our company is offering free credit monitoring for one year for every employee whose information may have been affected. To claim your free credit report from TransUnion credit bureau, call 1 (877) 322-8228 or visit their website through this link at http://www.annualcreditreport.com. If you provide them with your name, we have already set up a fund for your credit report to be paid for in full. In addition, we urge you to be proactive and check regularly with your bank(s) to see if any fraudulent activities have occurred.

Closing refers to future interaction and puts reader into action

We are committed to ensuring your information stays secure and hope you will utilize the services provided. We will have more information about this situation soon and will be contacting you with updates through email. In the meantime, you can also check our website's recent news for further updates.

Best Regards,

Sean Harrison

Director of HR

Tone—Indifference or Empathy; What Do Your Words Convey?

You have probably gathered that tone plays an important role in delivering bad news successfully. Applying the "You" Attitude in the buffer helps to establish common ground. Using passive voice and avoiding the "you" pronoun when it denotes blame helps to explain the reason behind a decision in an acceptable manner. Presenting the bad news in more positive terms or implying it reduces the impact it has on the reader. Finally, closing the message with a sincere goodwill effort establishes your concern and willingness to assist.

So, What Do You (the Writer) Have to Gain?

All of these strategies work together to create a message that will allow your reader to move forward into the solution instead of staying stuck in the problem. This, in turn, will help you (and your company) maintain a positive image with all stakeholder groups involved.

Now that you understand the "code book" for how to write direct informative, persuasive, and bad news messages in the workplace, put some of these strategies to the test. Regardless of your audience or the type of message, you'll find that these are easy strategies to memorize and put into practice. While you continue to develop and deepen your approach, you will find that your own messages will become more targeted and polished. More and more, you'll find you reach the mark. There is now only one strategic area left for you to master in business writing: it is time to learn about document design.

Chapter *3-4*

Document Design

Maximum Effectiveness, Minimum Effort

It does not matter how solid your strategy or how thorough your content: if you deliver information in ugly, inaccessible, or incomprehensible ways, your message will be confusing or worse, ignored. Consider all of the reading you are doing for this and other classes. Your authors (and the army of designers employed by our publisher) dedicated considerable effort to making this textbook as visually appealing as possible. We did this not just because we like pretty things, but because we know the truth about communication: how we organize and present information is just as important as the information itself. Effective information design helps achieve two goals: that your intended audience will actually read your documents, and that they will best understand what they read.

Information design is integral to what is commonly known as readability, or the ability of readers to understand information presented. Most common readability scores, such as Flesch Reading Ease and Flesch-Kincaid Grade Level, rely on calculations using the average sentence length and average number of syllables per word. Though this is a rich field of research, it is only important right now that you know that most Americans can read at the eighth or ninth grade level, for a Reading Ease score of roughly 60 to 70.

Documents with longer sentences and longer words will lower a document's Reading Ease score while increasing its Grade Level score. If one of your goals as a business communicator is to ensure your writing is both read and understood by as large an audience as possible, it behooves you to find the right balance between too long and too short. If your writing is too short, you run the risk of more sophisticated readers—often those in positions of authority—not reading what you've written. If your writing is too long, you damage the ability of everyone to understand your meaning.

As key components of readability scores, word, sentence, and paragraph length directly affect the amount of space taken by text on a page. Therefore, if you want to improve readability—and you absolutely should want to do that—you must consider how much space on the page your content takes and how it is arranged. The amount of space not taken up by text or other content is called white space. You can set yourself up for white space success by configuring your document's layout before you type a word. Start with the page margins, which are the spaces between the four edges of a page and the content on the page.

Margins

If your margins are too small, your readers might feel overwhelmed by how much text is on the page. If your margins are too large, your readers might think that you have not been as thorough as you could have been in generating your content. A good rule of thumb is to set your margins between ½ inch and 1 inch on all four sides; we advise against setting margins less than ½ inch or more than 1 inch. You may find that you need to occasionally make small adjustments to margins to accommodate a headline or a footnote, or to move the last word of a paragraph off a second page that is otherwise blank. Use this tactic sparingly. If the last few words of a paragraph have gone onto the next page, try to cut something from the rest of the paragraph first before adjusting margins.

Paragraphs

At this point, you have read a sizable portion of this textbook. You have certainly read other textbooks before this one. You also likely read websites, magazines, perhaps newspapers. Think about all of your reading experience to date. What is your initial reaction whenever you come to a page and see a very long paragraph? If you are anything like your authors, one of your first impulses might be to stop reading right there. Perhaps you get grumpy that the author of that wall of text was very inconsiderate for not making the paragraph easier to read. You might even be less inclined to believe the author of that big block or to follow a request they make.

Here's some cold, hard truth for you: those negative reactions are exactly what you will elicit with giant monoliths of solid text. As a drafting technique, it is perfectly acceptable for you to get as many thoughts as you can onto paper or a computer screen; just make sure you break it up and revise before you package your document for its intended audience. A good rule of thumb is that your business paragraphs should be between five and seven lines long. Any paragraph shorter than five lines makes you look like you have not fully developed your ideas, while any paragraph longer than seven lines will make your audience tune out. The longer the paragraph, the faster they tune out.

With all of these rules for structuring paragraphs, you might start feeling like writing takes too much effort. Quality writing does take hard work, but we have one way to make it a little easier for you. One common convention of business writing is that we do not indent paragraphs. This is a quick and easy shortcut to help you save time as you write your business documents. Instead of taking the time to indent every paragraph, you can just happily type away, secure in the knowledge that you are contributing to a world full of sleek and elegant business documents.

There is, of course, an argument to be made for indenting paragraphs. Before the days of word processors and computers, it was common practice for one paragraph to start on the line immediately following the previous paragraph. When the paragraphs were grouped so closely together, indenting made sense as a visual signal to the reader that a new paragraph was starting. Now with the advent of electronic means for producing standardized layouts with consistent space between paragraphs—something old school typewriters could not guarantee—you can add an extra line break between them. This has the added benefit of adding a little more white space to every page.

With that mention of an extra line break between paragraphs, you might be thinking that it would be a good idea to add extra spacing between the lines within a paragraph. This is commonly known as double-spacing and is a staple of academic writing. If you did think that, you would be wrong. Remember one of the key differences between academic and business writing: the former asks you to fill a minimum number of pages, while the latter asks you to limit yourself to a maximum number of pages.

You cannot cover everything you need to cover when working within maximum page constraints when you double space your writing. To put it another way, your boss probably would not be happy if you were using twice as much paper as necessary (and spending twice as much on office supplies) to convey the same information. If you look at your single-spaced document and judge that the lines are just too close together, you can increase the line spacing to as much as 1.15 lines. Having a small amount of white space between lines does help with readability, but don't go overboard.

Words

Now that we have looked at the page and the paragraphs, we turn our attention to the words that make up those paragraphs on the page. We cover the crucial mechanics of grammar elsewhere in this text; here we will focus on the physical mechanics of the written word. Words are composed of letters, and those letters are represented in typefaces. Typefaces prescribe a set of common style rules for letters, numbers, and other characters. Variations on those styles can be grouped together into typeface families. When you apply a specific size to a typeface, it becomes a font.

The font you choose for your business writing does make a difference in the readability of your documents. Some typefaces are better suited to paragraph text, while others have more impact when used sparingly in headlines. There are two major varieties of typefaces: serif and sans-serif. The word *serif* has Germanic origins and roughly translates to "dash" or "line." A typeface with serifs is recognizable by the little hooks and tails that hang off of its letters. The most commonly recognized serif typeface is Times New Roman. In fact, serif typefaces are sometimes referred to as "Roman."

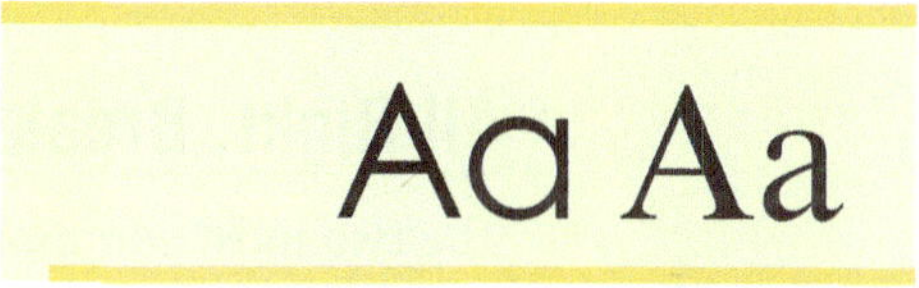

Figure 1 *Sans Serif (Century Gothic, left) vs Serif (Times New Roman, right) typefaces*

Conversely, sans-serif typefaces lack any of that additional ornamentation. These typefaces are also sometimes referred to as "Grotesque" or "Gothic." A recognizable example of a sans-serif typeface is Arial. Both serif and sans-serif typefaces are often styled in different weights or line thicknesses. Those weights can range from narrow or thin, through normal or regular, to semibold, thick, heavy, and bold. The typeface itself and the typeface weight you choose in any given business communication situation will depend on what you use the text for. Just like any other tool in your business communication toolkit, use the right one for the task at hand. Heavier weights work best when used sparingly, for emphasis; thinner weights may be difficult to read.

Merriam Webster's *Manual for Writers and Editors* reports that the people who study typeface readability have found that serif fonts are easier to quickly read and understand. For this reason, use serif fonts for paragraph text. Sans-serif typefaces are better suited for short bursts: headlines, titles, and anything that allows for a larger size or shorter length. Do be careful about mixing typefaces. We recommend using no more than one serif and one sans-serif typeface per document. The more typefaces you use, the more cluttered and unprofessional your document appears.

Not Words

You've likely heard that old bromide, "a picture is worth a thousand words." Though trite, it does hold some truth in business communication. Sometimes, our words just are not enough to inform or persuade our audiences. We might use a picture to illustrate a key point, a table to organize statistical data, or a graph to convey complex financial information. When using any of these elements, you must be just as strategic with them as you are with your words.

Interpreting visual elements can place a heavy cognitive load on your reader. This means that it may take more effort for a reader to switch from words to visuals, then interpret the visual material into understandable concepts. You can help alleviate this cognitive load by helping your audience pre-process the visual information. Never just drop a graph, chart, image, or other visual element into your document without first introducing it with text. Visual elements need context in order for the audience to understand how they support the bottom line of the document. Remember, it is your job as a business communicator to make your information as easy as possible for your audience to understand or follow.

Just as you need an introduction to visual material to provide context and ease your reader into this new form of content, you also should write a summative statement after the visual material to transition the reader back to the body text. See Figure 2 for an example of the context and summative statements used to bookend a visual element.

While visual elements like charts, graphs, pictures, and tables can help break up a document into easier to read and understand pieces, there are other document layout tools you can pull from your business communication bag of tricks to further this goal.

All Right, Break it Up

The two most common layout tools at your disposal are headlines and lists. Lists can come in two forms: bullets and outlines. Both of these tools serve two purposes: giving the reader a break from the cognitive stress of straight text and organizing information into discrete units. By creating these distinct sections and placing relevant information accordingly, you help your audience more quickly process the information.

Section Headings/Subheadings

One effective way of structuring the information you want to present is through "chunking," or breaking similar pieces of information into discrete sections. This organizational strategy helps your reader keep track of related information and helps you ensure that you control the flow of that information to maximize reader comprehension.

The easiest way for you to use this approach is to think about the major topics you want to cover. For example, let's say you are composing an industry report that seeks to provide your audience with relevant information about the size of the industry, recent trends, barriers to entry, and major players. These are all major topics that give you the opportunity to structure your information in an accessible way. To make the most of this strategy, you might start planning your message by creating a basic outline. Each outline level could then become a separate section, complete with its own heading.

The following chart shows the sales of widgets, doodads, and gadgets by region of the country.

As you can see from the chart, the western region dominated widget and doo-dad sales last year, while lagging behind the southern region in gadget sales.

© Kendall Hunt Publishing Company

Figure 2   *Context and summative statements bookending a visual element.*

For the hypothetical industry report above, you might create an outline as follows:

1. Introduction
2. Industry Size
3. Industry Trends
4. Barriers to Entry
5. Competitors
6. Conclusion

Note that in addition to the main topics to be covered, you also make sure to include an introduction and a conclusion to the document. Regardless of the length or type of document, always provide a frame for the message itself at the beginning and tie it all together at the end. If this was to be a short, one-page document, you might be able to succeed with dedicating one paragraph to each topic in your outline. As documents get longer and more complex, it helps to break up different sections. This is especially true when it may not be obvious where one topic is to end and the next is to begin.

Just as with newspaper headlines, section headings (and subheadings) indicate to the reader when a new topic begins. Your headlines should be on separate lines and set off in some way via formatting. For example, you might make the typeface of your headings bold or italicized, cast them in a different color, use a different typeface, change the size of the heading words. As with any other element of your formatting, just be consistent.

Subsections—and their corresponding subheadings—are considered part of larger sections, so they should be formatted similarly to the main section headings. Subheadings should also indicate their subordinate status to the main heading. For example, if you use a bold typeface for a main section heading, you might choose to italicize that section's subheadings. Since bold typefaces indicate prominence and italic typefaces indicate less strength than bold typefaces, your audience will automatically interpret the relative relationships of content falling under headings formatted with each respective style.

Since the use of section headings and subheadings is all about boosting audience comprehension through structural elements, make sure your line spacing is appropriate, too. Floating headings, in which there is equal white space both before and after them, make them look like orphans: neither the paragraph before nor the paragraph following want to claim ownership. Instead, eliminate the extra line break directly after a heading or subheading to clearly indicate to your reader that the paragraph that starts on the next line belongs to the heading immediately above it. To make the document as easy as possible to read, make sure that there *is* an extra break on the line immediately before each heading.

Section headings are an essential device in your effective communication toolbox, but they are supplemented by another tool that works like a magic wand for communicating lists of information in short, easily understood bursts.

Bullets and Outline Lists

You are probably used to creating outlines as a method for organizing your thoughts or preparing to write important documents. You probably also use lists in one form or another for helping you remember important items or tasks. Where would any of us be without our grocery and to-do lists?

One of the reasons that outlines and lists are so useful is because they provide the reader with a way to quickly visualize important information instead of having to read complete sentences or full paragraphs. Outlines and lists are the shortcuts on the path to audience comprehension. When used correctly, they save an audience time and make the information presented more accessible. It is possible to overdo the use of bulleted or multilevel outlines; neither can adequately substitute for genuine and thorough analysis and synthesis that can only be effectively conveyed through complete sentences and paragraphs.

Lists and outlines are shortcuts and should be treated accordingly. There is no point in sticking a bullet point in front of a paragraph that consists of two or more complete sentences. If you're writing a paragraph, let it be a paragraph. Bullet lists are best used for short thoughts: single words, succinct phrases, or brief clauses. If you find that you have written a bulleted list that consists of complete sentences at each level, you might as well just make that list a paragraph.

Sometimes, the information you seek to present consists of complex internal relationships. Not every piece of information is directly or equally related to every other piece of information. In these circumstances, you might choose to use a multilevel list or outline. Just as there are relationships between headings and subheadings, there are relationships between levels in a list or outline. All items in the top level of a list or outline should have equal relationship to the items on that same level.

There may be sublevels under those top-level items, and each of those sublevel items under each top-level item should have equal relationship to the other sublevel items under the same top-level item (though not to the sublevel items under other top-level items). That is a mildly confusing way of telling you to keep like information together. Sublevels must be related to each other and the top-level item under which they fall.

There is one more important point about bullet and multilevel outline lists. Items on any level can never exist in isolation. Avoid lonely bullets, the phenomenon of having only one bulleted item at a particular level of a list. You should not use bullet points or outline numbers if there is only one item on that level. In the case of outlines, that means that every 1 has a 2 and every a has a b.

> **AVOID LONELY BULLETS.**
> Every 1 has a 2 and every a has a b.

Since bullet lists and outlines are intended to help organize more than one piece of information, it does not make sense to use these formatting tools when you are only presenting one piece of information. If you have additional information you would like to use to elaborate on a bullet point, but there is not enough additional information to split into two sublevels, just include that information on the next line below the main point. Just do not use a bullet or letter/number; the additional information is part of the top-level item, not sufficient enough to justify its own sublevel.

This chapter helped you think through document formatting to make your writing both visually appealing and easier to understand. Part of any effective written strategy must include attention to document design. This is an element of writing strategy that is often overlooked, at the peril of the author or her causes.

Unit 3 References

Clark, B. (2015) How to Use the 'Rule of Three' to Create Engaging Content. Retrieved from http://www.copyblogger.com/rule-of-three/

Fadiga, L., Craighero, L. and D'Ausilio, A. (2009), Broca's Area in Language, Action, and Music Annals of the New York Academy of Sciences, 1169: 448–458

Holland, N. (2010). 3 Simple Rules for Writing That Match the Human Brain. Retrieved from https://www.psychologytoday.com/blog/is-your-brain-culture/201006/3-simple-rules-writing-match-the-human-brain

Maslow, A. H. (1943). A Theory of Human Motivation. *Psychological Review.*

Kincaid, J.P., Fishburne, R.P. Jr., Rogers, R.L., & Chissom, B.S. (February 1975). "Derivation of new readability formulas (Automated Readability Index, Fog Count and Flesch Reading Ease Formula) for Navy enlisted personnel." Research Branch Report 8-75, Millington, TN: Naval Technical Training, U. S. Naval Air Station, Memphis, TN.

Merriam-Webster. (1998). *Merriam-Webster's Manual for Writers and Editors* (Rev Sub ed.). Merriam-Webster.

Paiz, J., Angeli, E., Wagner, J., Lawrick, E., Moore, K., Anderson, M., Soderlund, L., & Brizee, A. (2016, May 13). *APA headings and seriation.* Retrieved from https://owl.english.purdue.edu

Pullam, G. (2009). 50 Years of Stupid Grammar Advice. Retrieved from http://chronicle.com

Quickster: Netflix to Split DVD Service into New Business (September 19, 2011). HuffingtonPost. Retrieved from: http://www.huffingtonpost.com/2011/09/19/qwikster-netflix-streaming-dvds_n_969135.html

Stelter, B. (October 10, 2011). Netflix, in Reversal, Will keep its Services Together. New YorkTimes. Retrieved from: http://mediadecoder.blogs.nytimes.com/2011/10/10/netflix-abandons-plan-to-rent-dvds-on-qwikster/?_r=0

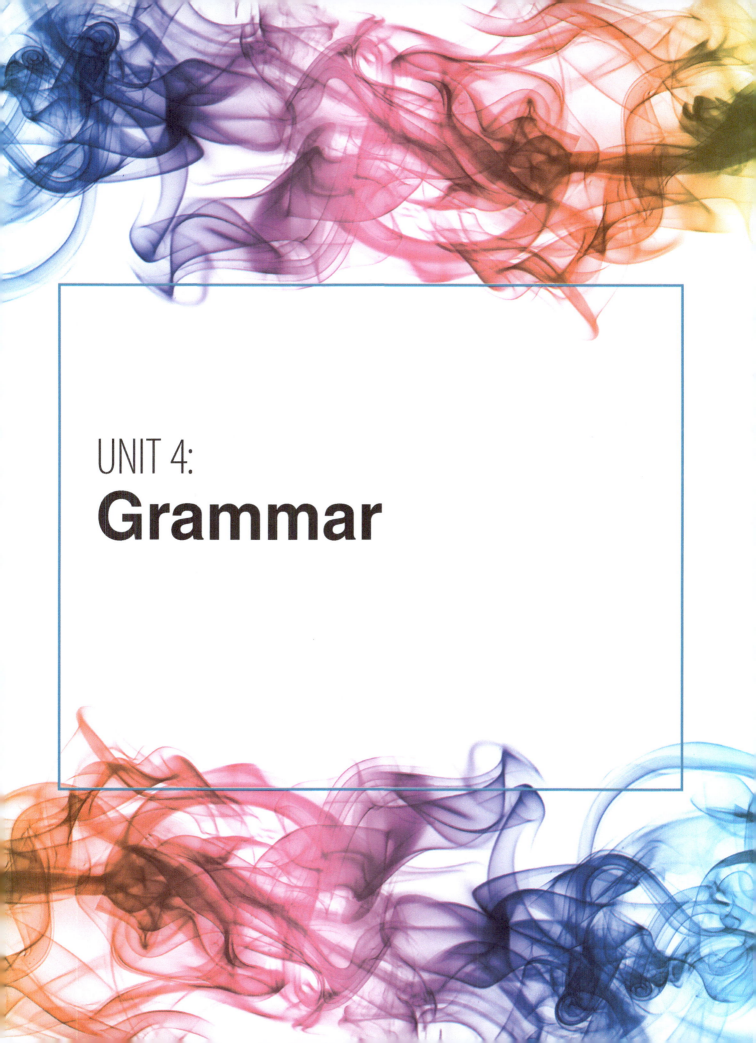

UNIT 4:
Grammar

Understanding Grammar

Communicating in the workplace includes producing written documents for a variety of audiences. As future business leaders, the level of proficiency that you demonstrate in your writing represents you and your brand. Your writing should evidence high standards and showcase your ability to think critically, to organize and reason logically, and to design documents effectively. In addition, your writing should be free of grammatical and punctuation errors.

Punctuating improperly or using sloppy grammar is like wearing lousy tennis shoes with a suit: you get ridiculed by those who know better—like bosses, like the people doing the hiring, like the manager in charge of your next promotion.

Writing well is a standard to which you should hold yourself, regardless of your native language. Many students in the United States are never explicitly taught grammar, so many have never learned the correct way to punctuate a sentence. It is never too late to learn; in fact, now is the optimum time to learn, since employers are actively seeking candidates with strong written communication skills.

You will project confidence when you know that your sentences and paragraphs are correctly

©Hidelight/Shutterstock.com

Figure 1 *Sloppy Grammar is Like Old Tennis Shoes: It Stinks!*

punctuated. Nothing compares to knowing that you are right. Good writers are few and far between, but it is a learnable skill and not a genetic gift. You have to learn the rules, and use them to revise your work.

Earlier in this book, you read about the types of errors most often made by those new to business writing: disruptive, credibility, etiquette, and accent. This unit will focus on the first two, disruptive errors and credibility errors, by giving examples of the most common errors that students make based on years of reading student work. This unit also boils down the basics of punctuation and effective sentence structures. By targeting key problem areas in student writing and describing standards that make writing effective and professional, this chapter will help you become a stronger writer. You will learn about writing concisely, choosing strong verbs, and properly punctuating different sentence constructions—areas of weakness in much student writing.

A Word about Concision

Above all else, be brief and to-the-point. Business writing has a specific purpose and audience. Both of these variables determine what you will write. How you write it will never change: get to the point clearly, quickly, and correctly. Your sentences should be fairly short, and your paragraphs should not be more than eight lines long. White space is important in helping the eye travel across the words and the brain process the incoming visual input.

Writing concisely is easier said than done. Similar to design concepts discussed earlier, removing distractors and keeping the lines clean and simple are good rules. With the exception of long reports, the majority of daily workplace writing is less than a page long. Like a sales pitch or an elevator pitch, you only have so much time and space to get your point across, so you need to distill your sentences to the fewest and best word choices. Business writing requires that you consider your **audience** and your **purpose**, and serve those two masters exclusively.

How do you write concisely? By rewriting. Most first drafts are wordy and wandering as you seek the best way to convey your message. It takes a lot of experience to knock out a clean first draft, even in a short email. Accept the fact that you will need to rewrite messages many times before they are audience-ready.

In the next section, you will learn the "Six Rules" to effective writing. Once you master these, you will write professionally and correctly.

Grammar

The Basics: Nouns and Verbs

When writing, you have few choices to make about the nouns you use, because the subject of the sentence is what it is. You can choose synonyms for the nouns, i.e. the manager, the girl, etc., or use pronouns like he/she/they/it, but you typically have to work with what you have. Not so with the verbs you use.

Verbs are the engine of the sentence, driving it toward meaning. You can speed, steer, careen, insist, detail, manage—all strong active verbs that allow the doer of the sentence to actually *do something*. The magic happens when you choose strong verbs.

Elena gave the report to her manager.

Elena, the subject of the sentence, is a noun and cannot be replaced by anything other than the pronoun *she* or maybe her title, "the sales manager." Nouns are people, places, or things and often act as the subject of a sentence. The verb is the action of the sentence. The verb tells the reader what happened and who did it.

Principle #1: Use Active Verbs

So, what is a strong verb? Active verbs are stronger and more impactful than passive verbs because they are doing something, not being done unto. The subject does the action of the verb in the sequence doer-action or doer-action-receiver of the action. Below are some examples of both types of sentence. Some of these sentences have a direct object, a phrase or noun that denotes the receiver of the action.

Subject + Verb + Who or What? = Direct Object

ACTIVE	PASSIVE
Sanjay threw the quarterly report.	The quarterly report was thrown by Sanjay.
Sanjay threw the quarterly report on his desk.	The quarterly report was thrown on his desk by Sanjay.
BP released the accident report.	The accident report was released by BP.
BP released the accident report to the press.	The accident report was released to the press by BP.
The manager ran the full-page ad.	The full-page ad was run by the manager.
The CEO quoted Mark Twain on a daily basis.	Mark Twain is quoted on a daily basis by the CEO.
Jeni wrote the most concise email to her boss.	The most concise email to the boss was written by Jeni.

The passive construction is not wrong; it's simply not as direct and does not link the action closely with the doer. Passive voice is used in science writing to maintain a sense of objectivity, and to keep the writer out of the conclusions drawn.

> **Incorrect:** *We found that genetically modified corn causes tumors in mice.*
> **Correct:** *The data suggest that genetically modified corn causes tumors in mice.*

> **Incorrect:** *My research suggests a correlation between hours slept and weight gain.*
> **Correct:** *Evidence suggests a correlation between hours slept and weight gain.*

Writers correctly use passive constructs when the doer or subject is unknown.

> **Unknown subject:** *The laptop was stolen.*
> *A bomb went off in the courthouse.*

A final suitable use of passive voice is to deflect attention from the doer or performer of an action. Examples of these include deflecting blame, avoiding responsibility, or delivering bad news. You often hear passive voice in press releases and in courtrooms where companies and/or people do not want to take responsibility for actions. Consider this from an oil company after a spill: "A few gallons might have been spilled." Or this from a serial speeder, "Posted speed limits were not always followed." By not having a subject or a doer, the focus is taken off of the actor of the sentence.

> **Deflecting blame:** *The window was shattered.*
> *The alibi was not corroborated.*

> **Avoiding responsibility:** *Mistakes were made.*
> *Shots were fired.*

> **Delivering bad news:** *Water will be shut off if payment isn't made.*
> *Ten points will be taken off for late submissions.*

A final reason business writing relies on active voice is for concision; the passive constructs are often longer than their active counterparts—and concision is the goal.

Thus, you can see that avoiding the passive voice and finding active verbs makes your sentences more immediate and less evasive. Likewise, avoid "to be" verbs as they, too, lack muscle and punch. Note: Using *to be* verbs is not wrong, but using too many makes for writing that lacks impact. The following chart shows the different tenses of the *to be* verbs.

	PRESENT	PAST	PERFECT	PROGRESSIVE
I	am	was	have been/had been	am/was being
he/she/it	is	was	has been/had been	is/was being
you/we/they	are	were	have been/had been	are/were being

Now, let's look at *to be* verbs used in sentences and compare them to the revised versions that use active verbs.

WEAK	STRONG
Those women **are** strong leaders.	Those women **emerged** as strong leaders.
The sales team **was recognized** as top performing.	Management **recognized** the sales team as top performing.
I **am** the supervisor of 15 full-time employees.	I **supervise** 15 full-time employees.
The owner **was being responsible** when she changed the locks.	The responsible owner **changed** the locks.

To be verbs are handy and familiar, so watch for them sneaking into your writing. Part of revising requires reviewing verb choices and working to make sentences stronger. This partial list provides some strong verbs you can use when feeling stuck:

save	eliminate	coach	implement	present
inquire	accomplish	represent	express	base
resemble	recruit	influence	regard	track
staff	consider	contradict	facilitate	educate
launch	process	transform	analyze	undergo
streamline	discuss	preserve	verify	negotiate
personify	challenge	eradicate	advise	embody
convey	exhibit	demand	produce	believe

When you consistently use strong, active verbs and revise to eliminate many *to be* verbs, your writing will improve significantly. Again, this takes practice and repetition, so keep revising and learning to spot the offending verb constructions when they arise. The process of revising deserves the effort.

Practice #1: Verbs

A. Replace the *to be* verbs in the following sentences with one of the active verbs in the chart above.

1. *Senator Robbins was loud in his request for more iced tea.*
2. *She was able to exert enough pressure to change public opinions.*
3. *Mr. Biocce is all about keeping tradition alive and well.*
4. *Benny is always fighting with his dad.*
5. *Meg was trying to help her students find a solution to the problem.*

B. Change one of the nouns to a verb and move it to the front of the sentence.

1. *Roger was exhibiting signs of agreeing to the merger.*
2. *The editor was eradicating the weak verbs from the manuscript.*
3. *He is always contradicting me.*
4. *Wembly is careful when he drives the bus.*
5. *Jorge is the star of the daytime drama.*

C. Combine choppy sentences to eliminate to be verbs and provide flow.

1. *Dumping toxic waste in the river would be in violation of environmental laws and officials are in acknowledgment of this.*
2. *The only responsibility that they were given by their professor was to turn their work in on time and not to plagiarize.*
3. *Kanye West was the musical artist who influenced my son the most and is the source of his inspiration.*
4. *There were shouting mobs in the streets, and they were breaking windows and looting stores.*
5. *Our department is managed by Dr. Begay, and she is the one who makes all of the big decisions.*

D. Front-load sentences by moving the doer to the beginning of the sentence and choosing a strong verb.

1. *The toxicology report was finished on Thursday by Dr. Gupta.*
2. *Results of the final exam were posted on the course site by Dr. Michaels early Friday morning.*
3. *Damning evidence in the case against the CEO were brought to light by the SEC.*
4. *The current economic crisis was explained to us by our uncle who is a financial advisor.*
5. *I want the quarterly report brought to me by you by 3 p.m.*

Principle #2: Use Concrete Nouns

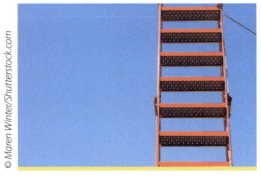

© Maren Winter/Shutterstock.com

Figure 2

Now that the importance of using active verbs has been established, it is equally important to use concrete nouns. Concrete rather than vague language is another consideration to writing with clarity.

S.I. Hayakawa, a linguist and semanticist concerned with inflammatory rhetoric and propaganda during World War II, studied the level of abstraction evidenced in some of Adolf Hitler's speeches. Hayakawa created a "ladder of abstraction" to categorize words from their most concrete and identifiable, to the highest levels of abstraction. Business writing aims for specificity and clarity; thus, choosing words from the lowest rung of the ladder is often the goal.

LEVEL OF ABSTRACTION	EXAMPLES
4 most	wealth, happiness, love, success, health, power, beauty, life form, vehicle
3	men, women, people, they, we, car, managers, directors, professionals, dogs
2	Lower class, pre-teens, married couples, romantic comedies, HR director, golden retrievers, German car
1 least	Knock Out roses, 12-year-old, Lydia, Ron and Rebecca Gardner, TV show *Friends*, my golden retriever, Benji, her father's BMW

With specificity, clear images come to the mind of the reader. If you write that a man drove a vehicle to his favorite store, the reader may imagine this in unintended ways. Perhaps they picture a thin old man driving a beat-up truck to the hardware store, when the writer meant her boss, the CEO of Whole Foods, driving a Prius to the Native Seeds store. Likewise, if you write that the company's sales were up from last quarter, giving specific numbers in context increases the chance that your reader will get the exact message you attempted to convey.

Practice #2: Concrete Nouns

Replace the abstract nouns in the following sentences with specific, concrete nouns that leave little room for ambiguity.

1. Some people were watching sports on a TV in a bar.
2. Pre-teens like to shop at the mall for various cheap items.
3. Happiness is achieved through harmonious activities.
4. True health comes from staying busy.
5. Our company exceeded its wildest dreams last year.
6. If we keep up with trends, we can take our start-up to the next level.
7. With a serious investment of capital, our company can reach its full potential.
8. I am seeking a job where I can move up quickly and have a generous benefits package.
9. My skills are many, and I am a good communicator and leader.
10. She became wealthy by investing and diversifying.

Principle #3: Avoid There is/There are & It is/It was

Though these are passive constructs, they deserve their own section because of their overuse by inexperienced writers. They are easy. It is true. The simplest solution is to look for these beginnings—and revise them. Again, revision is key to writing well. Sometimes, quick writing provides good content and ideas, but revision polishes them and makes them shine. Take the time to rid your writing of most of these constructs. How is this done? Again, by finding a strong, active verb.

Practice #3 There is/There are

1. There is little point to driving all the way to San Francisco when you can take BART.
2. It was the sales force that needed to be re-trained.
3. It is inevitable that attrition rates increase when student services are cut.
4. There are many positions at the company that require advanced degrees.
5. It was no one's fault that the copier finally broke.
6. There are a number of companies in China that do business with the United States.
7. It is best to let employees go on a Friday.
8. There were screaming kids running down the pier.
9. It was Connor who told his boss about the social media abuse in the office.
10. There is one explanation for the inconsistencies in the ledger sheets.

Principle #4: Avoid Why/How, The Reason For, Due to the Fact That

Using phrases like *the reason for, how, why, due to the fact that* to explain something is a common pitfall of the novice writer. Eliminate these from your writing by cutting straight to the point. Think of these words as little red flags signaling the necessity of revising the sentence.

Practice #4: How/Why

1. She couldn't explain the reason for its disappearance.
2. This document will provide information on how Costco can expand into Brazil and the reasons behind why this is a good decision.
3. As you requested, here is a report about management's proposal as to why India is the place to expand to.
4. I have outlined why I believe Costco is currently performing as one of the best in its sector of business, but I believe slight changes to our business plan is how we become bigger and better.
5. This analysis will inform you on the current successes of Nike, and why Nike through the years has always won globally where many others falter.
6. The reasons the corporate takeover failed are because no one anticipated the public backlash.

6. *The reason why employees resort to taking sick days is because they aren't given enough personal leave days.*

7. *Due to the fact that interviewees are nervous, interviewers should begin with a few easy questions.*

8. *She was fired due to the fact that she lied on her resume.*

9. *In light of the fact that he wrote the entire proposal, he should get the promotion.*

Principle #5: Watch Out for Misplaced and Dangling Modifiers

Misplaced Modifiers

Modifiers are words or phrases that, well, modify or change and amend something else. The placement of modifiers is critical: put them in the wrong place, and the meaning of the sentence is altered entirely. Perhaps the most common and familiar are limiting modifiers:

Just, only, nearly, hardly, almost, merely—or by the acronym, JON HAM.

An easy way to illustrate the importance of word order with limiting modifiers is with the word only.

1. *Ricardo only gave Izzy flowers.*

2. *Ricardo gave only Izzy flowers.*

3. *Ricardo gave Izzy only flowers.*

Figure 3 *An easy way to remember the most common and familiar modifiers is to misspell actor Jon Hamm's name: JON HAM.*

© Featureflash Photo Agency/Shutterstock.com

The first sentence means that the only thing Ricardo did with the flowers was give them to Izzy. He didn't throw them at her, nor did he eat them.

The second sentence means that the only person to whom Ricardo gave flowers was Izzy, not Izzy and Nola.

The third sentence means that Ricardo didn't give Izzy flowers and chocolate—flowers were the only thing he gave her.

Sometimes modifiers sit between two words and could modify either, thus causing confusion in the reader.

Incorrect: *Running quickly freaks out guard dogs.*

The ambiguity here is the reader doesn't know if someone who is running fast freaks out guard dogs, or if guard dogs freak out quickly when someone runs. A third possibility is that taking guard dogs for a fast run freaks them out. Depending on what was intended, these revisions are correct:

Correct: *When you run quickly, it freaks out the guard dogs.*

Correct: *When you run, the guard dogs quickly freak out.*

Correct: *When you take the guard dogs out for a quick run, they freak out.*

An easy way to use modifiers correctly is to place them next to the word they are modifying—not between two words they could possibly modify.

Dangling Modifiers

Modifiers need correct placement for correct meaning. Single words can be used as modifiers, but often mistakes are made with phrases that fail to modify what was intended, resulting in a dangling modifier, or, colloquially, a dangler. They are called danglers because they seem to be modifying a subject that isn't there; thus, they are just dangling in the sentence. The key to getting these constructs right is to name the person/doer immediately after the modifying phrase. Often, these phrases begin the sentence, so that is a good place to look when revising.

>   **Incorrect:** *After finishing dinner, the dog was eager for the scraps.*

In this sentence, the dog finished dinner, not one who presumably was going to give him scraps.

>   **Correct:** *After finishing dinner, Chad gave his eager dog the scraps.*

Remembering to follow an introductory phrase or clause with the noun or subject corrects most errors.

>   **Incorrect:** *Driving down the street, spilled oranges were everywhere causing Carlos to swerve.*

Written thusly, the oranges were the ones driving down the street.

>   **Correct:** *Driving down the street, Carlos had to swerve to avoid spilled oranges.*

Principle #6: Keep Structures Parallel

We have looked at a few ways that credibility errors can undermine your ability to write effective business messages. Next, we will look at disruptive errors. When disruptive errors are made, the reader is not able to read the message straight through. Disruptive errors cause a stop or pause followed by a rereading by the audience, literally interrupting the flow of reading. The danger with these types of errors is that the reader will not comprehend your message.

Credibility errors bring your competence into question, but disruptive errors bring the content into question because they can cause the message to be misinterpreted.

One common disruptive error concerns parallelism. What is parallel structure? We know parallel parking and have a passing familiarity with parallel lines from math, but what is parallelism in a sentence or bullets?

Like parallel lines, parallel examples in a sentence means that they line up evenly with one another. It also works a little bit like math–but that's a little later. First, let's look at non-parallel structures:

©Topuria Design/Shutterstock.com

1. *Ahmed enjoys computer science, communications, and doing math.*
2. *Roger redecorated his office with a new desk, chairs, and he painted the walls gray.*
3. *Lindy gets a panicked feeling when her homework is due, her room is a mess, and playing chess against her brother.*

These are wrong because they do not use parallel phrases or words. It's a rhythm issue too: "studying, testing, and memorizing" is parallel. All three use the gerund (ing) form of the verb.

Figure 4   *Keep It Parallel.*

Let's look at some of the same sentences when they are rhythmic and, therefore, parallel:

1. *Ahmed enjoys computer science, communications, and math.*
2. *Roger redecorated his office with a new desk, chairs, and gray walls.*
3. *Lindy gets a panicked feeling when her homework is due, her room is a mess, and her brother beats her at chess.*

Notice how the forms of the word are the same. As always, keep your eye on the verb. This is where the math comes into play. Do you remember how you solve this equation? $3(a+b+c)$ You have to distribute the 3 to the **a** and the **b** and the **c**.

You have to do the same thing with a verb that precedes a parallel list. In the following sentence the verb is acting like the 3 in the math example.

- *Our art teacher told us to draw a flower, a vase, and an apple. (draw a flower, draw a vase, draw an apple)*
- *When hitting a golf ball, you need to keep your head down, your eye on the ball, and your knees bent. (keep your head down, keep your eye on the ball, keep your knees bent)*
- *I like to draw, write, and cook. (to draw, to write, to cook)*

Keeping Bullets Parallel

Keeping bullet points parallel is a rule that is routinely broken. Elevate your game and hold yourself to the standards of proper grammar: Bullets must be parallel.

You can start them all with a verb.

Growing a garden is easy:
- choose quality soil
- find a shady spot
- buy heirloom seeds
- water sparingly

By following these simple instructions, you can easily grow your own garden.

You can start them all with a noun.

When choosing a career path, keep the most important considerations in mind:
- Opportunities for advancement
- Salary range
- Benefits
- Working conditions
- Corporate culture and climates

By keeping these considerations in mind, choosing the best job will be easier.

Parallel structures are just another way of staying consistent in your writing. Like most other grammatical points, the idea is to stick to a structure and a rhythm to make comprehension easy for your reader.

In sum, keep your writing right and tight and use strong verbs and parallel constructs to elevate the level of your messages. Writing correctly is a skill that will serve you well in the workplace.

Practice #6: Parallelism

Make these sentences parallel:

1. *It is harder to maintain a diet than starting one.*
2. *In the Army, you are told what to eat and to do so in the mess hall.*
3. *Olivia told her castmates that she bought new tap shoes and of her dream of being a dancer.*
4. *Robin liked dancing, talking, and the organization of big parties.*
5. *Delivering the cakes in a rain storm, the caterers thought it smarter to cover the cakes than walking with them in the rain.*
6. *Mr. Carlson begins every day by perusing the stock markets of foreign countries and then he checks the Nasdaq exchange.*
7. *Harvard Business School is selective about its candidates, and it is admitting only 4.5% of applicants.*
8. *I have a long to-do list: I have to skim the pool, to clean out my closet, and to pay the cable bill.*
9. *Once her check is deposited, Dolores puts money into her savings account, 401K, and credit card balance.*
10. *Andy hoped to get an extension on his paper, skip class, and to spend the morning kayaking.*

Create parallel bullets with the following non-parallel list:

- *Make sure you finish the assignment*
- *Proofreading is important*
- *Carefully edit your message*
- *D2L: Upload it here*
- *Don't forget to click "Confirm submission"*

Chapter 4-2

Understanding Punctuation

Punctuation

Credibility Errors

While earlier sections describe best practices and broad suggestions for stronger, more impactful writing, this next section describes credibility errors. Faulty subject/verb agreement and some punctuation and spelling errors, while they do not typically disrupt communication, do create doubt in the mind of the reader about the competence of the writer. Too many of these types of errors will cause the reader to lose confidence in the writer's basic credibility. Once lost, one's professional credibility is difficult to regain.

Sentence Structure

The English language uses four basic types of sentences. Here they are, in order of complexity:

SIMPLE SENTENCE	The dog ran.
COMPLEX SENTENCE	Whenever he had the chance, the dog ran.
COMPOUND SENTENCE	The dog ran around the park, and he sniffed every bush.
COMPOUND-COMPLEX SENTENCE	Whenever he had the chance, the dog ran around the park and sniffed every bush.

Four Ways of Combining Sentences

Not only does business writing consist mainly of these four types of sentences, but there are also four easy ways to combine sentences. Once you have mastered these four ways and the proper punctuation, command of the written word will be yours forever.

Way #1: Use Simple Sentences

This is self-explanatory. A simple sentence includes a subject and a verb and requires no punctuation. Beware of adding two simple sentences together with just a comma. This is called a comma-splice, and they are quite common in first drafts.

Incorrect: *Buffered Vitamin C wards off colds in the winter, it has immune building properties.*

Correct: *Buffered Vitamin C wards off colds in the winter. It has immune building properties.*

Though the second sentence is correct, you can see that stringing a bunch of simple sentences together sounds a lot like beginning reading books: See Spot run. Run, Spot run! Jane sees Spot run. Young children learn simple sentences first and gradually add more complexity as their brain's capacity increases. While they may understand complex structures, they do not begin actually using them until about age four. Since the goal of business professionals is to sound credible, be sure to vary your sentence structures and avoid placing too many simple sentences one after another.

Way #2: Commas after Introductory Phrases and Clauses

Sometimes, on a Sunday, people like to start their sentences with introductory phrases. The purpose of this little lead-in is to set the stage for the main part of the sentence. It usually tells **how**, **what**, **where**, **when**, or **why**.

> Introductory words and phrases set the stage for the rest of the sentence: What happened? Where and when did it happen? How did it happen and why?

They are perfectly correct and acceptable…except when you look back at your paper and see that every sentence begins with one.

Too many sentences structured the same way does not allow for variation that keeps the reader interested. In English, we have dependent and independent clauses. As the name implies, one can stand alone and doesn't need any support—the independent clause. It is a complete sentence. The dependent clause, on the other hand, cannot stand alone and needs to attach itself to an independent clause. Alone, the dependent clause is a fragment.

If you have an entire paragraph consisting of sentences that read—**dependent clause, independent clause**—it becomes distracting because of the repetitive tone. It would be nearly as distracting as ending all of the sentences with a question mark? Wouldn't it be? Don't you think it's annoying? Though few of us read out loud, we still "hear" the words in our head as we read, and we do note repetitive patterns that constitute the author's voice. Varying your sentence structures increases visual and auditory appeal.

Sentences that begin with an introductory word or phrase require a comma after that word or phrase and are called **complex sentences**. You know you have an introductory phrase or clause that requires a comma after it when you can remove it and the rest of the sentence can stand alone. Some examples of introductory words and phrases are presented here:

Although	That said	First	After…	Case in point
Besides	Last week	Yes	Before…	Until…
In addition	Consequently	Generally	Suddenly	Because

One way to spot introductory phrases is to look for the signal of any time phrase.

- *A couple of weeks ago,*
- *Last semester,*
- *Before World War II,*
- *During the blizzard,*
- *A week from Tuesday,*

Another way is to spot them is to watch for prepositions starting the phrase. Remember, prepositions are anywhere a cat can go: under, on, in, behind, next to, etc.

- *Under the shade of the striped umbrella,*
- *On any given Sunday,*
- *On the sandy beach under a towel,*

A final type of introductory phrase is a conditional phrase that begins with *If.*

- *If you would like to go,*
- *If I were the president,*
- *If we wanted to get in shape quickly,*
- *If you think about it long enough,*

Examples of Complex Sentences

The following sentences are complex sentences, as evidenced by the introductory phrase or clause followed by a comma.

1. *After leaving the office, Leila discovered she had forgotten her laptop charger.*
2. *When he heard a ding in the middle of the meeting, Matt ducked his head and realized that he had forgotten to put his cell phone on silent.*
3. *Last Friday, Sam was standing in front of the corporate offices in the pouring rain.*

> **Remember:** Moving a phrase to the end of the sentence is an easy way to check if you need to use a comma.

Another way to determine if you need a comma is by taking that beginning clause or phrase and moving it to the end of the sentence:

1. *Leila discovered she had forgotten her laptop charger after leaving the office.*
2. *Matt ducked his head and realized that he forgotten to put his phone on silent when he heard it ding in the middle of a meeting.*
3. *Sam was standing in front of the corporate offices in the pouring rain last Friday.*

If you can move the word or phrase from the beginning to the end of the sentence and it still makes sense there, then it is identified as an introductory phrase or clause. As such, it will need a comma *after* it when it begins a sentence. When in doubt, or if you become comma-shy, just move the word or phrase to the end of the sentence and leave it there—you will not need a comma. This slide to the end of the sentence is an easy comma test and a quick way to change your sentences should you become stuck with repetitive constructs.

Practice #1: Introductory Commas

Supply the necessary comma after the introductory words or phrases in the following sentences.

1. *Whenever it starts raining John starts singing.*
2. *In the past few months stock prices have fallen 4%.*
3. *After the most recent election the country is more polarized than ever.*
4. *Under the spreading branches of Africa's umbrella thorn tree a lioness dozed with her cubs.*
5. *On the sand nearest the cliffs clumps of wild flowers were blooming in a proliferation of reds and yellows.*
6. *During the hurricane families huddled together in interior rooms of their homes to avoid breaking windows and flying debris.*
7. *To raise enough money to go to Buenos Aires Brandon increased the percentage of his wages that were going to savings.*
8. *In order to better understand the behavior of the tsetse fly scientist hatch millions of larva each year in order to study them.*
9. *Without the help of stem cells spinal cord regrowth research would not have come as far as it has.*
10. *If you really feel like helping grab a shovel instead of just standing there.*

Way #3: Use Coordinating Conjunctions and Commas in Compound Sentences

Coordinating conjunctions are For, And, Nor, But, Or, Yet, and So; they can be remembered by the acronym FANBOYS.

Coordinating conjunctions are used to combine two complete sentences or independent clauses, thereby making **compound sentences**. You use compound sentences to lend more flow to your writing and to combine sentences that would otherwise sound choppy.

Here is the rule: Use a comma before a FANBOYS if both sides of the sentence can stand alone.

I like coffee and very sweet tea.

The best way to check your own writing when deciding whether to use a comma, try the "pinkie test" by covering over the FANBOYS "and." Can the part on the left and right of your finger stand alone as their own sentences? No? Then do not use a comma. That sentence is correct as it is written without a comma because "very sweet tea" is not a complete sentence and cannot stand alone.

I like coffee and I like really hot tea.

Now try it: I like coffee (pinkie finger here). I like really hot tea. Yes, they can both stand alone, so the FANBOYS needs a comma before it.

I like coffee, and I like really hot tea.

The tip-off is if you have a subject after the FANBOYS, you are going to need a comma.

I called the office looking for Steve and left a message for him.

I called the office looking for Steve, and I left a message for him.

April hates to write but loves presenting, peer tutoring, and working in groups.

April hates to write, but she loves presenting, peer tutoring, and working in groups.

Don't expect to get it right the first time. Always go back over your work, look for the telltale FANBOYS, and then use the **pinkie test** to see if you need a comma–or not. When sentences are thusly combined, they are called **compound sentences**.

The English language is infamous for having many exceptions to every rule. Fortunately, the FANBOYS rule has only one exception: Do not use a comma before so when it means *so that*—whether the word *that* is written or not.

> **Correct:** *She always carried her cell phone charger so she can keep her phone charged after a long day at the office.*

Even though the pinkie test would dictate that a comma before so was necessary since both sides can stand alone, because so in this sentence means *so that*, no comma is used.

Practice #2: FANBOYS Commas

Some of these sentences need a comma added or deleted, and some of them are correct. Edit them for correctness.

1. Sam appeared to wander around aimlessly but he knew exactly where he was going and why.
2. The files from the Castor Co. lawsuit were on Indira's desk, but she had no idea who had put them there.
3. Captain Ramsey piloted the ship through the tempest, and barked orders as the frightened crew slid around the slick deck.
4. I have found that female hermit crabs will come out of the shells when given a bath, but not all of them.
5. You can call the doctor or you can see to the wound yourself.
6. The professor appeared shy and somewhat aloof in meetings yet his student evaluations of his approachability were the highest in the department.
7. Ibrahim, the art gallery's curator, turned the stained glass lamp shade toward the light, so he could more easily study the subtle patterns and variations of color.
8. The thief never looked back for he knew the police were chasing him.
9. Crocodiles are meat eaters and it doesn't matter if the meat is fresh, or if it is rotten.
10. Reyk turned in his college applications minutes before the deadline, and nearly gave his parents a collective heart attack.

Combine these choppy sentences for flow using one of the FANBOYS. Add commas as necessary.

1. *He isn't honest. He isn't ethical.*
2. *Boston University is a beautiful school. BU has an excellent reputation.*
3. *New Year's resolutions are ineffective. They also put unnecessary pressure on people to be perfect.*
4. *Drinking too much coffee can upset your stomach. It can also help you stay up late to finish a paper.*
5. *Deandra recognized the handwriting immediately. She had been married to the man who wrote it for years.*
6. *North Korea has been testing rocket engines and heat-shields for an ICBM. North Korea has also been developing the technology to guide a missile after re-entry into the atmosphere.*
7. *Opera started in Italy at the end of the 16th century. Opera is part of the Western classical music tradition.*
8. *Cambodia is a large country in Southeast Asia with a population of almost 14 million. Tokyo, a city in a small country, has the same population.*
9. *She did not deny that she had seen the will. She did not confirm it, either.*
10. *Spiral notebooks are sturdy. Spiral notebooks come in regular and college ruled spacing.*

Choosing Compound or Complex Sentence Structures

In addition to knowing how to punctuate them properly, you also need to know when to use these two types of sentences. In business writing, you want the most important information to go in the independent clause. Compound sentences are more emphatic; complex sentences less emphatic. If you have bad news to give, you would be wise to deliver it in a complex sentence. If you have good news you want to stress, either put it in a simple sentence or a compound sentence. The complex sentence is indirect and lulls the reader by slowly getting to the point.

GOOD NEWS	BAD NEWS
Simple Sentence: You have won the lottery!	Simple Sentence: You did not win the lottery!
Compound Sentence: You have won the lottery, and you will be rich forever!	Complex Sentence: Although you play your last $20 every single week, this week the lottery was won by a grandfather in Michigan.
Complex Sentence: Since you have the right numbers on your lottery ticket, you have won the lottery!	Compound Sentence: You did not win the lottery, but a lucky grandfather in Michigan did!

In the bad news examples, using a complex sentence and leading with disarming information can soften the blow for the bad news that follows. Many times bad news messages start out with a buffering sentence or paragraph. Just as in the movies when the police knock on someone's door in the middle of the night, they don't yell, "There's been a horrible accident!" at the bewildered homeowners. They lead with a buffer like confirming the homeowners' names, asking if they own a White Honda Accord, requesting permission to come in . . . they take their time and deliver the bad news after a respectful lead-in. Keep this in mind when you consider the purpose of your message or sentence and your reader's reaction to it.

So remember: Use a comma after an introductory phrase or clause. Use a compound or simple sentence to deliver good news fast using FANBOYS and a comma to combine them. Use a complex sentence structure with an introductory word or phrase and a comma to soften and delay the delivery of bad news.

Way #4: Using Semicolons: Comma's Snobby Cousin

Once you have learned to properly use the introductory comma and FANBOYS comma properly, you can move on to another way to combine sentences for flow and variety. Knowing how to properly use a semicolon will also help you avoid credibility errors in your writing. First, actually *look* at the semicolon.

A semicolon is a pause longer than a comma but shorter than a period or colon.

The semicolon asks you to wait for the ending of the point you are making, but it's not as exciting as a colon. A semicolon says, "Wait, there's more . . ." A key consideration is that you have to stay on the same topic. You cannot use it with two unrelated sentences.

> Ronnie is worried about punctuating longer sentences; however, he just needs to grasp the use of the semicolon.
>
> Or . . .
>
> Ronnie has trouble figuring out how to punctuate longer sentences; he has yet to meet the semicolon.

You can use it with a transitional word like **however, therefore, moreover**, as long as you put a semicolon before the word and a comma after it. The most common transitional words and phrases used with semicolons are listed below.

accordingly	eventually	in any case	on the contrary
afterwards	evidently	in any event	on the other hand
again	finally	in fact	otherwise
anyhow	for example	in like manner	perhaps
as a result	for instance	in short	possibly
at last	for this reason	likewise	still
at the same time	furthermore	meanwhile	that is
besides	hence	moreover	then
consequently	however	namely	therefore
doubtless	indeed	nevertheless	thus
due to this	in addition	next	coincidentally

Incorrect: *Andrea neglected to let her bank know that she would be traveling in China, consequently the ATMs in Shanghai rejected her card.*

Incorrect: *Andrea neglected to let her bank know that she would be traveling in China; consequently the ATMs in Shanghai rejected her card.*

Correct: *Andrea neglected to let her bank know that she would be traveling in China; consequently, the ATMs in Shanghai rejected her card.*

You can combine closely-related complete sentences with a semicolon and no transition word:

Never use a semicolon and a FANBOYS. Think of FANBOYS as being too little to handle a semicolon. Little words need a little comma. After all, they are FANBOYS, not FANMEN.

- *Some bosses are hot-headed; anyone in their path risks drawing their wrath.*
- *Tamara did not return the internship leader's phone call; she was playing hard to get.*
- *That PowerPoint was good; I've seen better*

Remember, like the use of the comma before a FANBOY, both sides of semicolon have to be independent clauses able to stand alone. This means they also have to pass the "pinkie test." Cover the middle with your pinkie. If both sides can stand alone, use a semicolon.

Correct punctuation with FANBOYS: We are planning a catered feast for the company picnic, and we have hired a talented mariachi group to perform.

If you are going to use a semicolon and a transition word, it has to be a big beefy word like *moreover, therefore,* or *however*. A fun way to remember this is, if you feel like you should use a British accent when saying the transition word, you probably need a semicolon.

Correct punctuation with a transitional word: We are planning a catered feast for the company picnic; moreover, we have hired a talented mariachi group to perform.

Don't be afraid to use semicolons; however, as with a (phony) British accent, don't overdo it.

Practice #3: Semicolons

Combine the following sentences by using a semicolon and a transitional word:

1. *The chef's specialty is seared swordfish. It is not available on the lunch menu.*
2. *The man pleaded not guilty. He claimed to know the identity of the mastermind behind the jewel heist.*
3. *You need to clean the leather with a soft damp cloth. You need to let the cowboy boots dry completely before you apply the polish.*
4. *Brandon was calling his boss. His boss was emailing him telling him that they needed to talk about the system outage.*
5. *The fishermen caught their limit of sockeye salmon. They roasted the biggest one over the open fire on a spit.*
6. *The caterer bought twenty pounds of lean hamburger meat. She bought 30 hamburger buns.*
7. *Tickets to Iceland are cheap in the winter. You could have a honeymoon that doesn't go over your budget.*
8. *Mountain climbers know the dangers of changing weather conditions on Mt. Everest. That doesn't stop them from attempting to summit the mighty mountain year after year.*
9. *You may not be a good ball striker when you first learn to play golf. With enough practice and time at the range, you will improve.*
10. *I can never remember how to use lay and lie. I have problems with my lefts and rights.*

Colons: The Real Story

We have covered commas and semicolons; let's now look at the colon and its uses. The key takeaway to remember about the colon is that it has to follow a complete sentence. Again, misusing colons also brings your credibility into question.

Incorrect: *The things I want are: money, fame, and a closetful of shoes.*
Correct: *I want the following: money, fame, and a closet full of shoes.*

Incorrect: *You may want to bring: sunscreen, music, water, and something to eat.*
Correct: *You may want to bring a few essentials to the beach: sunscreen, music, water, and something to eat.*

Also note, you do not capitalize the first letter of the first word in a list following a colon. However, if what follows the colon is a complete sentence, you must punctuate it as such and capitalize the first letter of the first word.

My colleague always cautioned against excessive worry with a standard warning: Don't borrow trouble.

The professor reminded the students of the plagiarism rule at least five times: Do not use your roommate's paper!

Finally, you can use a colon to introduce a list that is either bulleted or numbered. It is a judgment call whether you will capitalize or punctuate. The important takeaway is that you must be consistent.

I want an assistant who can do the following:

1. screen phone calls
2. compose memos quickly
3. deal with difficult clients
4. keep me on schedule

I will only consider an assistant who can handle all four of these things at once.

Use colons after complete sentences when introducing a list or bullets, and punctuate consistently. Following that simple rule will allow you to use colons sparingly but with confidence.

Putting It All Together

Though it seems a daunting task to produce professional documents in the workplace, this chapter enumerated the finer points of making certain your writing is taken seriously. Errors of any kind bring into question your abilities and, ultimately, your credibility. You should review this chapter anytime you are ready to deliver a piece of writing and want to ensure that you have polished and revised down to the smallest of punctuation marks.

Practice #4: Putting It All Together

Putting together all that you have learned about punctuation, grammar, and concision, revise the following paragraphs until they are concise and correct:

Nike, Inc. is struggling in one of the most important markets in the world, Greater China. Nike is failing to target and accommodate to the athletic Chinese consumer. China's population stands at 1.3 billion people which is why the Chinese market has an immense influence on the world's economy. Not properly marketing and adapting to the wants Chinese consumers have creates a huge loss of potential sales for Nike, Inc. In 2012, Nike, Inc. predicted China sales to reach $4 billion by 2016 (Forbes). This issue is now recognized as a priority for Nike since competitors like Adidas and Under Armour are gaining ground on Nike in a crucial market for the corporation's success.

Google's goal is to have produced the first completely autonomous car to a public market. In reaching this goal it is critical that Google progresses the product on a strict timeline. The first stage of their timeline is the completion of their cars current research and development. Google can not release a vehicle that is subpar, meaning that their car must be completed before presenting it to potential partners. Forging a partnership is the next step, as once they have teamed up with a major car manufacturer they can begin the final two steps in the collaboration of both design and safety.

At the core of our issue is the relationship Aetna has with the government, specifically, the Affordable Care Act. While this piece of legislation has made business difficult for us, we realize the position that we are in. We know for the future of our company we must work with local and federal governments in order to have long-term success in any market. Our recommendation is to create a group within our company that solely maintains a positive relationship with the United States Department of Health. This benefits our company in many ways including knowledge of current and upcoming legislation, constructive meetings, and having productive dialogue between our entities.

This recommendation report follows our previous SBA report, where we covered issues regarding Aetna's collaboration with the Affordable Car Act and the affects of these dilemmas. Our team has researched and reported the dilemmas Aetna faces and now, below, provided recommendations and costs pertaining to our plan for fixing these issues. Topics below consist of reduction of labor hours, cost cutting for shareholders, Aetna and the government (ACA), and, lastly, bettering public relations. The overall cost of our team's implemented plan is approximately $31,060,000. This total cost is broken down and dispersed under each section below, for a better understanding on how our team reached this totaled cost.

Finally, if you are ready to put all you have learned to use, revise, edit, and proofread the following cover letter. Use all of your skills to hone it to a concise message. Do not worry about changing the content—do so as needed.

Dear MS …

I have been waiting for an opportunity like this to write to you. My name is Rick Wagner. Please take into consideration my application for the position of Goldman Sachs financial analysis. I have dual degrees in finance and accounting. I am good at analyzing financial markets and I can identify the relationship between market trends and current events.

I am an excellent student and a hard worker. I always read the money market news in the Wall street Journal. And some time buy some equity and financial derivative in the stock track. In the CME challenger competition, our team got a 8% holding period return during the 2 week's future trading. I try my best to conquer my human emotion bias. And I really want to be a financial analysis in the Goldman Sachs. I believe I can write some high qualified researches in this perfect company.

In that regard, I would appreciate the opportunity to meet with you to discuss my qualification and the possibility of joining your organization. Please find enclosed my resume for your review. I look forward to hearing from you.

Sincerely,

Good Student/Bad Writer

For additional grammar help, these sites provide excellent advice.

GRAMMAR GIRL	http://www.quickanddirtytips.com/grammar-girl
GRAMMAR MONSTER	http://www.grammar-monster.com/
GRAMMAR BOOK	http://www.grammarbook.com/

Chapter 43

Sample Messages

Now that you have learned the planning, writing, documentation, formatting, and editing of your own writing, this chapter offers sample documents of all the strategies covered in the previous chapters. The samples in this chapter can serve as models that you can use to organize and format your own deliverables.

Email

Email is an important type of message that is used frequently in the workplace. Your communication through email in the workplace requires more formality than posting on social media. Emails can be sent internally within your organization or externally to individuals in another organization. Email may be used as follows:

- To deliver direct or indirect messages
- To deliver positive, neutral, or negative information
- To persuade

To: managingdirector@companya.com
From: corporatevp@companya.com
Date: September 1, 2014
Subject: New Company Initiative

Dear Mr. Voss,

We appreciate your desire for excellent customer service and increased profitability. Our corporate goal is to build and maintain customer satisfaction at all of our properties. With enhanced customer satisfaction, our company is able to thrive and increase profits. I am glad to inform you of new changes to our sustainability initiative, GREEN. These changes will increase our customer satisfaction and fuel your property's profitability.

Benefits of GREEN

According to source 1, our company is currently ranked number one in the industry in terms of market share. However, we are ranked third in terms of sustainability measures. Both Company B and Company D lead the industry in sustainability initiatives. Therefore, they enjoy the benefits of increased public relations and profitability for their properties.

With our new initiative, your property will also have the opportunity to increase public engagement, customer loyalty, and overall profitability. Recently, we have found that customers care about an organization's sustainability, and almost 75% of people consider the company's sustainability efforts when making a booking.

Research shows that initiatives such as GREEN increase employee morale. Our employees are passionate about the program, resulting in higher efficiency and decreased turnover. Initiatives such as GREEN have also been shown to increase operation efficiency and enhance brand recognition. These benefits will enhance your public relations and increase profitability for your property.

Managing directors at our other properties have found GREEN is easy to initiate and sustain. They also save resources through the initiative. For instance, water is one of the easiest resources to save. We can reduce water usage at our properties in a variety of ways, from watering property landscapes with reclaimed water, to allowing guests to reuse towels and linens during their stay. There are various techniques to implement GREEN on your property.

The new standard for Company A includes linking 10% of your base salary and 100% of your annual bonuses to your progress toward a 5% reduction of water usage by the end of 2015. This is an attainable goal that can increase your salary and bonus. With this new change, we can be more profitable as a company. In addition, you can be more efficient as a property manager, keeping both employees and customers satisfied.

Action Item

Please choose a representative to send to our corporate-wide training about the best way to reach these goals and meet the key GREEN performance measures. Please email me at corporatevp@companya.com or call me at 999-888-7777, to sign up your representative. I look forward to hearing from you.

Sincerely,

Student A

Letter

A letter is a formal workplace message. Letters can be sent internally within your organization when the communication needs to be official, such as with HR notifications. However, letters are typically used for external communication. Letters may be used as follows:

- To deliver direct or indirect messages
- To deliver positive, neutral, or negative information
- To persuade

Tina Van Smith
66 Big Train St
Tucson, AZ 85721

February 2, 2014

Mayor Colin Kline
1 City Hall Square
Tucson, AZ 85701

Dear Mr. Kline,

On behalf of the Organization X, we congratulate you as the new Mayor of Tucson. We appreciate your dedication to the growth, safety, infrastructure, and people of Tucson. Organization X also cares about the enrichment of Tucson. We are excited to provide accessibility and exposure to the arts to all Tucson residents. I am writing to introduce you to our new membership program catered to lower-income patrons.

This lower-income patron membership program aims to reduce crime rates in Tucson, by enriching the lives of Tucson residents through exposure to the arts. Research has shown that poverty is directly related to crime. Tucson has a high poverty rate of over 20%; this program is an opportunity to reduce the poverty and crime rates in the city. This initiative will allow lower-income patrons to have the opportunity to be better involved in the Tucson community.

Enriching the lives of Tucson residents will also lead to positive publicity for you. In turn, more people will be educated about your initiatives and will want to support you. Your support of these efforts will allow you to become a more proactive figure in Tucson. Most importantly, through this venture, Tucson will become a better city.

We would like to partner with you on this new program. In order to make this initiative a success, we need funds to subsidize discounted membership rates for lower income patrons. We ask for your assistance to help underwrite this program. Please email me at director@artsorg.com for more information. I look forward to hearing from you soon.

Sincerely,

Jane Smith
ArtsOrg Executive Director

This student uses a letter to send an indirect persuasive message to an individual outside the writer's organization.

Alignment—presents a common goal and gives the reader a reason to keep reading.

Information—provides key information based on the audience's needs and wants.

Direct Benefit—shows reader what they can gain.

Call to **A**ction—makes ask and provides next steps.

Memo

With the popularity and efficiency of email, memos are not used as often in today's workplace as they were in the past. Memos are generally used internally, though on rare occasions can be sent externally to individuals in another organization. Memos may be used as follows:

- To deliver direct or indirect messages
- To deliver positive, neutral, or negative information
- To persuade

MEMORANDUM

To: Fred Jones
From: Kali Corner
Subject: Project Overview
Date: 8/4/14

This memorandum will summarize the problem that Company XYZ currently faces, the key stakeholders involved, and the unique situational variables. I will inform you of relevant information and explain key concerns of the project. This information will allow you to evaluate my progress throughout the project.

Company XYZ's new product is an excellent concept which needs to be brought to market. However, the company is attempting to launch with limited funds. In order to increase the startup funds, my team will develop a marketing strategy that will allow the company to pitch its concept to prospective venture capitalists. In addition, we have the added challenge of developing an actionable marketing plan that will appeal to the end users of the new product. It is our goal to create the necessary framework for Company XYZ to use to obtain funding and bring the product to market.

Stakeholders
The major stakeholders in this project are the founders of Company XYZ, venture capitalists who decide to invest in the company, and end users.

Venture Capitalists
Venture capitalists will want a strong, comprehensive marketing initiative to make the product sell. They are concerned with receiving a return on investment.

End Users
The end users include school districts, administration, teachers, students, and parents. End users will want to know how the new product can augment their needs. If successful, we could change the direction of technology in the classroom and enhance learning and teaching in modern education.

Situational Variables
Company XYZ anticipates that the product will be at the beta stages in December 2014. The product is designed to be the first of its kind on the market. Therefore, we will not have direct competitors. Our team must conduct research to better understand the industry Company XYZ competes in and the target markets that the new products will appeal to.

It will be our responsibility to develop a strong marketing strategy based on best practices and extensive industry research, giving the company a solid base for product launch. Company XYZ is developing a revolutionary product. Our team is ready to conduct the research to bring this new concept to market through a strategic approach. You should now have a sense of my current status and intended direction on the project. Please contact me at kali@companyxyz.com if you have any questions.

This student example uses a memo to send a direct informational message to an internal recipient within the sender's organization.

The introduction includes the message purpose, frames the information for the audience, and forecasts key information.

All information is analyzed for the audience in the body of the message.

The writer concludes the message with a summary, repeating her bottom line, and an invitation to inquire.

Note: Do not use a salutation, closing, or signature in a memo.

Industry Report

The following two documents are student examples of industry reports. These are informative reports written for larger audiences and designed to provide readers with a concise but comprehensive overview of a particular industry. Therefore, they feature a more formal layout than routine correspondence messages, and the introductions and conclusions are not addressed to a particular receiver. In addition, the authors avoid using the first and second person voicing more common in shorter, exchange-driven communication.

CORRECTIONAL FACILITIES
INDUSTRY REPORT

Course Number

Date

Strong information design &
color coordination.

Introduction frames and
forecasts, but reflects excess
"to be" phrasing.

Interesting and effective use of
color to identify subheadings.

Introduction

The largest in the world, the United States Correctional Facilities Industry has shown a positive increase in population prior to the 2000s. Recently, the Correctional Facilities industry has been showing more consistent trends, especially in the last three to five years. Topics that will be covered are segments, products and services, target markets, market drivers, major players, financial performances in domestic markets, presence in international markets, industry trends, and industry opportunities.

BREAKDOWN OF PRODUCTS AND SERVICES

- Community Correctional Facility
- Minimum Security Prisons
- Medium Security Prisons
- Maximum Security Prisons

0.061 0.026
0.277
0.636

Source: IBIS World Database

Products and Services

There are a total of 4 main services the industry offers. The first are Community Correctional Facilities that make up 27.7% of total revenues (O'Hollaren, 2016, p. 5). Community Correctional Facilities have very few restrictions and do not have correction officers. Facility workers are not allowed to use force or anything physical to restrain inmates. Inmates in these facilities, inmates can leave for job related opportunities but must return to the prison later in the evening ("U.S prison populations: Trends and implications," 2013, para 12).

Minimum Security Prisons represent 6.1% of total revenue of the entire Prison industry. These facilities have dorm-like living, and the staff to inmate ratio is comparably low to the other prison facilities. In addition, many inmates in minimum security prisons can be released early with transitional programs ("U.S prison populations: Trends and implications," 2013, para 12).

Medium Security Prisons represent the largest proportion of the revenue of the Correctional Facility Industry, making up 63.6% of total revenues. Housing in these facilities are mostly cell-type, but with the overcrowding problems with these facilities some cells are dorm style. These facilities have higher staff to inmate ratios than minimum security prisons ("U.S prison populations: Trends and implications," 2013, para. 12). Maximum Security Prisons represents the smallest proportion compared to the other services making up 2.6% of total revenues. These facility house either one or two inmates per cell, and most are unable to leave their cell for longer than one hour a day. These facilities have the highest staff to inmate ratio, but provide the least amount of trainings for their staff.

Major Markets

There are a total of four major markets that are a part of the Correctional Facilities Industry, and below is a pie chart representing each market and how much revenue they contribute in the industry.

The Federal Bureau of Prisons makes up the smallest proportion of the Correctional Facilities Industry with only 13% of total revenue from the industry. The Federal Bureau of Prisons was founded in 1930, and their mission is to have more humane prisons. The BOP over sees 170,000 inmates and almost 40,000 employees.

The US Marshals Services was founded in 1789, and is the enforcement arm in our federal courts. The USMS's main responsibilities include protecting the federal judiciary, selling assets from criminal activities, and housing detainees before they are sentenced to jail.

The United States Immigration and Customs Enforcement was the outcome of a merger in 2003 between the United States Customs Services and the Immigration and Naturalization Service. The ICE is in charge of protecting the US with border controls, immigration, and other related activities.

State and Local Governments, on the other hand, are in charge of local criminal activities. States with a large number of prisoners with tight budgets expand their market right after the recession. Since tax receipts increase with the growing and improving economy, the correctional facilities are under less pressure to budget and spend less money.

BREAKDOWN OF MAJOR MARKETS

- Bureau of Prisons
- US Marshals Service
- Immigration and Customs Enforcement
- State and Local Governments

Source: IBIS World Database

Author rendered charts to coordinate with the color scheme — a very nice touch.

Market Drivers

An Incarceration Rate represents the amount people in prisons. As this incarceration rate increases, prisons start to become more overcrowded, and becomes more likely to higher people at these correctional facilities. The incarceration rate is expected to increase in 2016, according to IBIS World Data base (O'Hollaren, 2016, p.3).

Since privately owned correctional facilities gain revenue from federal and state government contracts, so changes in Government Consumption and Investment will change demand for correctional facility industry services. An increase in government consumption and investments will increase demand for services. The government consumption is expected to increase in 2016 and that will present more opportunities for the Correctional Facilities Industry (O'Hollaren, 2016, p.3).

Increases in Crime Rate will intuitively increase the arrest and prison occupancy rate, and inevitably will raise demand for these industry services. The crime rate is expected to decrease in 2016, which will result in a threat for the industry growth (O'Hollaren, 2016, p.3).

Major Players

The first major player in the Correctional Facilities industry are the Corrections Corporations of America, founded in 1983 in Nashville Tennessee. CCA currently holds a market share of 34.9%, they are the largest owner in private correctional facility industry. The second major player in this industry is The GEO Group with a total market share of 27.1%. Their headquarters is in Boca Raton, Florida. As of the end of 2015, The GEO Group currently control 64 correctional facilities in 19 states and the Dominican Republic. Some other companies in this industry include the Management & Training Corporation, and their estimated market share is less than 5%. This company is privately held, and was first established in 1981. Their headquarters are located Centerville, Utah, and they operate a total of five main business segments: job corps, corrections, international workforce development, MTC works, and MTC medical (O'Hollaren, 2016, p. 7).

Financial Performance in Domestic Markets

There has been a steady growth in revenues for the GEO Group, Inc. throughout the past five years. The Correctional Corporation of America, has stayed stagnant for the past five years, but still generates more revenue than the GEO Group. According to Marketline (2016), the GEO Group, Inc. has not only been working domestically, but also internationally with Australia. They are planning large-scale projects soon that are projected to increase revenue. Given this information, I predict that the GEO Group will reach, if not surpass, the revenues of the Correctional Corporations of America within the next five to ten years.

Source: Annual Report and IBIS World

Presence in International Markets

This section is weak as it offers very little information.

While the United States Prison Industry is the largest in the world, Russia and South Africa are closely following behind. Since the Correctional Facility Industry is mostly service based, international trade is limited.

Industry Threats

Use of color adds to skim-friendliness.

Falling profit: Since most costs for the Correctional Facility Industry are fixed, there really isn't much room for growth in revenue for this industry for the next five years. As the incarceration rates begin to fall slowly, the costs for each prisoner continue to rise and revenue also decreases. This inevitably causes profits to decrease leaving little room for new employees and growth in the industry (O'Hollaren, 2016, p. 4).

Public Image: In early 2015, prison inmates in Willacy County Correctional Center in Texas went on strike to protest a poor Medicare plan for prisoners. According to former inmates and guards responded to this protest by shooting prisoners with rubber bullets and other weapons. This peaceful protest soon turned into a riot (Tyx, 2015, para. 3). Events like these start to create a negative image of these privately owned correctional facilities and people start to question where the line is drawn between humanity and being a correctional facility in these prisons.

Prison Overcrowding: As the prison population continues to grow, these facilities are starting to become overcrowded and impossible to live in. Prison overcrowding is becoming a very large and concerning problem in the United States. The cause of this overcrowding is because of harsher sentences for unlawful activities, and changes in the law causing more people to be put in these correctional institutes. Overcrowding can cause problems such as more than one person per cell, misconduct of prisoners from having less personal space, and other psychological problems from having too many people in one jail facility ("Prison overcrowding is a growing concern in the U.S.," para. 3–5).

Attitudes toward Psychiatry Trainings: A study was conducted to discuss the attitude toward psychological problems within the prisons across the United States. The published paper states, "There is a critical need for psychiatrists in the correctional system, and the correctional system in many states is the largest mental health provider," (Furhrlein, Jha, Brenner, & North, 2014, p. 294). If the Correctional Facilities Industry continues to ignore mental illness as a serious problem, it will only cause more negative effects for the industry in its entirety.

Industry Opportunity
Special Cell Designs: A large problem mentioned earlier in Industry Threats gave insight into the prison overcrowding problem in the United States. While a standard prisoner is required by the American Correctional Association to have 80 square feet in their cell. This often creates many problems (see Prison Overcrowding). Richard E. Vehlow writes in his article that there is room for improvement, and gives specific ways to fix this overcrowding problem. As he states in his article, "For optimum performance of a duct network in an institutional environment, especially with regards to inmate cells, good register balancing is paramount" (2011). By following the plan that Vehlow has laid out, we can improve on the overcrowding problem which would also improve the industry public image as well.

Conclusion
The Correctional Facilities Industry is the owner, manager, and leaser of prisons, community correctional facilities, and juvenile detention facilities. With an annual revenue looking to increase by .06% in the next five years, the industry seems to have a positive outlook. As crime rates and incarceration rates start to decrease, there is less prison overcrowding. This creates less pressure for the industry to grow rapidly. As the United States Department of Justice start to move toward less privatize prison facilities, governments will hopefully follow.

References

Corrections Corporation of America MarketLine company profile. (2016, October). *Business Source Complete*. Retreived April 21, 2017, from EBSCO Host.

Fuehrlein, B. S., Jha, M. K., Brenner, M. A., North, C. A. (2014 April). Availability and attitudes toward correctional psychiatry training: Results of a national survey training directors. *The Journal of Behavioral Health Services & Research*. Retrieved April 15, 2017, from ABI/INFORM Collection.

O'Hollaren, K. (2016, November). IBIS World Industry Report 56121. Correctional Facilities in the US. Retrieved April 15, 2017, from IBISWorld database.

Prison overcrowding is a growing concern in the U.S. *Portland State University* Retrieved April 22, 2017, from http://online.ccj.pdx.edu/news-resources/articles/prison-overcrowding-is-a-growing-concern-in-the-u-s.html.

The GEO Group Inc. MarketLine company profile. (2016, December). *Business Source Complete*. Retrieved April 15, 2017, from EBSCO Host.

Tyx, D. B. (2015 March). Goodbye to Tent City. *Texas Observer*. Retrieved April 22, 2017, from https://www.texasobserver.org/south-texas-prison-riot-willacy-county-economic-future/

U.S prison populations: Trends and implications. (2003 May). *The Sentencing Project*. Retrieved April 22, 2017, from https://www.prisonpolicy.org/scans/sp/1044.pdf

Vehlow, R. E. (2011). Special design considerations for institutional and correctional facilities. *ASHRAE Transactions*. Retrieved April 15, 2017, from Business Insights: Essentials.

INDUSTRY REPORT: CORRECTIONAL FACILITIES

Student

Date

Headings are over-treated. Bold would be fine. No need for the underline.

Provides an introduction appropriate for a wide audience. It is well-framed for a larger readership and it reflects a stand-alone document, not a correspondence message.

Overview provides high-level description/definition of the industry.

Again, the headings are busy. Bold headings, then a non-bolded italicized subheadings heading would suffice.

Though copying a graphic directly from a source is fine as long as it gives credit to the original source, you should consider creating your own graphical elements using that data to match the overall document design. When you do create your own graphics based on data, still cite the original source of the data you used.

Introduction

The correctional facility industry is a mature and slow growing industry. Outsourcing prison operations and the incarceration rate are key demand determinants that drive sales and revenue. This document provides a detailed overview of various aspects and drivers of the correctional facilities industry. The key points highlighted in this memo are market segments/target markets, products/services, prevalent companies, presence in international markets, market drivers, industry challenges/threats, financial performance in domestic markets, and industry opportunities.

Overview

The correctional facilities industry is comprised of operators that own and or manage correctional facilities and halfway houses and generates $5.3 billion in revenue annually. The industry is expected to grow at a yearly rate of 0.6% from 2016 to 2021. Two key external drivers of the correctional facility industry are the incarceration rate and crime rate, both of which were projected to fall at 0.5% and 0.1% respectively. This, in combination with the public scrutiny surrounding the treatment of inmates has caused the overall profit margin to fall over the last five years (2011–2016). In the coming years until 2021, revenue is expected to reach $5.4 billion. However, with the continued fall in crime rates, the correctional facility industry remains exposed to downside risk, which ultimately complicates revenue growth (O'Hollaren, 2016, Industry Outlook).

Market Segments/Target Markets

According to the Ibisworld database's 2016 industry report, the correctional facilities industry receives all of its revenue from federal and state contracts. The four major customer segments for this industry are state and local governments, Immigration and Customs Enforcement, the US Marshals Service, and the Bureau of Prisons.

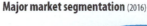

Major market segmentation (2016)

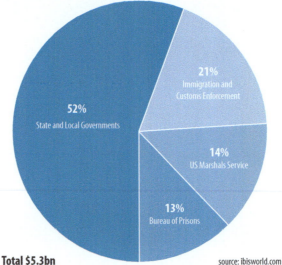

52% State and Local Governments

21% Immigration and Customs Enforcement

14% US Marshals Service

13% Bureau of Prisons

Total $5.3bn

source: ibisworld.com

State and Local Governments

State and local governments account for 52% of the overall industry revenue, which hire industry operators to house inmates and manage facilities. According to the Bureau of Justice, as of 2014, 30 states housed a portion of their inmates in private facilities, and seven states held at least 20% of their prisoners in private institutions (O'Hollaren, 2016, Major Markets). However, market research indicates that states are slowly eliminating the use of private prisons, and as the economy improves, state correctional departments feel less pressure to cut back on their budgets.

US Immigration and Customs Enforcement

21% of the total industry revenue is generated by US Immigration and Customs Enforcement (ICE), who is responsible for enforcing laws regarding border control, customs, trade, and immigration. Since the number of migrants (mainly from Mexico, Guatemala, Honduras, and El Salvador) increased by nearly 25% in the last ten years, major companies within the industry are considering expanding the capacity for housing illegal immigrants (ICE, 2016). Since ICE does not operate under the Department of Justice, the DOJ's recent policy change to slowly eliminate private federal prisons does not affect its use of private facilities.

US Marshals Service

The US Marshals Service (USMS) makes up 14% of the industry revenue. The USMS is primarily responsible for housing and transporting federal prisoners before they are sentenced or acquitted. Since the US Marshals Service does not own or operate any of its own correctional facilities, it relies completely on state, federal, and private prisons to house prisoners under its supervision and care. In 2014, 5.5% of inmates received by the USMS were kept in private institutions (O'Hollaren, 2016, Major Markets).

Federal Bureau of Prison

The smallest market segment, the Federal Bureau of Prisons (BOP), accounts for 13% of the industry revenue. The Federal Bureau of Prisons strives to provide "progressive and humane" rehabilitation to federal prisoners, and oversees the care of over 170,000 inmates (O'Hollaren, 2016, Major Markets). Though the BOP was reluctant to turn over entire facilities to private sectors at first, severe overcrowding led them to partner with private operators, such as The Geo Group. Revenue from the BOP is expected to fall in the coming years as the DOJ has elected to eliminate private federal prisons, and the total federal inmate population is declining.

Products/Services

The correctional facilities industry operates under different security levels depending on the type and number of inmates they house. The services offered by this industry are segmented into community correctional facilities, minimum, medium, and maximum security prisons, and halfway houses.

Products and services segmentation (2016)

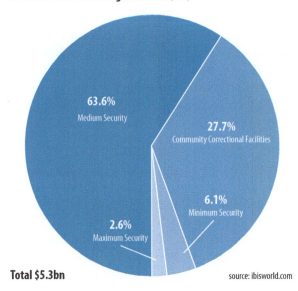

63.6%
Medium Security

27.7%
Community Correctional Facilities

6.1%
Minimum Security

2.6%
Maximum Security

Total $5.3bn

source: ibisworld.com

Community Correctional Facilities

Twenty-seven percent of total industry revenue is estimated to come from community correctional facilities. These facilities are much more lax than typical correctional facilities, and staff are not permitted to use force to restrain inmates. Inmates in this type of facility are often allowed to leave the grounds during the day for work, but must return to the facility at night (O'Hollaren, 2016, Products and Markets). As the use of private federal prisons is eliminated, community correctional facilities are expected to generate a larger share of total revenue.

Minimum Security Facilities

Minimum security facilities make up 6.1% of the total industry revenue. Minimum security institutions usually have dormitory style inmate housing, and have a low staff-to-inmate ratio. These facilities emphasize rehabilitation and are work and program oriented. However, with the new policy implemented by the Department of Justice to eliminate federal private prisons, the future of minimum security institutions is unstable (Business Insights, 2016).

Medium Security Facilities

Sixty-three point three percent of the correctional facility industry revenue comes from medium security facilities. This type of facility is characterized by high fences with detection systems or concrete walls, and cell-type housing. However, medium security facilities face challenges such as prisoner misconduct and violence, along with psychological damage to inmates due to prison overcrowding (Haney, 2006). Like minimum security prisons, medium security institutions also offer work and treatment programs, but the revenue is projected to remain relatively the same, as it is unaffected by the DOJ policy.

Maximum Security Facilities

Maximum security facilities account for about 2.6% of the overall industry revenue. Inmates in this type of institution are housed in single occupant cells, and are seldom let out during the day. Maximum security prisons have the highest staff-to-inmate ratio, and focus less than the other facilities on rehabilitation. Revenue for this segment is also expected to remain steady and relatively unaffected by the DOJ policy (Business Insights, 2016).

Prevalent Companies

The correctional facilities industry is divided into three segments, the Corrections Corporation of America making up 34.9% of the market share, The Geo Group making up 27.1%, and other smaller companies accounting for 38%.

This section overview is redundant; the same information is in the chart below.

Major Players (Market share)

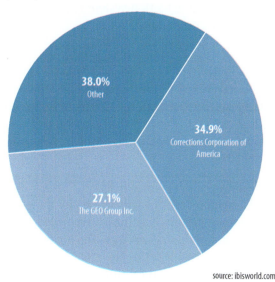

38.0%
Other

34.9%
Corrections Corporation of America

27.1%
The GEO Group Inc.

source: ibisworld.com

Corrections Corporation of America

The Corrections Corporation of America (CCA) is the largest owner and operator of private correctional facilities in the nation. As of 2016, the CCA managed 42% of all beds under contract with private operators and had more than 14,000 employees (MarketLine, 2016). In 2015, the CCA accounted for $1.7 billion of total industry revenue, and is expected to grow at an annual rate for 1.8% in the years following 2016. In response to the DOJ's effort to eliminate private federal prisons, the CCA is shifting their focus to partnering with state and local markets and expanding into the inmate rehabilitation market to bolster revenue and profits.

The Geo Group

The Geo Group (GEO) is a real estate investment trust that specializes in the ownership, leasing, and management of private correctional facilities and halfway houses. GEO is headquartered in Boca Raton, Florida, but operates internationally in the UK, Canada, Australia, and South Africa. In 2015, GEO reported total revenue of $1.8 billion, and controlled 64 correctional facilities. Since GEO's main customers are federal agencies, its revenue has steadily increased since 2011 due to higher demands for private facility operators and budgetary restrictions for federal and state governments (MarketLine, 2016).

Presence in International Markets

Given the nature of the correctional facilities industry, there is no international trade, and therefore low globalization rates. The only major presence in international markets comes from The Geo Group, the second largest industry player (MarketLine, 2016). As mentioned above, GEO currently operates in the US, UK, Canada, Australia, and South Africa. In 2012, 14% of GEO's total revenue came from international services (Mason, 2013). However, even though the United States currently maintains the highest number of privately detained prisoners, at least 11 countries including Australia, Scotland, England, and Wales are engaged in some level of prison privatization.

This section overview is more effective as it frames the content to come.

Australia

Australia's first private prison was owned and operated by Correctional Corporation of Australia, in international venture of the Corrections Corporation of America. As of 2011, five out of eight Australian states implemented some form of prison privatization (Mason, 2013). Like in the US and UK, Australian private prisons focus more on the detention of immigrants than on prison management. However, Australia's immigrant detention system is different because it is completely operated by for-profit companies.

South Africa

Prison privatization in South Africa is condensed into two main facilities, the Kutama-Sinthumule Correctional Centre, operated by The Geo Group, and the Mangaung Maximum Security Correctional Centre, managed by G4S, a UK based company. As of 2011, about 4% of South Africa's prison population was being detained by private facilities, in comparison to 19% in Australia, and 8% in the United States (Mason, 2013).

Market Drivers

The correctional facilities industry is heavily driven by the incarceration rate. As the incarceration rate grows, prisons become overcrowded, leading federal and state governments to expand industry services. The incarceration rate is projected to grow in the years following 2016. The rate of relapses back to crime from inmates also influence the correctional facilities industry, as prisons remain filled and industry demand grows. Another key external driver is the crime rate. Intuitively, as the crime rate rises, so should the incarceration rate. However, crime rate is expected to decrease in the years following 2016.

Incarceration Rate

According to Harris (2017), US penal authorities house "more than 2.3 million people in 1,719 state prisons, 102 federal prisons, 942 juvenile correctional facilities, 3,283 local jails, and 79 Indian Country jails as well as in military prisons, immigration detention facilities, civil commitment centers, and prisons in the US territories" (p. 119). The United States has the highest rate of incarceration among industrialized nations, due to "tough on crime" legislations that followed the logic of reducing crime by imprisoning as many perpetrators as possible. This approach has led to overcrowding in prisons and low recidivism rates.

Crime Rate

Supporters of the "tough on crime" approach argue that in locking up offenders, crime rate has been decreased. However, the rise in incarceration is only responsible for 25% of the decrease in crime, and that the overall crime rate is decreasing significantly. Harris (2017) maintains that in the years since 1991, the FBI reported that the number of violent crimes per year have decreased by more than 50% (p. 120). Dropping crime rates with increasing mass incarceration are just one of several reasons for public outcry and scrutiny against the correctional facilities industry.

Industry Challenges/Threats

Recent controversies involving prison riots over poor sanitation and treatment of inmates has challenged the stance of private prisons. In light of the policy implemented by the Department of Justice to curb and eventually eliminate federal private prisons, states are encouraged to reduce the number of inmates kept in private facilities to combat public opposition. In response to public outcry against mass incarceration due to the traditional "tough on crime" approach, federal and state governments are expected to use more progressive criminal justice policies in an attempt to reduce the prison population. However, in appeasing the public by implementing these changes, industry profit is threatened, and is expected to fall in the years following 2016, as there will be fewer prisoners and less revenue generated by private prisons (O'Hollaren, 2016, Industry Outlook).

Mental Health of Inmates

Mental health disorders in inmates have consistently been a prevalent issue in the correctional facilities industry. Despite court orders for access to adequate health care in prisons and public criticism, inmates' access to health care and mental health care have been extremely inconsistent (Gonzalez & Connell, 2014). Research done by Gonzalez and Connell indicated that inmates with untreated mental health conditions were at higher risk for rehabilitation treatment failure and were more likely to commit crime upon release from prison. While higher incarceration rates drive the correctional facility industry, research studies such as this one only fuel public outrage and drive the industry to make changes regarding treatment of inmates.

Mass Incarceration

The "tough on crime" approach implies that the more offenders are imprisoned, the lower the crime rate will be. However, research has indicated being incarcerated can have detrimental effects rather than restorative, rehabilitative ones. Compared with the non-incarcerated populations, incarcerated individuals were much more likely to catch infectious diseases, have chronic health conditions (such as hypertension, diabetes, etc.), problems with addiction, and mental health disorders (Wildeman & Wang, 2017). Since there is strong evidence linking mass incarceration with detrimental effects to inmates' wellbeing, there is high pressure on the correctional facility industry to reduce the number of inmates, which in turn threatens revenue and industry growth.

Financial Performance in Domestic Markets

As of 2016, the correctional facilities industry is considered to be a $5.3 billion industry. In the years preceding 2016, the industry was growing at a rate of 1.5% yearly, but is projected to have an annual growth of 0.6% annually in the five years following 2016. The correctional facilities industry generates an average annual profit of $591.7 million as of 2016 (O'Hollaren, 2016, Industry at a Glance). Due to strong demand for private institutions and services, this industry is expected to experience slow but continual growth over the next five years. Government contracts have also grown in size, promoting the growth of the major companies within the industry (Chatham, 2014). In particular, The Geo Group has grown significantly in the years since 2011 when they acquired Cornell Companies and expanded the number of facilities operated and managed by GEO. GEO's revenue grew at a rate of 8.1% annually from 2011 to 2016 (MarketLine, 2016).

Industry Opportunities

Since the correctional facilities industry is heavily regulated federally and by the state, it has high barriers to entry. New companies looking to enter the market not only face strict regulations, but also large capital costs and must receive accreditation from a national program, such as the American Correctional Association (O'Hollaren, 2016, Competitive Landscape). However, there is much more opportunity with lower barriers to entry for new entrants that supply supportive services to correctional facilities (i.e. doctors, educational services, psychologists, social workers), and do not own their own facilities. In 2015, McGraw-Hill Education addressed the need for accessible and high-quality testing materials for adults in correctional facilities. Research done by McGraw-Hill indicated that allowing individuals in corrections to obtain a high school equivalency degree can smooth the transition from prison to community life, as well as offer skills for future employment, and college prep (McGraw-Hill, 2015).

Summary

The correctional facilities industry is a mature, multi-billion dollar industry. Of the $5.3 billion generated in revenue, more than two thirds comes from two major companies in the industry, Corrections Corporation of America, and The Geo Group. These companies own and manage correctional facilities, and provide community facilities, and minimum, medium, and maximum security prisons to state and federal government customers. Faced with public backlash concerning the treatment of inmates and the fast growing number of incarcerated individuals, overall industry growth is projected to slow down in the next five years. While there are high barriers to entry within this industry, new entrants to the market can find their way in through supportive services.

Conclusion is written for a wide audience and does not include an invitation for inquiry as it would in a correspondence message.

References

Business Insights: Essentials. (2016). Correctional facilities. *Encyclopedia of American Industries*, 1, 1. Retrieved from http://bi.galegroup.com.ezproxy4. library.arizona.edu/essentials/article/GALE%7CRN2501400984/ aed4ac157fa9272d6bcbb2b1a8da6d13?u=uarizona_main

Chatham: Newstex. (2014). United States correctional facilities market: Demand for private facilities will grow as prisons remain overcrowded. *Newstex Trade & Industry Blogs*. Retrieved from http://ezproxy.library. arizona.edu/login?url=http://search.proquest.com.ezproxy2.library.arizona. edu/docview/1634882424?accountid=8360

Gonzalez, J. M. R., & Connell, N. M. (2014). Mental health of prisoners: Identifying barriers to mental health treatment and medication continuity. *American Journal of Public Health*, 104(12), 2328-33. Retrieved from http:// ezproxy.library.arizona.edu/login?url=http://search.proquest.com.ezproxy4. library.arizona.edu/docview/1628902908?accountid=8360

Haney, C. (2006). The wages of prison overcrowding: Harmful psychological consequences and dysfunctional correctional reactions. *Washington University Journal of Law & Policy, 22*, 265–293. Retrieved from http:// openscholarship.wustl.edu/cgi/viewcontent.cgi?article=1360&context= law_journal_law_policy

Harris, H. (2017). The prisoner dilemma. *Foreign Affairs*, 96(2), 118–129. Retrieved from http://ezproxy.library.arizona.edu/login?url=http://search. ebscohost.com/login.aspx?direct=true&db=bth&AN=121177806&site= ehost-live

MarketLine. (2016). Corrections Corporation of America. *MarketLine Company Profile*, 1–20. Retrieved from http://eds.a.ebscohost.com. ezproxy2.library.arizona.edu/ehost/pdfviewer/pdfviewer?sid=c1f49fdb- 8297-4470-bf81-26ed7a5ed86f%40sessionmgr4007&vid=4& hid=4113

MarketLine. (2016). The GEO Group, Inc. *MarketLine Company Profile*, 1–20. Retrieved from http://eds.b.ebscohost.com.ezproxy4.library.arizona.edu/ ehost/pdfviewer/pdfviewer?sid=c2dce433-4894-4a5a-aa2c-b9d1f55ab5f2%4 0sessionmgr102&vid=6&hid=117

Mason, C. (2013). International growth trends in prison privatization. *The Sentencing Project*, 1–12. Retrieved from http://www.sentencingproject.org/ publications/international-growth-trends-in-prison-privatization/

McGraw-Hill Education. (2015). McGraw-Hill Education expands accessibility for adult ed test preparation tools with new offline and Spanish offerings: Need for test prep accessibility for native Spanish speakers, rural students and adults in correctional facilities drives two new adult education solutions. PR Newswire. Retrieved from http://ezproxy.library.arizona.edu/ login?url=http://search.proquest.com.ezproxy2.library.arizona.edu/docview /1675009056?accountid=8360

O'Hollaren, K. (2016, November). IBISWorld Industry Report 56121. Correctional Facilities in the US. Retrieved from *IBISWorld database*.

US Immigration and Customs Enforcement. (2016). FY 2016 ICE immigration removals. Retrieved from https://www.ice.gov/removal-statistics/2016

Wildeman, C., & Wang, E.A. (2016). Mass incarceration, public health, and widening inequality in the USA. *The Lancet, 389*, 1464–1474. http://doi.org.ezproxy2.library.arizona.edu/10.1016/S0140-6736(17)30259-3

Direct Informational Memos with APA Citations

For the samples on the following pages, students were asked to summarize three articles in a brief, informative memo, and use APA format to cite sources. In each memo, students demonstrate their abilities to properly cite sources using APA format for in-text citations and a reference page. When citing in text, students used paraphrased and quoted material and integrated these elements with and without signal phrases.

MEMORANDUM

To: Zack Wilson
From: Student
Date: March 27, 2019
Subject: Footwear Information

In response to your request for information regarding the footwear industry, I have compiled the following document outlining important aspects of the market. This information will assist you in deciding whether to expand the University of Arizona Bookstore's presence in the shoe industry. I have included relevant data from IBISWorld, Investor's Business Daily, and Forbes.

IBISWorld

According to an IBISWorld Industry Report, the online shoe industry is profitable, but growth is slowing. The industry earns an annual $12 billion in revenue, of which $590.2 million is converted into profit (Hurley, 2016, Industry Performance). Online shoe sales have experienced rapid growth in the past few years, however, Hurley (2016) asserts that "growth will continue, albeit at a slower rate as the industry's markets become saturated" (Industry Performance). Amazon claims a large portion of this industry, but smaller online boutique shoe retailers are also increasing in popularity, and therefore, the online shoe business is highly competitive. Overall, Hurley predicts positive growth and continued interest in the online shoe industry.

Investor's Business Daily

A June, 2016 article from Investor's Business Daily analyzes the differences in footwear lines from Nike and Under Armour, based on which celebrities represent which shoes. Overall, a celebrity endorsement is an excellent way to boost sales of shoes, especially when that celebrity is a highly talked-about athlete. Nike partnered with Michael Jordan to create Air Jordans, which capture a 75% market share when compared to three other popular celebrity-branded shoes (Low, 2016). Different professional basketball players endorse multiple brands of popular shoes, and both Under Armour and Nike are profiting from these celebrities' increasing popularity.

Forbes

Forbes contributor Powell explored the footwear market in a June 2016 article. He found that while performance running shoes are losing popularity and lifestyle running shoes are gaining popularity, "total running sales are up in the low-singles" (Powell, 2016, para. 5). As of the June 2016, walking and outdoor sandals were experiencing low sales due to a wet spring (Powell, 2016). The market for these types of shoes is reactive to weather, which can be risky to manufacturers and investors. Overall, Forbes predicts slow but steady returns for those in the footwear industry.

As shown in the above information from IBISWorld, Investor's Business Daily, and Forbes, the footwear industry is diverse and profitable, if approached in the correct way. Online retailing, celebrity endorsements, and producing lifestyle running shoes are all viable options for the UA Bookstore. Thank you for the opportunity to compile this document. If you have any further questions, please contact me at student@email.com

Data are broken down by publication — a slightly less sophisticated approach. The author has organized the information clearly, but he/she did not identify common themes nor distill the overall message.

Author cites source without page #s, and uses paragraph # instead.

Summarizes and ends with invitation for further inquiry.

References

Hurley, M. (2016, September). IBISWorld Industry Report OD5093. Online shoe sales. Retrieved from IBISWorld database.

Low, E. (2016, June). Under Armour's golden boy vs. Nike's lifetime king: Whose shoes sell? *Investor's Business Daily*. Retrieved from EBSCOhost database.

Powell, M. (2016, June). Sneakernomics: What's really happening in the U.S. sneaker business? *Forbes*. Retrieved from https://www.forbes.com/sites/mattpowell/2016/06/06/sneakernomics-whats-really-happening-in-the-u-s-sneaker-business/2/#448d7c5a75e6

INTEROFFICE MEMORANDUM

to: Zack Wilson
from: student
subject: Footwear Industry Research Summary
date: March 22, 2019
cc: N/A

Introduction frames and forecasts.

As you requested, I have evaluated three articles pertaining to athletic footwear products and produced relevant summaries for your use. This document will give you the information to adequately procure an appealing line of athletic footwear in university bookstores. To guide your focus, I have separated the analysis into three distinct topics: superior footwear brands, footwear ecommerce trends, and economic factors.

Superior Footwear Brands

Effective heading that accurately describes content.

Effective citation using a signal phrase.

Well-integrated quote with a signal phrase.

One of the foundations to maintaining revenue streams in retail is the proper brand selection. Low's (2016) article compares Under Armour and Nike as they compete for top market share in footwear. Nike's top lines are based off of basketball stars Michael Jordan and Lebron James. Under Armour has created its most recent shoe line based on current basketball prodigy, Stephen Curry. While the two companies leverage athletes as their primary foundation for footwear design the factor important to our business is overall sales trends. According to Low (2016), "a Slice Intelligence report that examined sales of the top four NBA-player shoes, Curry kicks are in vogue, but Nike is still king of the cash register" (p. 1). The information in the article shows that in regard to longevity and consistency of sales, Nike is the primary brand we should offer in broad capacity at our bookstores.

Footwear E-Commerce Trends

Content is clearly organized and logically grouped.

University of Arizona bookstores currently offer online shoe retail, however, many challenges still remain in ensuring that our e-commerce sales portals are in adherence with modern retail trends. In her industry report on online shoe sales, Madeline Hurley demonstrates the growth of shoe retailers online and industry trends. According to Hurley (2016), online footwear retail has increased from 7.0% in 2011 to 14.2% in 2016. The reason for the growth of the industry online lies in consumer information trends. Over the past five years, online shopping has become increasingly consumer friendly. With a growing number of online operators, consumers can increasingly compare prices, read product reviews and browse merchandise with virtual ease (p. 6). Overall, the offering of consumer options and comparable product reviews increases online traffic.

Economic Factors

Effective quote without signal phrase.

Economic factors that contribute to cyclical sales trends and retailer insolvency are crucial data points that our bookstores need to take into account. A Forbes article highlights data for the upcoming quarter in the shoe retail industry. He stated, "With 10 percent of the sporting goods retail space closing by Labor Day, the remaining market will be stronger and healthier" (Powell, 2016, p. 2). In our division, we can use this data to procure athletic shoes after Labor Day to minimize costs and stand out from the degrading competition in the retail space.

This summary analyzed three articles and their relevance in enhancing our footwear procurement division: superior footwear brands, footwear e-commerce trends, and economic factors. The outcomes of my analysis demonstrate that with a culmination of proper brand selection, e-commerce consumer accommodation, and seasonal sales focus our athletic shoe revenues can reach new highs. Thank you for letting me analyze these documents and formulate conclusions that can improve our footwear division. Feel free to contact me at student@gmail.com if you have questions.

Conclusion clearly summarizes and invites inquiry.

References

Hurley, M. (2016, September). IBIS world industry report OD5093. Retrieved March 19, 2017, from http://clients1.ibisworld.com/reports/us/industry/default.aspx?entid=5093

Low, E. (2016, June 02). Under Armour's golden boy vs. Nike's lifetime king: Whose shoes sell? *Investors Business Daily*. Retrieved March 19, 2017, from http://www.investors.com/news/under-armours-golden-boy-vs-nikes-lifetime-king-whose-shoes-sell/

Powell, M. (2016, June 06). Sneakernomics: What's really happening in the U.S. sneaker business? *Forbes*. Retrieved March 19, 2017, from https://www.forbes.com/sites/mattpowell/2016/06/06/sneakernomics-whats-really-happening-in-the-u-s-sneaker-business/#40a57f311dc3

Annotated Bibliography

An annotated bibliography is a list of citations to books, articles, and documents. Each citation is followed by a descriptive and evaluative paragraph (the annotation). The purpose of the annotation is to summarize the content of the source and to inform the reader of the relevance, accuracy, and quality of each of the sources cited.

Cook, D. (2012). OtterBox profits in providing protection. Northern Colorado Business Report, 17(17), 5B—14B.

Summary
This article describes more of the history of OtterBox and their strategies that led to the success of the company. The founder and CEO, Curt Richardson, had built $350 million in revenue and even after the recession, he managed 106% in revenue growth from 2010 to 2011. He also increased the number of employees that work for him, which now ranges near about 500 employees. This article describes how the company targets emerging markets like Apple, Nokia, and Blackberry to maintain their position in the front of other manufacturers of cases. It describes in the article how OtterBox has gained the reputation as "worth the money."

Quality and Accuracy
The source is reliable because it is a widely-cited, respected publication.

Relevance
This article will provide the background of OtterBox our team needs to effectively build on previous success. We can analyze the various strategies used to increase revenue and to maintain a competitive advantage. This will ensure that we maintain corporate integrity and add value to the company in our upcoming report.

Graziano, D. (2012, June 22). Smartphone accessory revenues valued at $20 billion in 2012. BGR. Retrieved September 10, 2014 from http://bgr.com/2012/06/22/mo-bile-accessories-revenues-Increase-smartphones/

Summary
This is the article where the information about the smartphone industry as a whole was accessed. The smartphone accessory industry was expected to earn about $20 billion in 2012 making it a very profitable industry to get into. There was a study done that showed per device, each consumer spent about $56.

Quality and Accuracy
The source is a noted leader in technology journalism.

Relevance
This article will provide the evidence we need to persuade current and potential investors that this industry is strong and will continue to grow.

Professional Photo & Video Tripods, Heads, Lighting, & Bags. Manfrotto. (n.d). Professional Photo & Video Tripods, Heads, Lighting, & Bags. Manfrotto. Retrieved September 10, 2014, from http://www.manfrotto.us/

Summary
This is the main website for Manfrotto, from which I received information about their product that was competing against the lightstrap. Their product is the KYLP+ and is the first all-in-one photographic set for the iPhone 5/5s. It discusses the features of this product with its ability to shoot in low light scenarios and includes three interchangeable lenses allowing the

customer to shoot in fisheye, landscape, and portrait. It also describes the parts that it comes with which include a tripod and small kickstand to help with stability in the photo.

Quality and Accuracy
The source is likely highly accurate but does demonstrate obvious bias toward Manfrotto products because the source is the Manfrotto website.

Relevance
This article will enable us to post detailed product descriptions as we build our company's new Facebook page.

Stern, J. (2014, March 12). The only way to double your phone's battery life. Wall Street Journal (Online). p. 1.

Summary
This article compares products that all increase battery life. Mophie is not the only product anymore that expands battery life. The way the article describes it, Morphie also may not be the best anymore as far as recharge speed and quality goes. The article describes how it is hard to stand out against competitors, so Mophie constantly tries to stay ahead. It talks about providing a one-year warranty and that there are products under Mophie for both Androids and iPhones.

Quality and Accuracy
The source is reliable because it is a widely-cited, respected news publication. It was accessed through Business Source Complete, a popular academic database at the University of Arizona.

Relevance
This article provides an objective view of Mophie and its potential risks moving forward. This will allow us to research and propose new ways to stay ahead of the competition.

Strauss, K. (2013). From a barn to a $200 million enterprise: Mophie. Forbes Com, 7.

Summary
This article describes how Mophie became a competitor in the high-value phone accessory industry from its start in a barn. The co-founders, Daniel Huang and Shawn Dougherty, started this business in 2006 by making speakers and cases for iPods and other types of mp3 players. This company had made about $200 million in 2013, which really solidified its success. Mophie makes builds not only for Apple, but for Samsung, HTC, and other smartphone companies. This article discusses their transition from simply making speakers to making intelligent cases.

Quality and Accuracy
Accessed through the University of Arizona library website from Business Source Complete, a notable online database.

Relevance
This article shows the various distribution channels Mophie utilizes to reach its target market. This will be useful as we anticipate next quarter's sales.

Vuong, A. (n.d.). Case logic, otterbox top competitors in tough case business. –The Denver Post. Retrieved September 10, 2014, from http://www.denverpost.com/ci_20553796/case-logic-otterbox-top-competitors-tough-case-business

Summary

This article describes the top competitors in the smartphone accessory industry with OtterBox being one of them. It contains information about the industry as a whole as well, which is where the statistics about the revenue growth came from. In 2010, the mobile accessory revenue grew 18% and close to half of mobile phone buyers also get an accessory at the same time of purchase. It assesses the business and says that manufacturing cases for iPhones and other phones are continuing to boom, but the market is so competitive that it requires companies to stay on their toes or else they will drown in the competition. This article also references OtterBox being the market leader in terms of revenue and describes how they even have a new division in their company that specifically deals with forecasting what products will be popular and what their design might look like.

Quality and Accuracy

The Denver Post is an award-winning and well-respected daily newspaper, so it likely that this article is accurate and reliable.

Relevance

This article shows the strength of the smart phone industry and the market position of OtterBox. This will add evidence to the claims that the company is worth the investment.

Wolf, A. (2013). Manfrotto broadens U.S. business, outsources distribution. TWICE: This Week In Consumer Electronics, 28(9), 33.

Summary

This article describes Manfrotto's decision to target the pro-digital imaging and video production accessories in order to appeal to a wider range of consumers in the mainstream consumer market. The rise of social media is what inspired the company to join the competitive race to be on top among other accessory manufacturers. Manfrotto has its products in retail stores such as Target, Best Buy, and Walmart. This article also talks about how their company likes to let the staff focus on new products and emerging markets that the company can break into.

Quality and Accuracy

The article was accessed from Business Source Complete, a database on the University of Arizona's library website.

Relevance

This information will be useful in selecting the most profitable distribution centers and in developing a marketing campaign that reaches a wider demographic.

Griffin unveils new pattern cases for iPhones. (2009, October 26). Retrieved September 9, 2014, from http://eds.a.ebscohost.com.

Summary
This source was used to get a better understanding of Speck's competitive advantage and strengths. It was published in 2009, which shows that this company has been making cases since the iPhone 3 was on the market. The article was concise, yet informative, as it promoted and informed the reader on the company's durable mobile phone cases.

Quality and Accuracy
EBSCO Host is a respected and reputable database offered through the University of Arizona library.

Relevance
This article will be useful in determining which iPhone accessories have been most popular so that we can recommend development of our current line.

Moldvay, C. (2013). IBISWorld Industry Report 81331. Conservation & Human Rights Organizations in the US. Retrieved September 21, 2013 from IBISWorld database.

Summary
This on-line article sheds light on Belkin's competitive advantage in the smartphone industry. It was interesting to find that the company provides not only a wide variety of smartphone accessories, but promotes other smart appliances as well.

Quality and Accuracy
IBISWorld is another University of Arizona-offered database, so I have high confidence in this source's reliability, accuracy, and quality.

Relevance
This information will be useful when contracting new distributers for our Belkin products.

In this unit, you learned about audience and tone, professionalism and editing, formatting and polishing. Revisit this unit when you either need a refresher explanation or an exemplary sample. By following the processes outlined, you can ensure that your writing is targeted at the right audience, hits the proper tone, uses the appropriate strategy, and is error free. Using the information in this unit, you will be well on your way to writing professional documents reliably, time after time—an ability that will serve you well in the classroom and in the workplace.

Unit 4 References

Conciseness: Reducing wordiness in your writing. (February 2013). Purdue OWL—Online Writing Lab.

Heath, C., & Heath, D. (2008). *Made to stick: Why some ideas survive and others die*. New York, NY: Random House.

Kamalani Hurley, P. (2007). *The you attitude and reader-centered writing*. Leeward Community College, University of Hawaii. Retrieved from: http://emedia.leeward.hawaii.edu/hurley/modules/mod2/2_docs/you_attitude.pdf

Purdue University Online Writing Lab (1995–2017). *Conciseness*. Retrieved from https://owl.english.purdue.edu/owl/resource/572/01/

University of Wisconsin Madison Writing Center (2009). *3a. The best misplaced and dangling modifiers of all time*. Retrieved from http://writing.wisc.edu/Handbook/CommonErrors_BestMod.html

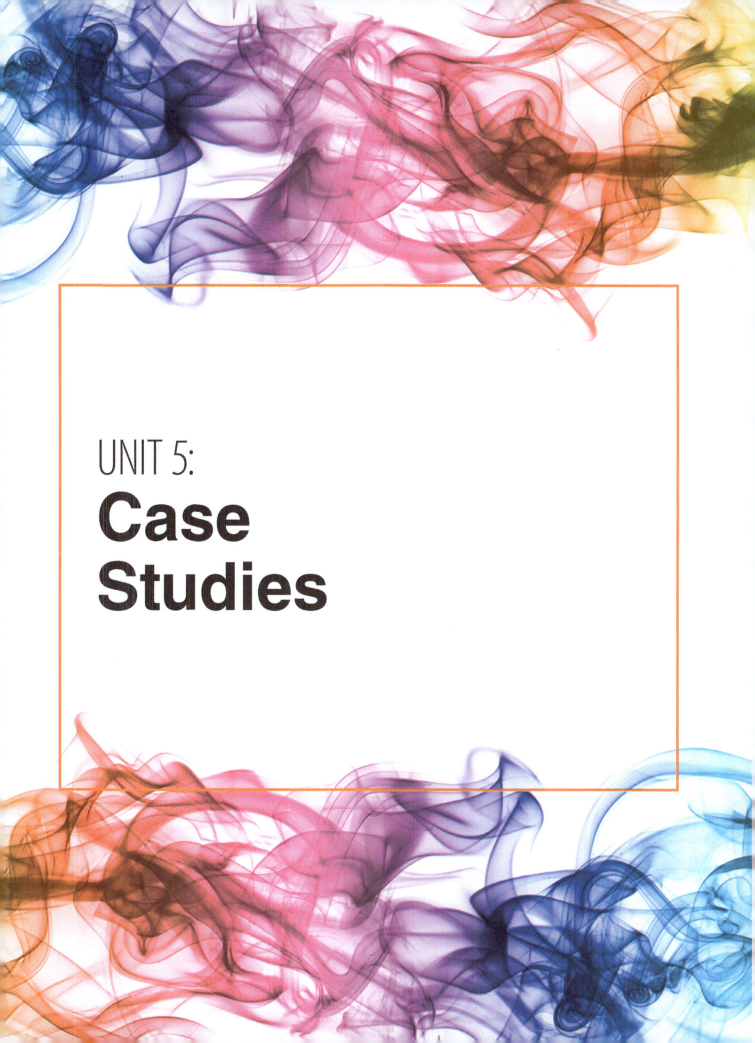

UNIT 5:
Case Studies

This unit includes five real-world case studies designed to help you practice different forms of written business communication. Each case includes a synopsis of the situation, the context in which you will be completing your tasks, and different assigned writing tasks with sample responses. The different forms of written communication covered are:

- Direct Informative
- Indirect Persuasive
- Bad News
- Direct Persuasive
- Direct Persuasive Instructional
- Letter of Intent/Cover letter
- Stakeholder Analysis

All of the case studies are based on real-world events. Some of the tasks, however, are created simply for the purposes of the assignment, and do not necessarily reflect actual events. As you move through the cases and assigned tasks, try your hand at composing the assigned document before reading the sample response.

Chapter 5-1

Chipotle Case Study

Fast Casual Chain Sickness Scandal Heats Up

2015 was not a good year for Chipotle Mexican Grill. The popular "fast casual" chain was linked to norovirus outbreaks in California and Boston that sickened more than 100 people and E. coli outbreaks that caused illnesses for customers in nine states. Sales and stock prices suffered a heavy blow due to the incidents, with 4th quarter reporting indicating a 30% drop in sales compared to 2014.[1]

Timeline of Outbreaks

- July 2015: E. coli virus sickened five people (Washington)

- August 2015: Norovirus outbreak sickened 98 customers and 17 employees (California)

- August/September 2015: Salmonella outbreak sickened 64 people (Minnesota)

- October 2015: E-coli outbreak sickened 53 people (spanning nine states)

- December 2015: Norovirus sickened 153 people (Massachusetts)

©Ken Wolter/Shutterstock.com

Figure 1

---

[1] Elizabeth Whitman "Chipotle (NYSE:CMG) Stock Price Falls Nearly 4% After Employee Diagnosed With Norovirus" March 9, 2016, International Business Times

Legal Woes

As a result of these incidents, the company was served with a federal grand jury subpoena in January 2016 relating to a criminal investigation connected to the norovirus incident in California. The company later received an additional subpoena that expanded the investigation.

Chipotle's co-Chief Executive Steve Ells has acknowledged that 2016 will not be an easy year for the company. The subpoena that was served in January sought information about company-wide safety practices dating backing to 2013. This inquiry could focus on what leadership at the company knew about the conditions of the restaurants nationwide.[2]

Chipotle Responds

Chipotle has worked hard to mitigate the impact of these incidents. They closed all of their locations on February 8, 2016 for a company-wide food safety meeting for all employees. They are seeking to lure customers back with offers of free burritos,[3] and are revamping their food safety testing procedures, using an independent consulting group.

IEH Laboratories, the consulting group that Chipotle asked to design a stricter food safety program, has put forth a series of protocols that seek to ensure food safety from the farm to the fork. These safety measures include DNA testing of ingredients before they are shipped to the restaurant, end of shelf life testing, and improved training for employees on safe food handling and preparation.

Media Response

According to an article by Jason Mudd in the online magazine *The Business Journals,* Chipotle must take the following measures to mitigate the damage caused by these events:

---

[2]Subrat Patnaik and Siddharth Cavale "Though CDC probe over, Chipotle Faces Criminal Investigation" February 6, 2016, ClaimsJournal http://www.claimsjournal.com/news/national/2016/02/05/268629.htm

[3]Tonya Garcia "Chipotle is giving away millions of free burritos to lure back wary customers" March 18, 2016, MarketWatch http://www.marketwatch.com/story/chipotle-is-giving-away-millions-of-free-burritos-to-lure-backwary-customers-2016-03-16

1. **Use the good reputation it has already earned**

Chipotle is known as a restaurant chain that puts people before profits, as evidenced when it removed an item from its menu because no ingredient suppliers could meet its high standards. Chipotle must keep the focus on the customer and not be afraid to remain honest and admit mistakes, even in the face of losing revenue.

2. **Communicate, communicate, and communicate**

The company needs to raise the bar with proactive communications, both when responding to customer concerns and in the information distributed on the website and to news media. Additionally, regular updates are required.

Consumers are more likely to forgive when a company addresses a problem and is transparent about its next steps.

3. **Be consistent in communications**

The company issued press releases explaining that it's impossible to eliminate all food risks, but then the co-CEO, Steve Ells, went on national television promising that Chipotle will become the "safest place to eat."

4. **Work to find the true nature of the crisis**

Chipotle is known for using fresh, ethically-sourced ingredients, which makes it particularly susceptible to such incidents, and it can be challenging to pinpoint an exact cause. During the outbreak at Taco Bell, the green onions it uses were found to be the culprit.

5. **Present solutions**

It's fine to give all details related to what went wrong, but consumers will really want to know what's being done to fix the issue and ensure it won't happen again. This is the way to rebuild trust. Chipotle must quickly announce what changes are happening now to avoid future incidents.

Chipotle must discover where and how the contamination occurred in the process of getting the food from the farm to the customer. The sooner customers are reassured that the issue is handled, the quicker the company can bounce back.[4]

Jason Mudd©2016 American City Business Journals. All rights reserved. Reprinted with permission.

There is obviously evidence of continued mistrust. According to a survey of 6,500 teens conducted by Business Insider, teenagers are losing interest in the chain.

"While Chipotle remained the second most preferred brand among upper income teens and ties for top five among average income teens, . . . it did cede share sequentially across both gender and geography categories," analyst Nicole Miller Regan wrote in the report.[5]

It is under these circumstances that you begin your internship with Chipotle.

[4]Jason Mudd, "5 Steps Chipotle must take immediately to fix its brand and reputation," January 7, 2016, The Business Journals http://www.bizjournals.com/bizjournals/how-to/marketing/2016/01/5-steps-chipotle-must-takeimmediately.html?page

[5]Kate Taylor "Chipotle's most desirable customers are ditching the brand", April 13, 2016, Business Insiderhttp://www.businessinsider.com/teens-are-ditching-chipotle-2016-4

Practice Assignments Context

Congratulations! You have been selected for a highly desirable internship with Chipotle at their Headquarters in Denver, Colorado. You are excited to be working for such a fresh and innovative business. See below for Chipotle's website and HQ information.

You have been assigned to the Chairman and Co-Chief Executive Officer. As such, he has many people working for him, and he will assign you different tasks in different departments during your eight-week internship.

While you are very honored to have been chosen for this internship, you are aware of the recent problems that have plagued Chipotle. You know that there will be some difficult choices to be made within the coming weeks and everyone will be on edge. You will want to make sure that all the work you present is the best it can be.

Chipotle Website:
https://www.chipotle.com/company

Headquarters Information
http://www.headquartersinfo.com/chipotle-headquarters-information/

Use the information contained in this case study and information on Chipotle's website to inform your writing as you move through the various types of message structures.

Practice Assignments

1. Direct Informative Message

   You have just started at Chipotle Headquarters for an eight-week internship. You were chosen for this important position because word of your excellent writing skills reached the higherups at Chipotle, so you want to ensure that you live up to your reputation.

   The Chariman and Co-Chief Executive Officer's assistant has sent you an email with your first task. Mr. Jack Lemon has just joined the Board of Directors of Chipotle. Mr. Lemon is the husband of a major stockholder. Like all members of the Board, he is interested in having as much information as possible. It is your job to get him up to speed on the current situation.

   Compose a neutral summary report for Mr. Lemon regarding the norovirus incidents and the recently filed federal criminal investigation. Your report should not be more than two pages. You have not been asked to provide any recommendations at this juncture. Just deliver the facts in a clear and logical fashion.

2. Indirect Persuasive Message

   The Chariman and Co-CEO was impressed with your Neutral Summary Report. Good job!

   Because of so much negative press regarding the criminal investigation and customers getting sick at various Chipotle locations, the executive team is very concerned that the company is losing some of their core customers. These customers are the loyalists—the ones with the frequent burrito cards—your CORE CONSTITUENCY.

   A new Facebook group called "SO LONG CHIPOTLE!" popped up and is filled with images of customers tearing their frequent burrito cards in half and posing in front of Panera.

The Chariman and Co-Chief Executive Officer has asked you to draft a persuasive letter to these customers asking them to come back to Chipotle (you have their email addresses because they agreed to share that information when they registered for the frequent burrito card).

You can offer them one free burrito for the first three months if they reinstate their customer loyalty card. You also want to assure them that Chipotle is taking aggressive steps to ensure the safety of the food the company serves.

Craft a persuasive letter to these customers from your boss. For purposes of this assignment, you can address the customer as Ms. Jane Doe, as the computer system will fill in their specific addresses.

3. Bad News Message

Your boss and the CFO have asked you to work with the Investor Relations (IR) department this week. As you are aware, the stock prices of Chipotle have lately taken a severe hit.

The IR team knows that some of the bigger investors are well aware of the criminal investigation over the Norovirus issue, but they are concerned that not all stockholders know of the issue. In an effort to be as transparent as possible, the IR teams wants to deliver an email to ALL stockholders informing them of the investigation.

Your assignment is to craft an email informing the stockholders of the criminal investigation. Because this is a sensitive topic, you will want to use the indirect approach to deliver the bad news.

Compose an email on behalf of the Head of the IR team. You may address this to Ms. Jane Doe, as the computer system will supply the specific email addresses.

4. Direct Persuasive Message

The fallout from the federal criminal investigation and sickness caused by Chipotle food continues. It has come to the Chairman and Co-CEO's attention that your childhood friend is a senior member of the editorial staff at the *Denver Times*. The *Times* is considering writing an editorial suggesting that Chipotle close ALL of its Denver locations until the criminal investigation is completed.

This would obviously be a disaster for the company. Your boss has asked you to reach out to your good friend and attempt to convince her to hold off on writing the editorial.

Compose a letter to your friend asking that she hold off on running the editorial. You can use reasons from the information provided above. Because she is a good friend of yours, you will want to use the direct persuasive structure.

Your friend's name is:
Ms. Susan Young
1 Newspaper Way
Denver, CO 00990
You are the author of this letter.

5. Direct Persuasive Instructional Message

Your good work is being noticed. Now the Human Resources (HR) Department has asked you to come work with them in crafting a memo to all employees regarding new procedures to be used at all Chipotle locations.

The executive team has instituted new polices to ensure the safe handling of food. One of these new policies requires that all employees set up monthly wellness checks with a Chipotle approved doctor.

Your task is to draft a memo to all employees informing them of this new policy and directing them to set up their first monthly visit by February 26, 2016.

The memo can be sent via email and should be addressed to "All Employees" and from "HR Department."

Chapter 5-2

Facebook Case Study

Emotions Run High

Facebook, the leader of all social media, is constantly striving to improve the experience for their users and increase their advertising revenue. For many years, users of Facebook have pressed the company to add on to the LIKE button, as they felt that the simple "thumbs up" icon was limiting their ability to accurately express their reactions to posts.

In an effort to address the concerns of their users, Facebook created five new "reactions." They unveiled the new reactions on February 24, 2016. "By popular demand, Facebook is going beyond the ubiquitous thumbs-up button with a new shorthand to express your thoughts and feelings. Acknowledging that 'like' isn't the right sentiment for every occasion, the giant social network is offering new options. Reactions, five emoting emojis, started rolling out to Facebook's nearly 1.6 billion users around the globe Wednesday."[6]

The "reactions" consist of five emojis, each depicting a specific sentiment: love, haha, wow, sad, and angry. Facebook, in a press release announcing the new "reactions," explained that they had been conducting research using focus groups and surveys for more than a year before releasing the new user tool. The Product Manager for Reactions, reported that in test markets, the "Reactions" elicited a positive response. To view Facebook's press release, please go to http://newsroom.fb.com/news/2016/02/reactions-now-available-globally/.

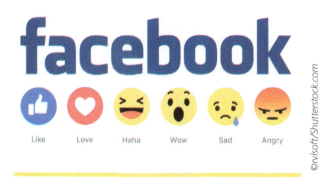

©rvlsoft/Shutterstock.com

Figure 1

---

[6] Jessica Guynn, "Meet Facebook's new emoting emojis: Love, haha, wow, sad and angry." February 25, 2016 USA Today http://www.usatoday.com/story/tech/news/2016/02/24/facebook-reactions-launch/80803468/

Users generally had a positive response to the introduction of the new "reactions." However, some disgruntled posters still clamored for a "Dislike" button, but Facebook has consistently insisted that a dislike button would not fit in with the community that Facebook has created.

"Facebook CEO was against a thumbs-down emoticon—that's not what the community really wanted, he claimed. 'Our community has been asking for a dislike button for years, but not because people want to tell friends they don't like their posts. People wanted to express empathy and make it comfortable to share a wider range of emotions,' the Facebook CEO posted on Facebook after the global release of Reactions."[7]

Industry analysts note that Facebook has not only launched the "reactions" in response to consumer demand, but also to increase ways by which they can obtain user data to better target advertisements. "Facebook will tell you that the new reactions are all about giving users new ways to communicate and express themselves. No doubt that's part of it. Users have long complained that like doesn't feel appropriate in a lot of circumstances, such as when a friend's loved one has died or an acquaintance posts a political screed that you find interesting but also troubling. But, like almost everything Facebook does, there is a double purpose at work here—and that second purpose involves data. Specifically, Facebook is now going to be able to collect, and profit from, a whole lot more of it."[8]

It is under these circumstances that you begin your internship with Facebook.

Practice Assignments Context

Congratulations! You have just been offered an internship with Facebook at their new Headquarters in Menlo Park, CA. Over the next eight weeks, you will be working for several members of the senior leadership team at Facebook, including the COO of Facebook, the Product Manager, and the VP of Human Resources and Recruiting.

This is a dream internship for you, as you love Facebook and would like to see it engage more with the younger generation. Your goal is to secure an offer of full time employment upon graduation from the University of Arizona. In order to achieve this goal, you know that you need to deliver top quality work in a fast paced environment.

Facebook has recently launched their new "reactions" buttons. A great deal of thought went into this new product. However, as with any new product, there are people who are not happy with the change. Your work over the next eight weeks will primarily be focused on delivering messages to various stakeholders regarding the "reactions" product.

Use the information contained in this case study and information on Facebook's website to inform your writing as you move through the various types of writing structures.

Best of luck as you embark on this exciting opportunity!

---

[7]Kerry Flynn, "Facebook Users Show Range of reaction to new Love, Haha, Sad, Angry, Wow, Emoticons" February 25, 2016,International Business Times http://www.ibtimes.com/facebook-users-show-range-reactionsnew-love-haha-sad-angry-wow-emoticons-2323629

[8]Will Oremus, "Facebook's Five New Reaction Buttons: Data, Data, Data, Data, and Data" February 24, 2016, Slate.com, http://www.slate.com/blogs/future_tense/2016/02/24/facebook_s_5_new_reactions_buttons_are_all_about_data_data_data.html

Practice Assignments

1. Direct Informative Report

   You have just started at Facebook Headquarters for an eight-week internship. You were chosen for this important position because word of your excellent writing skills reached the higher ups at Facebook, so you want to ensure that you live up to the reputation that precedes you.

   The COO of Facebook has directed her assistant to assign you your first task. Here is the email you receive on your first day:

   TO: Student
   FROM: Jack Draper, Asst to the COO
   DATE: 3/7/16
   RE: Your first assignment

   Welcome!

   Here at Facebook, we hit the ground running. The COO has asked me to give you your first assignment.

   Facebook has a new person on our Board of Directors. Mr. Tom Greene, a retired Stanford Professor of Economics, joined the board late last week. In order to get Mr. Greene up to speed on the new "reactions," the COO has asked you to draft a neutral summary report explaining to Mr. Greene how and why the "reactions" were developed and what the news coverage has been.

   You are writing this report on behalf of our boss, the COO, so attach transmittal email, and then compose your report. Your report should not be more than two pages (three with the email.) You have not been asked to provide any recommendations at this juncture. Just deliver the facts in a clear and logical fashion.

   The COO needs this on her desk by 11:59 p.m. on 3/11/16.

   Thanks,

   Jack

2. Indirect Persuasive Message

   The COO was impressed with your neutral summary. Good work!

   As you can see from the readings, many people have embraced the new "reactions." However, there is a group of Facebook users who have been asking for a DISLIKE button for years. They have written many letters over the years to the Facebook CEO asking for the dislike button. As you are aware, the Facebook CEO has his reasons for not including a dislike button.

   It has come to the attention of Facebook leadership that this group—we can call them the "DISLIKERS"—have started a boycott Facebook campaign on Twitter.

   The COO has asked you to draft a persuasive letter on behalf of the Facebook CEO to these customers asking them to end their boycott of Facebook. You can offer these former users a chance to participate in an online forum of VIPs to discuss expanding the "reactions" buttons.

Craft a persuasive letter to these customers from your boss, the Facebook CEO. For purposes of this assignment, you can address the customer as Ms. Jane Doe, as the computer system will fill in their specific addresses.

Because this is a sensitive topic, you will want to use the indirect persuasive structure.

3. Bad News Message

The clamor for a DISLIKE button continues. Now the newest Board Member, Mr. Tom Greene, has indicated that he is strongly in favor of adding a thumbs down button to the expanded "reactions." He has reached out to the employees of Facebook and has urged them to lobby the leadership team for a DISLIKE button. Because Mr. Greene is on the Board of Directors of Facebook, his message has resonated with some of the employees.

As you know, the Facebook CEO will not include a DISLIKE button. The Vice President of Human Resources, has asked you to draft a letter to the employees informing them of Facebook CEO's final decision on this matter.

Craft a letter to the employees, on behalf of the VP of HR, informing them of the bad news (the fact that a DISLIKE button will not be implemented). Because this issue was first raised by a Board Member, you must deliver this bad news carefully. Use the buffer, reasons, bad news, goodwill closing structure.

Address this letter to Employee A (the computer system will insert the specific employee's name).

4. Direct Persuasive Message

The interest and chatter about the new "reactions" continues. It has come to your attention that a dear friend, who happens to write for the Los Angeles Times, is planning on authoring an editorial implying that the new "reactions" will be disastrous for the stock prices of Facebook.

This seems counterintuitive to you, but you know you must address it and try to prevent him from writing such an ill-advised editorial.

The COO of Facebook is aware of your friendship with the writer for the Los Angeles Times. She has asked you to write a letter, directly from you, to your friend asking him not to write the editorial.

Compose a letter to your friend asking that he hold off on running the editorial. You can use reasons from the reading above. Because he is a good friend of yours, you will want to use the direct persuasive structure.

Your friend's name is:
Mr. Stan Smith
1 Newspaper Way
Los Angeles, CA 00990

5. Direct Persuasive Instructional Message

Your good work is being noticed. Now the HR team has come to you again and has asked for your assistance.

A few weeks ago, the Facebook CEO posted an internal memo about employees crossing out "Black Lives Matter" and replacing the slogan with "All Lives Matter" on the company's Wall at Facebook Headquarters.

Now the Wall at Headquarters has been covered with huge handwritten THUMBS DOWN images. The Facebook CEO has had enough. He has decided to implement a new policy prohibiting any employee from posting on the Wall at Headquarters. The Wall will now only be used by the Facebook CEO himself for messages he wishes employees to see.

Your task is to draft a memo to all employees informing them of this new policy.

The memo can be sent via email and should be addressed to "All Employees" and from "HR Department."

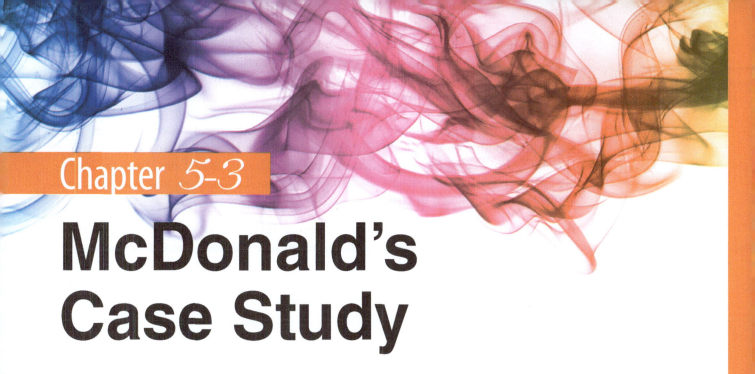

McDonald's Case Study

McDonald's Millennial Angst

McDonald's has dominated the fast food industry for many years with more than 36,000 stores globally. Since its inception in 1955, it has grown in popularity and has become the standard bearer for fast food as we know it. Recently, however, the fast food market has become increasingly competitive, and McDonald's has been struggling to keep up.

The mega chain is feeling the strain of such changes in their pocketbook. With the rise of fast/fresh—and ostensibly healthier—rival fast food franchises, McDonald's has seen a significant drop in sales. Its March 2015 quarterly report indicated:

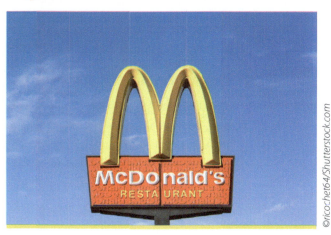

Figure 1

- Global sales were down 2.6%
- Asia-Pacific/Middle East region sales were down 8.3%
- Total revenue was down 11%, to $5.96 billion
- Net income was down 32.6%, to $812 million[9]

---

[9]P.A. Watson, McDonald's getting crushed by healthier fast food companies like Chipotle, Natural News, April 26, 2015 http://www.naturalnews.com/049495_McDonalds_Chipotle_fast_food.html#ixzz3uUgzknjC

The most lucrative demographic for takeout food is arguably the millennial generation. Unfortunately for McDonald's, millennials are turning their back on the Golden Arches. According to an article in Al Jazeera America, "[millennials] are a leading force in the good food movement, with national networks such as Real Food Challenge, which was founded just a few years ago and now enlists tens of thousands of college students to push for better food on college campuses, and Food Corps, a national AmeriCorps training program that fosters youth school garden educators. Books such as Michael Pollan's *The Omnivore's Dilemma*, films like *Food Inc.* and advocacy groups such as Food & Water Watch are inspiring young people to ask questions about where their food comes from and raise hell about antibiotics and hormones in meat."[10]

In an attempt to turn McDonald's future around, industry analysts suggest focusing on the millennial generation. "Generally speaking, millennials love food and dining out, and yet their preferences—customizable options, transparency, and fare that's healthier, more sustainable, and altogether superior compared to any cheap cookie-cutter fast food joint—are the exact opposite of what McDonald's is known for."[11]

McDonald's Responds

CEO Steve Easterbrook took the helm in early 2015 and has grappled with these issues. A 47-year-old British national, Mr. Easterbrook has spent nearly his entire career in Europe, most of it with McDonald's. He is credited with turning around the company's 1,200-store business in Britain in part by doing things—reducing the salt in fries, adding organic milk—that appealed to a more health-conscious consumer.[12] In an effort to turn the tides, Mr. Easterbrook announced some changes.

"In recent years, many restaurants have stressed improvements in food quality and customization, and CEO Steve Easterbrook acknowledged in a recent video detailing the turnaround that change outside the company has moved faster than it has at McDonald's during the past five years."[13]

In a press release dated March 4, 2015, McDonald's announced some changes to their menu policies. McDonald's U.S. President Mike Andres stated that new menu sourcing plans included only sourcing chicken raised with antibiotics that are important to humans and offering jugs of milk that was not treated with rbST, an artificial growth hormone.

[10]Anna Lappe, Millennials aren't lovin McDonalds, March 4. 2015 America Aljazeera http://america.aljazeera.com/opinions/2015/3/millennials-arent-lovin-mcdonalds.html

[11]Brad Tutlle, 5 Things that will Challenge McDonald's No Matter who's CEO, Money, January 29, 2015 http://time.com/money/3687899/mcdonalds-problems-new-ceo/

[12]Stephanie Strom, McDonald's Seeks its Fast Food Soul, March 7, 2015 http://www.nytimes.com/2015/03/08/business/mcdonalds-seeks-its-fast-food-soul.html

[13]Katie Little, McDonald's has a big problem in uphill turnaround. CNBC May 5, 2015. http://www.cnbc.com/2015/05/05/mcdonalds-has-a-big-problem-in-uphill-turnaround.html

Practice Assignments Context

Congratulations! You have just begun your dream internship with McDonald's, the world's leading fast food franchise. You are working in Oak Brook, Illinois at McDonald's Headquarters.

McDonald's has hired a team of university students for the winter semester in an effort to gain insight into the desires of the millennial generation (most researchers and commentators use birth years ranging from the early 1980s to the early 2000s to describe this generation). Over the course of 2015, McDonald's has suffered some blows, including lowered stock prices, accusations of unfair employment policies, and demand for healthier food and more transparency regarding the origin of said food. It is also clear that McDonald's is failing to attract the younger millennial generation, arguably the most important demographic group because of their spending power and social media savvy.

You will be working primarily with the Vice President of Customer Experience, the Senior Vice President, Chief Marketing Office, and the Senior Vice President, Menu Innovation. Over the course of your internship, any one of these executives may assign you tasks.

This is your opportunity to shine! As you work on each assignment, remember the unique perspective that you bring to the table as a member of the millennial generation. You not only want to do your best work, you also want to stand out from the other millennial interns in hopes of receiving a full time job offer upon graduation.

McDonald's Website: http://www.mcdonalds.com/content/us/en/home.html

Use the information contained in this case study and information on the McDonald's website to inform your writing as you move through the various types of writing structures.

Practice Assignments

1. Direct Informative Message

   You have arrived in Oak Brook at McDonald's Headquarters. You are about to embark on a four-week long internship and are eager to impress the executives you will be working under. The Senior Vice President and Chief Marketing Officer has called you into her office and has asked you to compose a SUMMARY REPORT outlining the problems that McDonald's currently faces. She would like you to focus on the relationship between the millennial generation and the company.

   The Sr. VP CMO has not asked you for any recommendations at this point, so make sure you compose your report in a neutral fashion. Use the data from the readings and video to inform your writing.

   Your report should not exceed two pages.

2. Indirect Persuasive Message

   The Sr. VP CMO was impressed by your summary report and she has shared it with some of her peers.

   The Senior Vice President, Menu Innovation, is in charge of adding new items to McDonald's menu. You know that he is considering a variety of new items as he is concerned that McDonald's is losing out to perceived "fresh fast food" establishments such as Chipotle and Panera.

You have been thinking about this issue for a while. You believe the inclusion of a veggie burger and eggplant fries will attract the highly desirable millennial crowd. Craft a persuasive email to the Sr. VP Menu Innovations advocating for the inclusion of these items on the menu.

Because the Sr. VP Menu Innovations is your superior and this email is unsolicited, you will use the indirect persuasive structure.

3. Bad News Message

The Senior Vice President, Menu Innovation, has decided AGAINST including veggie burgers and eggplant fries to the permanent menu at this time.

Unfortunately, one of his junior executives had already contacted ALL ABOUT EGGPLANTS and made a verbal commitment to order 100 cases of frozen eggplant fries. Of course, the Sr. VP Menu Innovations immediately fired the junior executive for this error.

The Sr. VP Menu Innovations has asked you to craft a letter to Ms. Jane Nightshade, CEO of ALL ABOUT EGGPLANTS, informing her that McDonald's will not be needing the eggplant fries at this time. He has specifically told you NOT to mention the error of the junior executive because it would make it seem as if he was not in control of his team. You must inform Ms. Nightshade that McDonald's cannot honor the verbal contract because focus groups revealed that eggplant fries would not be big sellers.

Compose a bad news message to Ms. Nightshade from the Sr. VP Menu Innovations. Remember, you want to continue to have a good working relationship with this company because McDonald's may choose to use eggplant fries in the future. For this reason, use the indirect bad news structure (buffer, reasons, bad news, goodwill close). Also, choose the information you use carefully in your reasons section so as to avoid offending Ms. Nightshade.

The recipient's address is:
Ms. Jane Nightshade
CEO
ALL ABOUT EGGPLANTS
1 Eggplant Way
Newport, CA 09821

4. Direct Persuasive Message

Your internship with McDonald's is going very well. However, you have heard through the grapevine that PETA (People for the Ethical Treatment of Animals) is planning an ad campaign attacking McDonald's for not offering veggie burgers.

You happen to be close friends with the President of the Illinois chapter of PETA, Mr. Greg Waters. You and Greg are childhood friends, and while you appreciate his passion for animal issues, you do NOT want him to start a large ad campaign against McDonald's.

You have taken it upon yourself to write a letter to Greg asking him to hold off on any negative ad campaign. You believe that there is room for compromise and that McDonald's may choose to offer a veggie burger at some point in the future, but not if they are strong-armed by PETA.

Craft a direct persuasive letter to Greg. Remember, you are close friends, which is why you can use the direct approach (still AIDA, but with the ask in both the first paragraph and the final paragraph). Also, be mindful of your tone with Greg. He is your buddy.

His address is:
Greg Waters
PETA Illinois
1 Animal Way,
Oak Brook, IL 55781

5. Direct Persuasive Instructional Message

The Sr. VP Menu Innovations has realized that breakfast is the answer. He and his Menu Innovation team have decided to offer breakfast all day at all McDonald's stores. In the opinion of the Menu Innovation team, all day breakfast will capture the hearts and stomachs of the millennials and bring them back into the fold.

You have been tasked with crafting a memo to all employees of McDonald's informing them of the new policy of all day breakfast. Leadership wants all employees working the counter and drive in to now say "Welcome to McDonald's! We are now serving breakfast all day. What can I make for you today?"

Use the direct persuasive instructional structure (state directive, provide reasons, courteous closing).

For-Profit Colleges Case Study

New Life or Burnout?

The once bustling for-profit college industry has fallen on hard times. Marketed to "non-traditional students," these colleges appealed to older students, working parents, and those with full time jobs who sought to advance their careers. The colleges focused heavily on their ability to provide marketable skills that would allow the students to obtain good jobs. Enrollment in these colleges bloomed in the late 1990s and early 2000s. For example, "the University of Phoenix . . . enrolled hundreds of thousands of students across the country, earning billions of dollars a year. Between 1990 and 2010, the percentage of bachelors' degrees that came from for-profit schools septupled."[14]

Figure 1

Fast forward to 2016. The promised lucrative jobs failed to materialize. Students who were encouraged to take on significant debt to attend such colleges are defaulting on their student loans in record numbers. The number of current enrollees is dropping along with the stock value. For example, at the largest for-profit college in the United States, students are simply not signing up:

---

[14]James Surowiecki, "The Rise and Fall of For-Profit Schools", November 2, 2015, The New Yorker http://www.newyorker.com/magazine/2015/11/02/the-rise-and-fall-of-for-profit-schools

At the University of Phoenix, enrollment was at approximately 460,000 students in 2010. By 2016, the enrollment had dropped to a mere 213,000. The student enrollment numbers were not the only ones in decline. In March 2016, parent company Apollo Education Group (APOL) reported that its enrollment AND revenues sank 14% compared to 2015.[15]

This dramatic change in enrollment numbers is likely due to more than just one factor. Many students feel they were misled by the University. For example, Fox news conducted an investigation that revealed that although students were told they were enrolled in an accredited social work program, they were in fact ineligible for social work internships due to the unaccredited status of the University's program.[16]

Other students feel that they were promised high paying jobs that simply never appeared, leaving them with huge student loan debt and working in low paying jobs.

"Dependence on student loans was not incidental to the for-profit boom—it was the business model. . . . Since the schools weren't lending money themselves, they didn't have to worry about whether it would be paid back. So they have every incentive to encourage students to take out as much financial aid as possible, often by giving them a distorted picture of what they could expect in the future."[17] Students were told fantastical stories of how much they could earn. In one case, a potential student was told that he could earn $250,000 as a barber.[18]

Federal regulators became concerned with the sector's aggressive recruitment of veterans and predatory advertising to low-income constituencies. Multiple lawsuits by students and multiple restrictions placed on how for-profit colleges do business have made it hard for the industry to recover to its former glory.

Not only are students and regulators unhappy, stockholders are upset too. The University of Phoenix has faced multiple lawsuits, the most recent one concerning the recruitment of veterans. "Shareholders of Apollo Education Group Inc. (Nasdaq: APOL) have filed a class-action lawsuit against the Phoenix company over University of Phoenix's military recruitment activities. The complaint was filed on March 14 in the U.S. District Court for the District of Arizona, according to an 8–K filed with the U.S. Securities and Exchange Commission."[19]

Rising from the Ashes?

For-profit universities have had to come to terms with the mistakes they have made in order to stay afloat. The University of Phoenix is closing one-third of its locations, lowering tuition fees, testing students before admission to ensure that they are ready for college, and offering two-year Associates degrees. These measures are intended to bring back students and ensure that they graduate without crushing debt and scarce job prospects.

[15]Patrick Gillespie, "University of Phoenix has lost half its students", March 25, 2016, CNN Money, http://money.cnn.com/2015/03/25/investing/university-of-phoenix-apollo-earnings-tank/

[16]Meghan Dwyer, 'University of Phoenix under fire by federal government after deceptive marketing tactics,' March 25, 2015, Fox6Now, http://fox6now.com/2015/04/23/university-of-phoenix-doles-out-financialsettlements-after-misleading-students/

[17]James Surowiecki, "The Rise and Fall of For-Profit School," November 2, 2015, The New Yorker

[18]Ibid.

[19]Angela Gonzales, "Shareholders file class-action lawsuit against University of Phoenix parent," March 18, 2016, Phoenix Business Journal, http://www.bizjournals.com/phoenix/news/2016/03/18/shareholders-file-class-actionlawsuit-against.html

The parent company of the University of Phoenix, Apollo Education Group (APOL), has expressed that it plans to address the difficulties the University of Phoenix faces, include educating prospective students about the true costs of student loans, focusing coursework on skills important to potential employers, and closing smaller physical locations to focus more on larger metropolitan markets. Apollo Education Group's CEO, Greg Cappelli, credited increased competition and federal oversight for a "transformation." According to Cappelli and his fellow executives, the "new" University of Phoenix will be judged not by its enrollment numbers, but by the proportion of students who graduate and land jobs.[20]

The University of Phoenix mission statement is that it "provides access to higher education opportunities that enable students to develop knowledge and skills necessary to achieve their professional goals, improve the performance of their organizations, and provide leadership and service to their communities."

It is under these circumstances that you begin your internship with the University of Phoenix.

Practice Assignments Context

You are applying for an internship with the University of Phoenix. Access to education is very important to you, as your mother was unable to attend college because of child rearing obligations and low paying jobs. You are a strong advocate of institutions that help the "non-traditional" student attend college and earn a degree. Your first task will be to write a Letter of Intent/Cover Letter to the President of the University of Phoenix.

Practice Assignments

1. Letter of Intent/Cover Letter

   Compose a letter to the President of the University of Phoenix expressing your desire to be an intern with the University of Phoenix.

2. Indirect Persuasive Message

   CONGRATULATIONS! Your application to become an intern has been accepted and you have just begun an internship with the University of Phoenix.

   You will be interning for the President of the University of Phoenix. Because he is committed to giving his interns a comprehensive internship experience, you will also be doing work for the Senior Vice President, Chief Marketing Officer, and the Human Resources Officer. Throughout your internship, you will be assigned various tasks requiring different types of written communication.

   You are aware of the troubles that have plagued the University of Phoenix and the decline in student enrollment. There is a group of individuals who expressed interest in the University via an online form, but have since been unresponsive to follow up emails from the student enrollment office.

[20]Christina Estes, "Apollo Education Group CEO: 'None Of Us Are Happy With The Performance," January 19, 2016, http://kjzz.org/content/253484/apollo-education-group-ceo-none-us-are-happy-performance

The President has asked you to compose an email to this group of potential students urging them to enroll. You should use the information above to inform your arguments and to address any anticipated pushback from the potential students.

Address the email to Mr. John Doe, as the computer system will input the specific addressee information. Use the indirect persuasive message structure.

3. Direct Persuasive Message

As part of the University's efforts to improve their reputation and enhance the educational experience, they are closing several physical locations across the country in order to reinvest in higher performing metropolitan markets. This has led to confusion and angst among instructors at the locations scheduled to close. Some of these instructors have been meeting and are scheduling a "sick-out" (an organized period of unwarranted sick leave taken as a form of group protest, usually as a measure to avoid a formal strike) to protest the closure of the smaller locations.

The Human Resources Officer, has asked you to draft a letter on her behalf asking this group of instructors to not engage in a sick-out. If these instructors agree with her request, she will ensure that they are given priority consideration when applying for the online teaching positions that are opening up. Because these are employees of the University, you may use the direct persuasive message structure.

Address the letter to Employee X, as the computer system will fill in the specific details.

4. Bad News Message

In response to the heightened scrutiny by regulators and the public, the University of Phoenix has raised its admission requirements to ensure that all students accepted into the school are indeed ready for college-level work. No longer will a high school diploma or GED be the sole requirement for admission. Prospective students must now pass an exam to enroll in the University.

Unfortunately, 200 students who did NOT pass that exam were erroneously sent letters of admission. They must be informed of this mistake and be told that at this time, they will be unable to enroll at the University. This is not only extremely unfortunate for the students, it is also a marketing nightmare. The Senior Vice President, Chief Marketing Officer has asked you to draft a letter on her behalf informing the students of this bad news.

You may address the letter to Student X, as the computer program will supply the names and addresses. Use the bad news structure (buffer, reasons, bad news, goodwill closing) for this letter.

Lyft Case Study

Driving Toward Success

The car-for-hire business has changed drastically over the last decade. Where once the only non-public transpiration options were taxicabs or rental cars, there now exists a booming car-for-hire industry. Peer-to-peer ridesharing companies, such as Uber and Lyft, are part of the growing sharing economy in the modern business market.

With success often comes controversy. For example, Uber has struggled with violent incidents involving both drivers and passengers, leading industry analysts and consumers alike to question the validity and vigor of Uber background checks. However, Uber has defended their vetting practices.

©360b/Shutterstock.com

Figure 1

"'Unlike the taxi industry, our background checking process and standards are consistent across the United States and often more rigorous than what is required to become a taxi driver," according to Uber spokesman Taylor Bennett. Uber uses a private company called HireEase to conduct background checks.

"Ours cover courthouse records, county, state, and federal records," Bennett said. "We cover the gamut in terms of what we look at."

There have been several reports about loopholes that have led to Uber approving drivers with criminal histories including felony convictions. And the Fair Credit Reporting Act limits the amount of information HireEase is able to uncover.[21]

---

[21]Adrienne LaFrance and Rose Eveleth, "Are Taxis safer than Uber?," March 2, 2015, The Atlantic. http://www.theatlantic.com/technology/archive/2015/03/are-taxis-safer-than-uber/386207/

Brief History of Uber Incidents

December 2013: Uber driver hits a family, killing one

January 2014: Uber employees order fake rides to sink competitor

March 2014: Uber driver accused of groping a passenger

June 2014: Uber driver charged for assault

September 2014: Uber passenger struck by Uber driver with a hammer

October 2014: Uber driver charged with battery and vandalism

November 2014: Executive suggests digging up dirt on Uber's critics

December 2014: Uber driver accused of raping a passenger

April 2015: Uber driver charged with robbery

November 2015: Uber rider attacks a driver

January 2016: Uber driver charged with rape

February 2016: Uber driver in Michigan goes on shooting spree[22]

March 19, 2018: Uber vehicle in self-driving mode kills Tempe, Arizona woman

In addition to the assault incidents, Uber, and other ride-sharing companies, such as Lyft, have experienced pushback from local governments and established traditional taxi services. "Uber is the subject of ongoing protests and legal action from taxi drivers, taxi companies, and governments around the world who are trying to stop Uber from operating in their areas. These groups say that Uber presents unfair competition to taxis because the company does not pay taxes or licensing fees; that it endangers passengers; and that drivers are untrained, unlicensed and uninsured."[23]

Finally, both ride hailing services face competition with each other. Not only are they courting clients and market share, they are also in a race for drivers. In this race, it comes down to how the drivers feel. National Public Radio spoke with more than 20 people who worked for both Uber and Lyft.

> ". . . consistently, these drivers say: In Lyft there are fewer expectations. It's more touchy-feely. Passengers are supposed to hop in the front seat and be friendly because, as the motto goes, the driver is 'your friend with a car.'"
>
> "I have very few problems with Lyft passengers," Christopherson says. "They're generally very nice. Or if they're not nice, they're quiet." Uber started as a luxury brand. Its motto is "everyone's private driver." So, Christopherson says, for people like him—people who drive super-part time, who have other jobs—it's not a great feeling when passengers expect a chauffeur.
>
> "They don't really kind of care about what you think of them. And so it's a little more fraught," he says."[24]

It is with this information that you begin your internship with Lyft.

---

[22]Daniel Roberts, A brief history of Uber scandals, February 22, 2016 Yahoo Finance http://finance.yahoo.com/news/uber-scandals-timeline-michigan-shooting-140035801.html

[23]Uber (company) Wikipedia https://en.wikipedia.org/wiki/Uber_(company)

[24]Aarti Shahani, "In the battle between Lyft and Uber, the focus is on drivers," January 8, 2016, National Public Radio http://www.npr.org/sections/alltechconsidered/2016/01/18/463473462/is-uber-good-to-drivers-it-s-relative

Practice Assignments Context

Congratulations! You have just landed a much-desired internship with the company Lyft (https://www.lyft.com). Located in beautiful and exciting San Francisco, Lyft is your dream company. Your internship is for a mere two months, so you want to ensure you make the most of this incredible opportunity.

Because of Lyft's collaborative corporate nature, during your internship you will be moved around to different departments depending on the needs of the company. Your main point of contact—your boss—is the Director of Retention and Trust and Safety.

The Director of Retention and Trust and Safety is very concerned that Lyft does not make the same mistakes that Uber did over the past few years. Her goal is to build a deep sense of trust with her clients, her drivers, and the governments of the cities in which Lyft operates.

To that end, she will routinely task you with various projects.

Use the information above and information on Lyft's website to inform your writing as you move through the various types of writing structures.

Practice Assignments

1. Stakeholder Analysis

   You have begun your internship with Lyft. Congratulations! It is Day One and the Director of RTS has called you into her office to greet you and to give you your first assignment.

   As you know, she is very concerned that Lyft differentiate itself from Uber. She sees the problems that Uber experienced in the past few years as instructive in terms of what to avoid.

   As a way to get started about thinking how to avoid making the mistakes Uber did, and to proactively build trust among the various stakeholders, she has asked you to complete a stakeholder analysis.

2. Indirect Persuasive Message

   The Director of RTS was impressed with your Stakeholder Analysis. She has spoken of you to her colleagues in the Government Relations Department of Lyft.

   Lyft wants to operate in every large city in the United States. However, some cities are resistant to Lyft because of their allegiance to Uber. One of the many responsibilities of the Government Relations Department is to convince cities to allow Lyft to operate in their region.

   Lyft has their eye on a smaller city in Maine. The Vice President of Lyft's Government Relations team would like you to draft a letter from him to the Mayor of Belfast, trying to get the Mayor to support Lyft's application to operate in Belfast.

   For this assignment, you will want to use the indirect persuasive structure.

   Remember, you are drafting this letter for him so you should attach an email transmittal to the letter letting him know that you are completing his request. Then, attach your letter addressed to the Mayor of Belfast, from Mr. Estrada.

3. Bad News Message

   Good work on drafting the letter for the VP of Lyft's Government Relations team. News of your hard work is spreading throughout the company, and you have been called in to the office of the Vice President of People at Lyft.

   Lyft receives many applications for drivers each day, and under normal circumstances, the VP of People at Lyft would not be personally involved in accepting or rejecting these applications. However, one of his dear friends has a daughter, Lisa Race, who has applied to be a driver for Lyft. The problem is that Ms. Race is only 17 years old, and according to Lyft policy, drivers must be at least 18 years of age.

   He has asked you to send a letter to Ms. Race informing her of the news that Lyft cannot hire her at this time. Because Ms. Race's father is such a good friend of his, and because you know that this bad news is unexpected, you will want to use the indirect bad news structure. Recall from earlier chapters that the indirect bad news structure calls for buffer, reasons, bad news, and goodwill close.

   There is no need for a transmittal email for this assignment. Simply draft the letter to Ms. Race from him.

4. Direct Persuasive Message

   During your internship with Lyft, you have seen how lucrative it can be to be a Lyft driver. You have a spotless driving record, a clean car, and the desire to make some extra money on the side while completing your unpaid internship with Lyft.

   Your task is to write a letter to the VP of People of Lyft persuading him to allow you to drive for Lyft. You have developed a good working relationship with him, and he appreciates directness. For these reasons, you have chosen to use the direct persuasive structure.

   Write a letter to him urging him to allow you to drive for Lyft. Don't forget to include all of the elements of the AIDA structure. The difference between the indirect structure and the direct persuasive structures is where you place your ASK.

After working through this unit, you have undoubtedly gained fluency in various forms of written communication. Using the structures presented here will ensure that your writing is clear, informative and persuasive.

The following appendix contains sample responses to the prompts given in the preceding chapters. You may use these as a guide when writing your own practice responses.

Sample Practice Messages

Chipotle Sample Practice Messages

©Ken Wolter/Shutterstock.com

Sample Chipotle Direct Informational Message

Chipotle's Norovirus Incidents and Federal Criminal Investigation
This document contains the executive summary of Chipotle's most critical issues, the recent norovirus incidents and the company's current federal criminal investigation. The extensive research presented will incorporate background knowledge regarding the affected population, virus, and subpoena details. Furthermore, this report will highlight the financial ramifications of Chipotle's recent business operations. The information will assist you in determining next steps for Chipotle.

Frame, Forecast, WIIFY

Norovirus Incidents
Norovirus is the primary source of sickness from contaminated foods, impacting up to 21 million individuals in the United States each year. This virus typically

Body

lasts a few days and affects the gastrointestinal tract. The first recorded Chipotle norovirus incident was discovered in August of 2015 in Simi Valley, California. Once it was discovered that numerous Chipotle employees and customers reported norovirus symptoms, the infected restaurant temporarily shut down until it was properly cleaned.

According to the FDA, between the months of August and December, roughly 150 individuals were impacted by norovirus, and more than fifty individuals in nine states were affected by a separate E. coli virus. After the initial August outbreak, Chipotle has received negative publicity for various health related incidents, with the most notable events listed below:

- More than 150 customers sickened by Norovirus in Massachusetts.
- More than 50 people sickened by E. coli in nine states.
- More than 60 people sickened by Salmonella outbreak in Minnesota.

Federal Criminal Investigation
In the wake of the Simi Valley norovirus epidemic, Chipotle disclosed in an SEC filing that a federal grand jury has officially served them with a subpoena. This is because the number of individuals affected from this specific incident was determined by district agents to be greater than originally reported. The examination is being directed by the FDA Office of Criminal Investigations, along with the US Attorney's Office for the Central District of California. However, Chipotle representatives have assured the public that they will cooperate properly in the examination. In their SEC filing, Chipotle stated that the subpoena requested them to provide a "broad range of documents." In late January of 2016, Chipotle received a broader subpoena requesting information regarding food safety policies dating back to January 2013.

Financial Ramifications
Not only are sales and shares plummeting, but also many investors are losing faith and patience in the company. In addition, Chipotle's short-term future does not look bright as analysts are predicting record low earnings. Chipotle's financial woes have been publically documented and were displayed in their SEC filing. 2015 4th quarter reporting indicated a drop of 30% in sales compared to 2014.

Conclusion
Chipotle has suffered from various health-related outbreaks including incidents of norovirus, e-coli, and salmonella making customers and employees sick. Because of these incidents, Chipotle has been served with a federal grand jury subpoena seeking information about food safety policies within the company. Chipotle is committed to fully cooperating with the government in this matter. Stock prices have suffered because of these health-related incidents.

Conclusion

Sample Chipotle Indirect Persuasive Message

To: Jane Doe
From: The Chairman and Co-Chief Executive Officer
Date: Month, Date, Year
Subject: Logo Design Initiatives

Dear Ms. Jane Doe,

Thank you for being a part of Chipotle's frequent burrito card program. It is because of loyal customers like you that Chipotle has had the success it does today. I would like to offer our deepest apologies regarding the recent health scares and express Chipotle's commitment to providing the safest, freshest ingredients for you to enjoy.

Alignment

Loyal customers like you have a powerful impact on our company because our success depends on providing you with the best quality food and service. Despite recent incidents, since Chipotle's beginning, all of our food safety programs have met or exceeded industry standards. In order to achieve our goal of establishing the best practices in food safety, we collaborated with preeminent food safety experts to develop a state of the art comprehensive food safety program that significantly reduces risk on our farms, throughout the supply chain, and in our restaurants.

Information

I understand your concern regarding the safety of our products given the recent incidents. However, we have already begun to implement high-resolution sampling and testing of many of our ingredients to prevent contaminants, including E. coli, from getting into our restaurants. Because you are such a truly valued customer, I am pleased to offer you one free burrito for the first three months if you reinstate your customer loyalty card and come dine with us again.

Direct Benefit/
Deflect Pushback

Working together with food safety experts I want to assure you that Chipotle is taking the most aggressive measures to ensure the safety of the food the company serves you. I ask that you consider reinstating your frequent burrito card and visit Chipotle in the near future for your free burrito. For further information, please contact me at Steve.Ells@customerservice. Chipotle.org. Thank you for your time, and I look forward to hearing from you.

Ask

Sincerely,

The Chairman and Co-CEO

Sample Chipotle Bad News Message

To: Ms. Jane Doe
From: The Head of the IR Team
Date: February 2, 2016

Subject: Chipotle News

Ms. Jane Doe,

Buffer

I would like to thank you for your support as a shareholder of Chipotle. Without individuals such as you, Chipotle would not be able to provide the excellent food, service, and environment that we offer to our customers around the world. In order to keep our valued shareholders informed, we felt it was necessary to personally reach out to you regarding a few current incidences.

Reasons

Since Chipotle's opening in 1993, our employees have always strived to provide the best food and service in the fast food industry. Unfortunately, Chipotle has experienced several food-borne illness incidents across the country and has been scrutinized lately for these incidents. In 2015, over 200 customers and employees were sickened due to various food borne illnesses at our stores.

Bad News

Because of these incidents, the US Attorney General's office is currently conducting an investigation to find the reason for the outbreaks. This investigation has led to a decrease in customers, which has ultimately led to a decrease in share price. Chipotle is working diligently to revamp our health standards and ensure that incidents such as these will no longer occur.

Goodwill Closing

We are doing our best to make sure our valued customers feel safe and satisfied every time they step into our store. We are very confident that our new rigorous health policies will lead to an increase in customer satisfaction, as well as an increase in our share price. If you have any questions regarding the investigation, our new health policies, or any other matter, please feel free to contact me at tomshark@chipotle.com. We are happy to have you as a shareholder and hope that you continue to enjoy everything that Chipotle has to offer.

Sincerely,
Head of Investor Relations

Sample Chipotle Direct Persuasive Message

1401 Wynkoop St. Ste. 500
Denver, CO 80202

MONTH, DATE, YEAR

Ms. Susan Young
Denver Times
1 Newspaper Way
Denver, CO 00990

Dear Susan,

Congratulations on the recent promotion to senior member of the *Denver Times*! I am certain that your work educating and informing readers about important issues of the day is very rewarding. It has come to my attention that you are considering running an editorial suggesting that Chipotle close all of its Denver locations until the current criminal investigation is completed. I am writing you today to ask that you hold off on writing such an editorial.

Align/Ask

No one can deny that the recent food sickness and federal criminal investigation of Chipotle is most unfortunate, not just for the company but especially for the customers and employees of our establishments. However, as a result of these incidents, we have taken aggressive action to implement industry-leading procedures for the handling of our food, not just with our company, but also the vendors with whom we do business. These standards have been adopted nationwide since December 2015 and, according to IEH Laboratories and Consulting Group, lowers food risk to a nearly non-existent level.

Information

I understand your concern for the citizens of Denver and that you may be skeptical of the safety of Chipotle foods. Our newly implemented DNA-based tests far exceed current regulatory requirements and industry standards. Nonetheless, you may still be concerned with ingredient contamination after their arrival and while they are in storage. We have addressed this issue through two key policies: the first is that we are enhancing the training of our employees to ensure proper compliance with our standards and uniform handing of food across our locations. The second policy is to further test the ingredients throughout their storage and shelf life. Holding off on writing an editorial that suggests closing all of our locations will benefit you by maintaining your creditability as a writer, and further solidify your reputation as a journalist who reports the facts.

Direct Benefit/
Deflect Pushback

Please do not write an editorial suggesting Chipotle close its Denver locations. If this letter does not convince you of the safety of the food served by Chipotle, are you available to meet after work to discuss the issue? Many thanks for your consideration of my request.

Repeat Ask

Best,
Student X

Sample Chipotle Direct Persuasive Instructional Message

MEMORANDUM

To: All Employees
From: HR Department
Date: February 15, 2016
Subject: New Policy regarding ALL employees

Directive

This memo is to inform all employees of Chipotle of the new required monthly wellness checkups to further ensure the safe handling of food in our restaurants. Your first checkup will need to be completed by **February 26, 2016**.

Information

In order for Chipotle to ensure the safety of our customers, it is imperative that all employees follow the new policy. Please read the following further requirements related to the policy:

- Checkups must be completed once per month
- Checkups must be completed by a Chipotle-approved doctor
- The first checkup has to be completed by February 26, 2016

When followed correctly, this new policy will dramatically increase the safety of our food and the wellbeing of our customers and employees.

Courteous Closing

Thank you for your cooperation with this policy. You are very important to us and we want to ensure that you are healthy. We appreciate your continued hard work for Chipotle.

Facebook Reactions Sample Practice Messages

Sample Facebook Reactions Direct Informational Report

Meet Facebook's Newest Feature: Reactions

Facebook continues to dominate the cyber world with billions of daily users. With their launch of the new "reactions" feature, Facebook has more than just a "like" button. This innovative addition allows users to choose a new emotion when commenting on a status update with a simple click of a button. Overall, these emojis give greater variety in expressing what a user is thinking or feeling about posts on Facebook.

This document explores how Facebook "reactions" were created, why this feature was introduced, and the current news coverage from the public. This information will assist you as you explore next steps for Facebook.

In-depth Facebook Research

Facebook researchers, engineers, and specialized product teams spent more than a year preparing to launch "reactions." According to a 2016 report found on CNNMoney.com, the research consisted of:

- Performing different surveys
- Working with specific focus groups
- Consulting with sociologists
- Determining final emotions for product release

Need for Expression

Facebook wanted to give users a way to respond to posts in a more authentic way. The like button limits users to expressing a single emotion in regards to a post. Before emoji "reactions," liking a sad or angry post put users in uncomfortable positions. However, the "reactions" feature solved this problem. The new "reactions" allow users to express whether they are sad, serious, impressed (wow), funny, or happy.

The Six Reaction Emoji

According to a recent report from USAToday.com, Facebook users already interact via emoji on Facebook and other social media and messaging outlets. These added Facebook emoji "reactions" are designed to be an extension of the like button feature rather than a replacement. The six emotions found on Facebook are like, love, haha, wow, sad, and angry (See Figure 1).

Title

Frame, Forecast, WIIFY

Body

©rvlsoft/Shutterstock.com

Figure 1

Global Launch

Before releasing the "reactions" in the United States, Facebook launched pilot programs in various other countries. It took more than a year's worth of searching for alternatives for the common known "like" button. Overall, consumers are using "reactions" more frequently. Facebook product manager Sammi Krug selected seven countries to represent a range of cultures and languages to ensure "reactions" would be understood universally; they are:

- Colombia
- Chile
- Ireland
- Japan
- Philippines
- Portugal
- Spain

Facebook CEO's View

Facebook CEO felt the need to create a sort of "empathy" button and eventually formed a team to address this problem. According to Forbes.com, the Facebook CEO wanted to resist the idea of a "dislike" button so users would not encourage criticism towards other users. Instead, "reactions" involves a different type of interaction that allows users to express a variety of feelings towards user posts. Universal expressions and comments were studied in order to pick the top few that could be used on Facebook globally.

User Feedback

The global Facebook community is expressing mixed emotions to the new "reactions" feature. According to a recent 2016 report issued by IBTimes.com, some users pointed to the negative possibility of trolling and complained about how the emojis looked. However, some publishers also love the new feature and currently enjoy having a variety of emotions to react to posts with. The "love" reaction has been the most popular globally across countries.

Conclusion

The "reactions" feature is proving to be one of the biggest changes to the Facebook platform globally. It is an attempt to deepen people's attachments and emotions toward other user's content. The six reaction emojis are like, love, haha, wow, sad, and angry. Despite some users' desire for a "dislike" button, Facebook has declined to include one because it would create a judgmental atmosphere that does not reflect the company's philosophy. Facebook researchers will continue to gather a variety of data and feedback from their users in order to perfect the feature.

Sample Facebook Reactions Indirect Persuasive Message

Dear Ms. Jane Doe,

Thank you for your letters to our corporate offices. Because of your time and efforts, we have cultivated innovations here at Facebook while keeping our customers in mind. We are committed to creating the greatest social media experience on the Internet, and because of your suggestions and ideas, we are moving closer to our goals.

Alignment

Facebook's goal is to provide an environment where people can authentically react to posts by their friends and family. We have continued to foster a positive space for people to share their lives with friends and loved ones. While some users, including you, have urged us to include a "dislike" button, we feel that the inclusion of the five new "reactions" (love, sad, haha, wow, and angry) more accurately meet the needs of our users to expand their reactions to the posts of others.

Information

We have noticed your boycott of Facebook. While we understand that you are displeased that we have not included a "dislike" button, we want you to continue to enjoy the sense of community that is Facebook. If you suspend your boycott, we would like to invite you to help us continue to develop our social media experience. We are developing an online forum of VIPs to discuss expanding our current reaction buttons. Although the dislike button may not be in Facebook's future, we are sure you can help us figure out what will be.

Direct Benefit/
Deflect Pushback

Please suspend your boycott of Facebook. Working with Facebook and promoting our positive company values to create new reactions will be beneficial for both you and the company. I ask that you seriously consider joining our VIP discussion group. For further information, please contact me at facebookceo@facebook.com. Thank you for your time and your passion. I look forward to hearing from you.

Ask

Sincerely,
Facebook CEO

Sample Facebook Reactions Bad News Message

Dear Employee A,

Buffer

On behalf of the entire Facebook Executive team, we want to thank you for your loyalty and commitment to this company. Without individuals like you, we would not be able to create the positive atmosphere at Facebook. We appreciate the work you have done thus far and the work you will continue to do for this company.

Reasons

One of the most important attributes that the Facebook CEO wants to cultivate at Facebook is a sense of a supportive community. This sense of positivity must be evident in the workplace and our Internet platform. We want our users to feel welcomed and supported. The last thing we want to do is create a hostile environment that drives our users away from the site.

Bad News

For these reasons, the Facebook CEO has made a final decision to exclude the "dislike" button from Facebook. While many of you have felt strongly about the "dislike" button, the Board of Directors has concluded that it goes against our company's philosophy and counteracts all the work we have done to cultivate a positive environment.

Goodwill Close

I personally want to thank you for your input and encourage you to continue to bring things to our attention. Your unique perspective on these issues is something we respect. Thank you for your support and excellent work.

Regards,
Director or Human Resources

Sample Facebook Reactions Direct Persuasive Message

April 4th, 2016

Stan Smith
Los Angeles Times
1 Newspaper Way
Los Angeles, CA 00990

Dear Stan,

I hope you are well and enjoying your work with the *Los Angeles Times*. I understand that you are planning on authoring an editorial indicating that the new "reactions" will be catastrophic for the stock price of Facebook. Our team has devoted years of research into implementing the new "reactions" in order to build revenue and increase user communication. As a close friend of yours, I ask that you hold back on your planned editorial regarding your predicted negative correlation between the new "reactions" and Facebook's stock price.

Align/Ask

The new "reaction" buttons provide a boost of engagement and allow users to more authentically engage with other posters. These new "reactions" also will provide data that can be used to inform advertisers and increase ad prices, both of which will positively affect Facebook stock. For example, in the past if a user did not like a post he or she could not express her empathy. Now, that person can express her anger or sadness with one of our reaction buttons. This leads to more user communication as well as more specific data that can be passed on to advertisers.

Information

Writing an editorial expressing the opinion that the "reactions" will negatively affect Facebook stock is counterintuitive and in direct opposition to the positive media that the "reactions" have enjoyed since Facebook launched them. I would be happy to arrange a conversation with you and our "reactions" product manager, Sammi Krug, so that you can get a first-hand account of the development of this exciting new product. As a close friend, I honestly think this will make for a much more interesting article.

*Direct Benefit/
Deflect Pushback*

Please do not move forward with writing the editorial regarding negative impacts that "reactions" may have on Facebook stock. I am happy to discuss this with you further, as well as set up that conversation with Ms. Krug. Please give me a call at xxx-xxx-xxxx. Thanks Stan, I hope to hear from you soon.

Ask (Again)

Sincerely,
Student

Sample Facebook Reactions Direct Persuasive Instructional Message

TO: ALL EMPLOYEES

FROM: HR DEPARTMENT

SUBJECT: NEW POLICY PROHIBITING ANY EMPLOYEE FROM
               POSTING ON THE WALL AT HEADQUARTERS

DATE: MAY 9, 2016

Directive

The Facebook CEO has issued a new policy that prohibits employees from posting on the Wall at our Headquarters. This new policy has been issued for all employees. The only person now permitted to post on the Wall is The Facebook CEO.

Reasons

The Facebook CEO has noticed lately that some employees have been causing a negative environment by posting hurtful things on the Wall. For example, a few weeks ago someone posted "black lives matter" and another employee replaced it with "all lives matter." This was an insensitive action due to the ongoing problems in this country with racism. Recently, the Wall has been covered with huge handwritten "thumbs down" images. This does not reflect the positive atmosphere that The Facebook CEO seeks to foster at Facebook.

Courteous Closing

Thank you for your cooperation with this new policy. We appreciate your hard work and dedication to Facebook.

McDonald's Sample Practice Messages

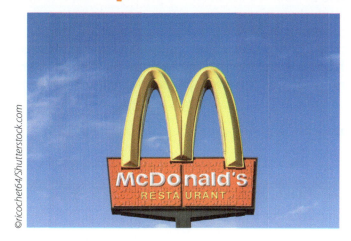

©ricochet64/Shutterstock.com

Sample McDonald's Direct Informational Message

McDonald's and Millennials Summary Report

Title

For decades, McDonald's has led the fast food industry in sales and popularity. Since 2013, however, net profit has declined. In order for McDonald's to attract key demographic groups, such as the millennial generation, the company must explore new concepts. Careful analysis of the challenges facing McDonald's and specifically the millennial generation market provides information about these issues. This report will cover the challenges McDonald's currently faces as a company, challenges McDonald's faces with the millennial generation, attempts McDonald's has made to combat these challenges, and finally the outcome of those efforts for McDonald's.

Frame, Forecast, WIIFY

McDonald's Company Challenges

Some now view McDonald's as cheap, unsafe food that is a major contributor to problems such as obesity, much like how Morgan Spurlock's 2004 documentary *Super Size Me* portrayed the company. Aaron Allen, a restaurant industry consultant said that due to bad imagery of McDonald's food, "people are ashamed to eat there." CNBC journalist Katie Little refers to McDonald's as: "The poster child of fast food. All that is good and all that is bad." She goes on to say that one of their main problems are that they are "reactive and not proactive" when it comes to solving problems. This lack of proactive problem solving to challenges like the aforementioned bad imagery has created several major companywide issues that McDonald's will need to find solutions to:

Body

- Customer visits fell 4.1% domestically in fiscal year 2014 according to CNBC
- Quarterly sales fell in 2013 for the first time in almost 20 years reported PR News Blog
- Investors losing confidence in the brand as evidenced by the February, 2015 Gates Foundation divesture of $1 billion of McDonald's stock

McDonald's Millennial Focus

CEO Steve Easterbrook has made it a priority to recapture the millennial market. The millennial generation is now eating at brands that are more concerned about the environment, workers' wages, and animal welfare. Having income, but perhaps not the responsibilities of families, millennials have the discretionary income to eat out. While this group often eats out, they are not willing to compromise on certain standards of the food they are eating or the company that prepares it. Millennials want:

- Customizable options
- Transparency
- Healthier food
- Food that is better than "cookie-cutter" fast food
- Companies that treat and pay employees fairly

Millennials are spending their money at "fast-casual" restaurants such as Shake Shack or Chipotle instead of McDonald's. While McDonald's saw a decrease in millennial interest, these other restaurants saw an increase of 2.3% in 19-21 year olds, and a 5.3% increase in 22–37 year olds according to a *Wall Street Journal* article.

Attempted Solutions

According to an article in *Al Jazeera America*, millennials want to know where their food comes from and demand healthier food. McDonald's has made several attempts to recapture the millennial market as shown below:

- Customizable Options: McDonald's attempted a "Build Your Own Burger" kiosk in stores where customers could choose their patty, toppings, etc. and not be limited to predefined burgers.
- Transparency: The "Our Food, Your Questions" campaign was started in attempts to help McDonald's back the story of their new food practices. For example, customers can watch videos that prove a fresh egg is used in every Egg McMuffin, and also learn exactly what is in a chicken nugget.
- Healthier Food: CEO Steve Easterbrook is leading from the top regarding sourcing healthier food by stating that within two years all the chicken served at its restaurants would be free of antibiotics.
- Non Cookie-Cutter Food: Since the early 2000's, McDonald's has attempted to achieve higher quality food by expanding their menu and adding premium items such as the Premium McWrap, Angus Deluxe, and Chicken Selects.

Conclusion

This report provides information regarding McDonald's disconnect with the millennial market. Millennials desire transparency and healthier foods. McDonald's is losing the millennial generation as customers, which is affecting stock prices and leading to store closures. McDonald's is at a critical juncture to decide between the new healthier rebranding approaches as laid out by Easterbrook, versus the "hotter, fresher and faster" method that their empire was built on.

Sample McDonald's Indirect Persuasive Message

To: Senior Vice President, Menu Innovation
From: STUDENT X
Date: MONTH, DATE, YEAR
Subject: Menu Options

Dear Mr. Watson,

As Senior Vice President of Menu Innovation, your ideas have established McDonald's as a powerhouse in the food industry. Similarly, I am constantly searching for ways to reach the millennial generation. I think that changes to the menu at McDonald's can propel the company to the top again.

Alignment

The millennial generation has been distancing themselves from McDonald's. We are different from any other, and we value the quality of a meal rather than convenience. For example, fast-casual restaurants that are perceived to have quality food, such as Chipotle, have grown 2.5% in the same time period that McDonald's has fallen. This shift demonstrates that millennials have chosen quality over convenience. McDonald's can fight this with two minor additions to its menu.

Information

Adding a veggie burger and eggplant fries are small changes that can go a long way in reaching the millennial generation and most importantly help the profitability of the company. Currently, millennials are drifting toward companies that make them look savvy, healthy, and smart. An addition of a veggie burger and eggplant fries would help build McDonald's reputation as a healthy fast food restaurant and cement your legacy as the Senior Vice President of Menu Innovation. Due to the fact that McDonald's does not currently serve these products, the ingredients will have to be purchased. It may seem like this could be a costly addition to the menu, but I assure you that it will improve the overall profitability of the company. This seemingly small change will help McDonald's close the gap between the company and the millennial generation.

Direct Benefit/ Deflect Pushback

Adding the veggie burger and eggplant fries to the McDonald's menu will be beneficial for both you and the company. I ask that you add these specific items to the menu in order to bridge the gap between this generation and your company. For further information, please contact me at STUDENTX@ GMAIL.COM. Thank you for your time and I look forward to hearing from you.

Ask

Sincerely,
Student X

Sample McDonald's Bad News Message

Dear Ms. Nightshade,

Buffer

McDonald's and I would like to thank you and your team for your commitment to our new menu change. We understand that our order is large and that it is hard to organize and prepare for an order of this size. All About Eggplants is synonymous with quality eggplants, and that is why we contacted you to provide the ingredients for our eggplant fries.

Reasons

As a company McDonald's likes to research its new ventures to make sure that they will be successful and profitable. Because of this, McDonald's performs focus group studies on all of its new menu items. Through the focus group study we performed on the eggplant fries, McDonald's found out that they would not be as popular as previously anticipated.

Bad News

Due to this new information, we are sorry to inform you that we are unable to move forward with the purchase of your eggplant fries.

Goodwill Close

We will reevaluate our new menu options next year; while the eggplant fries do not work for the McDonald's menu at this time, they may in the future. We appreciate all that you have done and hope to continue to build a positive relationship with All About Eggplants. Please accept our sincere apologies.

Sincerely,
Senior Vice President

Sample McDonald's Direct Persuasive Message

Greg Waters
PETA Illinois
1 Animal Way
Oak Brook, IL 55781

Hello Greg,

I hope you are doing well and enjoying your work advocating for animals. I am not sure if you are aware, but I am currently interning for McDonald's and am enjoying working with the company to bring more millennials into our stores. I understand the PETA is unhappy with McDonald's lack of a veggie burger option. However, I am writing to ask that you do not proceed with the negative campaign towards McDonald's.

Align/Ask

I currently work with the Menu Innovation section of the company. McDonald's is trying many different options when it comes to changing and improving our menu to attract more customers. We are aware that our company lacks healthier menu options and Menu Innovation is working to implement changes that are mutually beneficial to our company, customers, and our suppliers.

Information

Offering veggie burgers is an option that we have strongly considered. McDonald's has been working with focus groups to determine what changes will be successful and beneficial overall. Postponing PETA's campaign against McDonald's will allow us more time to study the ramifications of adding a veggie burger. We would also like to work with PETA to explore different ways to reach consensus. Launching an attack campaign now would torpedo hopes of working together in the future.

Direct Benefit/
Deflect Pushback

I hope that you will reconsider and postpone any negative campaign against McDonald's. Please contact me at student@gmail.com to discuss how we can work together. I appreciate your time and your passion, and I am eager to get together soon.

Ask (Again)

Thank you,
STUDENT X

Sample McDonald's Direct Persuasive Instructional Message

TO: ALL EMPLOYEES
FROM: HR DEPARTMENT
DATE: November 3, 2015
SUBJECT: NEW POLICY REGARDING ALL DAY BREAKFAST

Directive

McDonald's will now be serving breakfast items throughout the day. In order to let our customers know about this exciting change, all counter and drive-through personnel, when greeting a customer, will now be required to say the following: "Welcome to McDonald's! We are now serving breakfast all day. What can I make for you today?"

Information

Leadership has found that millennials' favorite meal at McDonald's is breakfast. In order to attract more of this demographic to our stores, we will be offering these delicious breakfast items throughout the day.

Courteous Closing

Thank you for your cooperation. We appreciate your hard work and your commitment to providing our customers with the best experience possible.

For-Profit Colleges Sample Practice Messages

©kenwolter/Shutterstock.com

Sample For-Profit Colleges Letter of Intent/Cover Letter

President
University of Phoenix
1625 W. Fountainhead Way
Tempe, AZ 85282

Dear President,

I am very excited to write to you about my interest in the intern position with the University of Phoenix. Access to secondary education is very important to me, and I believe that the University of Phoenix provides access to non-traditional students who, without the existence of your wonderful institution, would be denied the chance to advance themselves in the academic world.

Opening Paragraph

While I was growing up, my mother worked two jobs in addition to taking care of my sisters and me. It was always her dream to attend college, but there was simply no way she could find time in her schedule to attend a traditional college. However, after seeing an ad for the University of Phoenix one night, she decided to enroll. I could not be more proud to say that she graduated in 2014 with a degree in Accounting. I have first-hand knowledge of the life-changing impact a University of Phoenix degree can have on an individual and her career. If awarded this internship, I will bring this knowledge and my enthusiasm for your programs to each and every task.

Body

I am eager to share my energy, hard work, and devotion to the mission of the University of Phoenix. I deeply appreciate your time and consideration of my application. My resume is attached. If I can provide any further information, please do not hesitate to contact me at student@gmail.com.

Closing

Sincerely,
Student X

Sample For-Profit Colleges Indirect Persuasive Message

TO: Mr. John Doe
FROM: President, University of Phoenix
DATE: May 1, 2016

RE: University of Phoenix opportunities

Alignment /Ask

Thank you for your interest in the University of Phoenix. When you filled out our online form, you took the first step toward an exciting academic career. I understand that you have a busy schedule and you may have missed some of our follow-up emails.

Information

The University of Phoenix provides access to higher education to people from all walks of life. Our mission is to reach out to those who feel that they don't have the time for college, or whose circumstances make it difficult or impossible to attend a traditional university. We prepare you to do more than get a job, we help you jumpstart a career. Our programs are designed to help you meet the demands of today's job market so that you can edge out the competition and get ahead in your chosen field.

Direct Benefit/
Deflect Pushback

Because of our many degree programs, we can help you get the right training so that you can get the job you want. You may have heard of issues that our institution has faced regarding student debt and job placement. We have heard these concerns and we have taken steps to address them. We have lowered our tuition rates so that access to our quality programs will not leave you with significant student debt. We have also tailored more of our courses to address exactly what employers seek in job applicants.

Ask

Please reach out to our student enrollment advisor and enroll today. We value you and want to help you realize your dreams. Call or email us at university@phoenix.com or 800-222-3333.

Sample For-Profit Colleges Direct Persuasive Message

Dear Employee X,

We are very fortunate to have quality instructors like you working to provide a unique educational experience for our students. Your dedication to excellence is what makes the University of Phoenix the leader in for-profit universities. We have learned of your concern regarding the closure of some of our physical locations and your plan to conduct a "sick-out." I am asking that you do not engage in such a disruptive activity.

The University of Phoenix has experienced some hard times recently. We have been accused of over-promising job opportunities, saddling students with significant student debt, and predatory marketing toward veterans. We must now refocus our energies so that we can fulfill our mission to provide quality education opportunities that enable students to develop knowledge and skills necessary to achieve their professional goals. As part of restructuring, we will be closing some of our smaller physical locations.

We understand your concern about these closures. Restructuring is never easy, and we are mindful that you are worried about your continued employment with the University. Working together to ensure the successful rebranding and polishing of our image will affect everyone associated with the University in a positive way. Staging a sick-out will give further fodder to our detractors. By presenting a united front, we will enroll more students. We will need to provide online classes to students in the locations where we are closing our physical campuses. If you stand with us, you will be given priority consideration when applying for these online teaching positions.

Please do not move forward with the sick-out. We value you and your work, and we want to continue to work together to provide our students with the best education possible. Please let me know of your decision by COB on Monday. I look forward to hearing from you.

Sincerely,
HR Officer

Align/Ask

Information

Direct Benefit/
Deflect Pushback

Ask (Again)

Sample For-Profit Colleges Bad News Message

Dear Student X,

Buffer

Thank you for applying to the University of Phoenix. We so appreciate your initiative and desire to further your education. Ambitious people like you are what make our school so exciting and successful.

Reasons

At the University of Phoenix, we are constantly striving to improve our educational experience for our students. We want to ensure that all of our students are at a place academically where they are primed for success. For this reason, we now require an entrance exam. You may recall taking this exam a few weeks ago. Due to its very recent implementation, our exam computer system has experienced some technical difficulties.

Bad News

Unfortunately, due to these technical issues, some students received notification that they passed the entrance exam when in fact they did not. You were one of the students affected, and I am sorry to inform you that you did not pass the entrance exam required for enrollment in the University of Phoenix. I am sure this is very disappointing, but we do have several orientation programs that you can take, free of charge, to get you ready to take the exam again in two months.

Goodwill Close

Again, we are very sorry for the confusion and disappointment this news has caused. Please do take advantage of our free orientation programs. If you have any questions, please do not hesitate to contact me at 1-800-222-3333. We look forward to seeing you at the next entrance exam.

Sincerely,
Senior Vice President, Chief Marketing Officer

Lyft Sample Practice Messages

©360b/Shutterstock.com

Sample Lyft Stakeholder Analysis

Lyft Stakeholder Analysis

Lyft and its counterpart, Uber, are in competition to expand their territory. Their expansion has presented many challenges to traditional taxicabs systems. Many taxi companies have joined together to sue Uber, alleging that they are operating unregulated livery companies. Uber's platforms are facing increasing regulatory scrutiny; philosophical debates are erupting concerning the validity of sharing as a viable alternative to private ownership, and trust among customers is difficult to build.

Introduction

Uber has also faced issues with insurance companies. According to the local governments, there are likely gaps that exist between the commercial and private passenger insurance periods. This could result in situations where drivers and passengers are not being covered at all.

Finally, there is deep concern regarding violent incidents perpetrated by Uber drivers. Customers and regulators are concerned for their safety and question the vigor of the company's background checks of the drivers.

By studying Uber's weaknesses, this report identifies stakeholders affecting the operation of the rideshare industry and recommends appropriate actions to address individual concerns. The stakeholders impacting the operation of rideshare industry include customers, government agencies, and employees. The following table lists the stakeholders with a summary of the related level of urgency, concerns, and recommended response.

STAKEHOLDERS	URGENCY	CONCERNS	RECOMMENDED RESPONSE
Customers	High	Trust; value of reputation; the impact of partner, stranger, or feedback networks on transaction frequency	Reassure and educate
Local and International government	High	Legal challenges; vehicle safety; driver qualification and background checks	Engage and convince
Employees	Moderate	Rating impact of company revenue; impact of text review on transaction price; driver compensation and working condition	Internal communication

Customers

Body

Customers must have faith in a company and trust the company to keep them safe if that company seeks to be successful. Trust is developed through centralized and scalable review systems enabled by the emergence of the Internet and personal computing. Features connected to rideshare include social media accounts, such as Facebook Connect, verification of memberships, and a verified government check. Customer reviews allow other customers to learn of peer experiences. Educating customers about good reviews and vigorous background checks should lead to increased trust by potential customers.

Recommendation: It is critical for Lyft to cultivate and maintain a relationship with the media (including social media), and through that, develop its image. Lyft should use media to deliver and educate the public about its services and the safety protocols Lyft employs to keep customers safe.

Local and international government

Most governments require companies to meet several regulatory requirements regarding the mechanical conditions of their vehicles. Requirements relating to vehicle condition and inspection have the following objectives that could enhance service reliability:

- Establish a baseline standard for what is necessary
- Provide safe transportation to the public
- Implement a mechanism that forces service providers to address mechanical issues

The rideshare industry is not regulated by the government, and the only information available regarding vehicle inspections is either provided directly by the company or through the company's website. Lyft has developed an internal inspection protocol that allows experienced Lyft drivers to inspect vehicles. Government regulatory agencies are concerned that the procedures that ride-sharing companies implement do not meet the high standards that traditional taxi companies meet.

Recommendation: Lyft should initiate dialogue with government agencies to convince them of the efficacy of Lyft's safety protocols. The goal of engagement is to encourage local and international governments to air their concerns so that Lyft can address those concerns.

Lyft engagement with government agencies will need to be far-reaching, inclusive, and balanced. Lyft engagement with regulators should be a process of consultation, communication, exchange, and dialogue. This approach is likely to improve ethical and social accountability and performance.

Employees

Employees are arguably the most important "face" of the Lyft organization. Ensuring that employees feel valued and safe will translate into more positive employee/customer interaction and better retention of employees. In addition, ensuring that Lyft drivers are safe, both physically and financially, will assist with attracting quality employees.

Recommendation: Communicating with employees about their value to the company is critical. Lyft should hold weekly webinars and send out weekly emails educating employees about current industry trends and focusing on a "driver of the week" to highlight how much Lyft cares about its drivers.

Summary

There are various challenges that Lyft should consider in order to avoid mistakes made by Uber. These include vigorous background checks of drivers, vehicle safety, insurance requirements, and workplace happiness initiatives.

By using social and other forms of media to inform potential customers about the safety and comfort of the Lyft riding experience, Lyft will see an increase in the number of riders. By engaging in dialogue with government regulators, Lyft can break down barriers that prevent Lyft from operating in certain locales. By ensuring that Lyft employees know their value, Lyft can attract and retain quality drivers. Armed with this knowledge, Lyft can begin formulating strategies to avoid the same mistakes made by its closest competitor, Uber.

Sample Lyft Indirect Persuasive Message

VP of Lyft Government Relations
2300 Harrison Street
San Francisco, CA 94110

November 4th, 2015

Mayor Ethan Strimling
389 Congress St.
Portland, ME 04101

Dear Mayor Strimling,

Alignment

Congratulations on defeating incumbent Michael Brennan in the mayoral race. The city of Portland has a lot to look forward to as you move to ensure "everyone's voice is heard." I would like to thank you and the city of Portland for your acceptance of peer-to-peer ride sharing services. As Mayor, I understand your interests are aligned with the safety of the people. In my business, safety is of paramount importance.

Information

In your inauguration speech, you mentioned your primary focus will be confronting affordability in the city of Portland. As the VP of Lyft Government Relations, it is my duty to inform you that Lyft offers solutions that align with your goals. Uber, the current ride-sharing service in Portland, charges as much as 700% to 800% more during periods of high demand while Lyft prices can only increase by 200%. If you are looking to save the citizens of Portland time and money, Lyft is the best solution.

Direct Benefit/
Deflect Pushback

Additionally, I would like to bring to your attention that Uber has recently been involved in scandals in which Uber drivers jeopardized the safety of their customers. Due to such occurrences, I would like to inform you that Lyft demands the highest level of customer safety, ensuring that all drivers undergo extensive background checks and carry valid driver's insurance. Unlike Uber, in order to provide the safest and most reliable peer-to-peer ride-sharing platform, Lyft offers a 24/7 emergency call center in case of disputes.

Ask

We believe it will benefit you and your city to permit Lyft to operate in Portland. This will secure the safety of the people at the most affordable rate. Lyft has capitalized and learned from Uber's recent mistakes, spending time and money to increase safety precautions. Establishing a relationship with Lyft will not only keep the citizens of Portland safe, but will also do so at dramatically lower rates than those of Uber.

Please allow Lyft to operate in your wonderful city. In order to move forward with establishing a thriving relationship between Lyft and the city of Portland, I would like to set up a meeting with you at your earliest convenience.

Greatest Respects,
VP of Lyft Government Relations

Sample Lyft Bad News Message

Vice President of People, Lyft
548 Market Street
San Francisco, CA 94104

November 8, 2015

Lisa Race
1306 Carlos Ave
Burlingame, CA 94010

Dear Ms. Race,

I wanted to personally thank you for your interest in a position with Lyft. It was great getting to know you through your application, and learning about your skills and experience. I can already see that you have great potential so early in your young adult career.

Buffer

In order to be employed as a driver at Lyft, certain qualifications must be met. One of our policies is that drivers must be at least 18 years old. The reason for this is that the insurance companies that insure our drivers do not provide coverage for those younger than 18.

Reasons

Because of this age requirement, I am sorry to report that we are unable to hire you as a driver at this time.

Bad News

I would, however, like to extend to you the opportunity of an internship position with our corporate office. Your personality, skills, and desire to work at Lyft makes you a great fit for our company. Until your 18th birthday, you would have the chance to build new skills, network with professionals, and become familiar with Lyft. After that point, we would invite you to apply again for a driver position. Please let me know if this internship is of interest to you. Thank you again for your interest in Lyft, and we wish you success in achieving your goals.

Goodwill Close

Sincerely,
Vice President of People, Lyft

Sample Lyft Direct Persuasive Message

Dear Vice President of People, Lyft

I would like to thank you and the Lyft organization for allowing me to participate in this semester internship; the opportunity has been a true privilege. Working for Lyft has made it apparent how lucrative driving for Lyft can be. The freedom that Lyft drivers have regarding the decision of when and where to work is an attractive benefit. Since we have developed a good working relationship over my time working for Lyft, I would like to ask you if the Lyft organization would permit me to finish the rest of my internship working as a Lyft driver on my off hours in order to acquire first-hand experience and make some extra money on the side.

Information

Driving for Lyft has interested me since the first day of my internship. The way in which you value your drivers is evident and makes driving for the company fun and rewarding. I promise to always represent the Lyft team to the best of my abilities, making sure that each customer is pleased and reaches their destination safely. I know the safety requirements Lyft demands and the level of respect to which each customer is entitled.

Direct Benefit/
Deflect Pushback

Driving for Lyft during my internship's off hours will not impact my work as an intern. I would only seek to work as a driver once my daily internship duties are fulfilled. At the age of 21, I exceed Lyft's required minimum age of 18. I am aware that all drivers are entirely liable for any unpleasant encounters with either law enforcement or customers. My driving record is spotless, I have valid insurance, and I am confident I will pass Lyft's extensive background check. Additionally, I own a very clean four-door Suburban (2010), which passes Lyft's vehicle requirement. I possess all the skills and requirements necessary to succeed as a Lyft driver.

Ask (Again)

Please allow me to work as a Lyft driver and make some extra money on the side while I complete my internship with you. May I schedule a meeting with you to discuss my proposal further? Please contact me at student@gmail.com to schedule this meeting. Thank you for considering my request.

Sincerely,
STUDENT X

Index

A

Academic writing, *vs.* business, 23
Accent errors, 9, 12
Active verb, *vs.* passive, 117
Adaptability, 4
Agility, 4
AIDA strategy, 83
Analysis, 6
Annotated bibliography, 169, 170–175
APA citation, in direct informational memo, 163, 164–168
Appendices, 48
Apple FaceTime, 21
Audience
    bad news messages and, 93–94
    channel and formats to reaching, 15
    example of analysis of, 25
    primary, 24
    receptive, 79
    resistant, 79
    response, approach to, 79
    secondary, 24
    strategy and, 14–15
Audience analysis, 24–26
Audience response
    to bad news message, 93
    matching approach to potential, 79
    to persuasive appeal, 79
Auditory media, 21

B

Back matter, in formal report, 48
Bad news message
    audience reaction to, 93
    Chipotle, 183, 208
    conveying, 91–92
    direct approach to delivery of, 94–95
    Facebook, 188, 214
    fight or flight reaction and, 94
    indirect approach to delivery of, 96–99
    Lyft, 204, 231
    McDonald's, 194, 220
    for-profit college, 200, 226
    resistant audience and, 93–94
    sample of direct, 96
    sample scenario and indirect, 99–102
    tone and, 103
    types of, 92–93
    writing, 94
Bibliography, 169, 170–175
Body
    direct persuasive approach, 80
    formal report, 47
    indirect persuasive approach, 84
    informal message, 74–75
Bottom line on or near bottom (BLOB), 16
Bottom Line on Top (BLOT), 7, 16
Brand awareness, 7
Bulleted list, 108, 111, 124

Business communication standards, 4–8
    application of, 9
    critical thinking, 5
    error interference, 8–9
    information design, 7–8
    logic and reasoning, 6
    structural coherence, 6–7
Business correspondence. *see* Correspondence
Business report
    conclusion, 37
    findings, reporting of, 36–37
    formal, 39, 46–48
    informal, 39–42, 44
    recommendations in, 37–38
    transmittal message and, 45
Business writing, 21–29
    vs. academic, 23
    employer expectations and, 22
    vs. other writing forms, 22–23
    purpose, identifying, 26–29
    rules to effective, 117–125
    tone setting in, 27–29

C

Car-for-hire business, 201. *see also* Lyft case study; Uber
Case studies
    Chipotle Mexican Grill norovirus outbreak, 179–184
    Facebook, 185–189
    Lyft, 201–204
    McDonald's, 191–195
    for-profit colleges, 197–200
Channel, 14–15
    selection considerations, 15
Chart, 108
Chipotle Mexican Grill norovirus outbreak, case study
    Chipotle's response, 180
    legal woes, 180
    media response, 180
    practice assignments, 182–184
    timeline of outbreaks, 179
Chipotle sample practice messages
    bad news, 183, 208
    direct informational, 205–206

direct informative, 182
direct persuasive, 183, 209
direct persuasive instructional, 183–184, 210
indirect persuasive, 182–183, 207
Chronological message structure, 70
Cisco, 6, 8
Coherence, 6–7
Collaboration, 4
Colon, 135
Comma, 128–132
Comparison message structure, 70
Complex sentence, 127, 128–129
Compound-complex sentence, 127
Compound sentence, 127, 130–132
    good news *vs.* bad, 132
Concision, 116
Conclusion, 37, 48, 73–74, 84–85
Coordinating conjunction, 130–131
Core message, 16
Correspondence
    composing business, 32–33
    defined, 31–32
    meeting invitation, 33–34
    questions of reader to consider, 32
    report writing, 34–35
    thank you messages, 33
Correspondence message, *vs.* report, 31
Credibility, 6, 8
Credibility errors, 9, 12, 123, 127
Critical thinking, 4, 5, 10–11
    skills measurement, 5
    team work and, 5
Curiosity, 4
"The Curse of Knowledge," 23, 25

D

Dangling modifier, 123
Data analysis, 6
Data dump, 6
Dell Corporation, 5
Design, 7–8. *see also* Document design
Direct bad news message, 94–96
    body, 95
    conclusion, 95
    introduction, 95
    sample of, 96

Direct informational memo with APA citations, 163, 164–165, 166–168
Direct informational report
    Facebook, 187, 211–212
Direct informative message
    Chipotle, 182, 205–206
    McDonald's, 193, 217–218
Direct informative report, Facebook, 187
Direct message, 16
Direct object, 117
Direct persuasive approach, 79–81
    body, 80
    conclusion, 81
    examples of, 81–82
    introduction, 80
    organizational patterns for, 80
Direct persuasive instructional message
    Chipotle, 183–184, 210
    Facebook, 189, 216
    McDonald's, 195, 222
Direct persuasive message, 200
    Chipotle, 183, 209
    Facebook, 188, 215
    Lyft, 204, 232
    McDonald's, 194–195, 221
    for-profit college, 200, 225
Disruptive errors, 8, 12, 123
Document design, 105–111
    bullets, 108, 111
    font, 106–107
    headings, 108–110
    lists, 108, 111
    margins, 106
    outline, 108, 111
    paragraphs, 106–107
    visual elements in, 108
    words, 107–108
Documents, workplace, 32–35. *see also* Correspondence

E

Email, 139, 140–141
Emoji
    etiquette errors and, 9
    Facebook reactions, 185–186
Employer expectations, 22
Error interference, 8–9, 10–11, 12
    accent errors, 9, 12
    credibility errors, 9, 12
    disruptive errors, 8, 12
    etiquette, 12
Ethos, 77
Etiquette errors, 12
Executive summary, 47
External message, 15

F

Facebook case study, 185–189
    practice assignments, 186, 187–189
    reaction emojis, 185–186
Facebook reactions emojis sample practice messages, 187–189
    bad news, 188, 214
    direct informational, 211–212
    direct informative, 187
    direct persuasive, 188, 215
    direct persuasive instructional, 189, 216
    indirect persuasive, 187–188, 213
Face-to-face communication, 15
Fight or flight response, 94
Figures list, 46
Findings, reporting of, 36–37
First-person pronoun, 31
Font, 106–107
Formal message, 15
Formal report, 46–48
    appendices, 48
    Under Armour, 49–64
    body content, 47
    conclusion, 48
    executive summary, 47
    figures list, 46
    introduction, 47
    references in, 48
    table of contents, 46
    tables, abbreviations and symbols in, 47
    title page, 46
Format, message, 15
For-profit colleges case study, 197–200
    practice assignments, 199–200

For-profit colleges practice assignments, 199–200
    bad news message, 200, 226
    direct persuasive message, 200, 225
    indirect persuasive message, 199–200, 224
    letter of intent/cover letter, 199, 223
Free writer, 24
Front matter, in formal report, 46–47

G

Geography/category message structure, 70
The Global Achievement Gap, 4
Google Docs, 14, 15
Google Hangouts, 21
Grammar, 115–125
    active verb, 117–119
    concision, 116
    concrete noun, 120
    dangling modifier, 123
    disruptive errors, 123–124
    misplaced modifier, 122
    noun, 116
    overused words to avoid, 121, 121–122
    parallelism, 123–125
    verb, 116
Graph, 108

H

Headings, 108
Hichert Partner's International Business
    Communication Standards (IBCS), 7

I

Image, 108
Imagination, 4
Indirect bad news message, 96–99
    body, 98
    conclusion, 98–99
    direct benefits and deflection, 84
    introduction, 97–98
    sample scenario, 99–100, 101–102
Indirect message, 16

Indirect persuasive approach, 83–86
    AIDA, 83
    body, 84
    conclusion, 83–84
    introduction, 83
Indirect persuasive message, 199
    Chipotle, 182–183, 207
    Facebook, 187–188, 213
    Lyft, 203, 230
    McDonald's, 193–194, 219
    for-profit college, 199–200, 224
Industry report, 146
    student example, 147–152, 153–162
Informal message, 15
Informal report, 39–42, 44
    research summary sample, 41–42
    strategy summary sample, 44
    types of, 40
Information analysis, 4
Information assessment, 4
Information design, 7–8, 10–11
Information gathering, 35
Informative message, 67–75
    defined, 67
    organizational patterns for, 70–75
    prewriting, 69
    structure, 69–70
Internal message, 15
Internet, 21
Introduction, 47, 71–72, 83
Invitation, 33–34

L

Letter, 142, 143
Letter of intent/cover letter, 199, 223
Levers, of persuasion, 78
Logic and reasoning, 4, 6, 10–11
Logos, 77
Lyft case study
    practice assignments, 203–204
    Uber incidents history, 202
Lyft practice assignments
    bad news message, 204, 231
    direct persuasive message, 204, 232
    indirect persuasive message, 203, 230
    stakeholder analysis, 203, 227–229

M

Made to Stick, 23
Margin, 106
McDonald's case study, 191–195
    McDonald's response, 192
    practice assignments, 193–195
McDonald's sample practice messages
    bad news, 194, 220
    direct informational, 217–218
    direct informative, 193
    direct persuasive, 194–195, 221
    direct persuasive instructional, 195, 222
    indirect persuasive, 193–194, 219
Medium, 15
Meeting invitation, 33–34
    checklist, 33
    example of, 34
Memo, 144, 144–145, 145
    direct informational with APA citations, 163,
        164–165, 166–168
Misplaced modifier, 122
Modifier
    dangling, 123
    defined, 122
    limiting, 122
    misplaced, 122
    placement, 122

N

Negative news. *see* Bad news message
Netflix, 92
Noun, 116, 120
    concrete, 120
    ladder of abstraction, 120
    practice assignment, 120

O

Oral communication skills, 4
Outline, 108, 111
Outliner, 24

P

Paragraph, 106–107
Parallelism, 123–125
    bullets, 124
    disruptive error and, 123
    practice assignment, 125
Passive constructs, 121
Passive verb, 117
Pathos, 77
Persuasion, 77–90
    audience response to, 79
    body and, 84
    conclusion and, 84–85
    direct approach, 79–81
    examples of direct, 81–82
    indirect approach, 83
    introduction and, 83
    levers of, 78
    message types, 78–79
    revision and, 89–90
    tone and, 87–89
Persuasive appeal, 77. *see also* Persuasion
Persuasive messages
    identifying types of, 78–79
Plan, in report writing, 35
    questions to ask yourself, 35
Preparation, writing, 21–24
Primary audience, 24
Problem statement
    articulating, 5
Professional writing standards, 10–11
Pronoun usage, 26, 27–28, 31
Punctuation, 115, 127–135
    colon, 135
    comma, 128–132
    complex sentence, 128, 129, 132, 133
    compound sentence, 132, 133
    credibility errors and, 127
    dependent clause and, 128–129
    independent clause and, 128–130
    introductory phrase and, 128–130
    semicolon, 133–134
    sentence structure and, 127–134
    simple sentence and, 128
Purpose, 15–16, 26, 26–29

Q

Questions
    in business correspondence, 32
    in report writing, 35

R

Reading aloud, 27
Recommendations, in report, 37–39, 48
References, in report, 48
Relevance, 25–30
Report, industry, 146, 147–152, 153–162
Report writing
    vs. correspondence, 31
    planning, 35
    process in, 34–35
    recommendations, 37–39, 48
    references, 48
    revising, 35
    writing, 35
Revision, 35, 121
    practice assignment, 136–137
Ridesharing, 201

S

Sample practice messages, 205–232
    Chipotle, 205–210
    Facebook, 211–216
    Lyft, 227–232
    McDonald's, 217–222
    for-profit college, 223–226
SBAR (Situation, Background, Analysis,
    Recommendations), 7
Secondary audience, 24
Second-person pronoun, 27–28, 31
Semicolon, 133–134
    practice assignment, 134
Sentence
    combining, 128–132
    complex, 127
    compound, 127
    compound-complex, 127
    parallel structure, 124
    simple, 127
    structure, 127–134
Sequence message structure, 70
Simple sentence, 127, 128
Skills, workplace, 4
Skype, 21
Stakeholder, 14
Stakeholder analysis, Lyft, 203, 227–229
Standards. *see* Business communication standards;
    Professional writing standards
Strategic business communication, 13–17
    approach to, 16–17
    audience and, 14–15
    purpose of, 15–16
Strategic organizational structure, 7
Structural coherence, 6–7, 10–11
Subject, 117
Synthesis, 6

T

Table of contents, 46
Tables list, 47
Teamwork, critical thinking skills and, 5
Thank you message, 33
Third-person pronoun, 31
Title page, 46
Tone, 27–29, 31, 87–89
    implied entitlement, avoiding, 87
    objective, maintaining, 89
    reader autonomy and, 88
Transmittal message, 45

U

Uber
    assault incidences, 202
    vetting practices, 201
Under Armour formal report, 49–64
    analysis, 51
    appendices, 59–64
    background, 51
    budget, 56
    communication, effective, 54

communication plan, 52–57
consumers, 56
executive management, 54–55
executive summary, 51
figures, 59–61
manufacturers, 55, 62
memorandum, 62
opportunity evaluation, 52–53
past, assessment of, 52
recommendations, 51
references, 58,64
retailers, 55–56, 63–64
situation, 51
timeline, 57

V

Verb, 116, 117–119
    active, 117–118
    active *vs.* passive, 117
    practice assignment, 119
Verbal message, 15
Visual elements, 108
    importance of, 7–8
Visual media, 21
VOIP, 21

W

WIIFY (What's in it for you), 35, 45, 71, 75, 82, 205, 211, 217
Workplace documents. *see also* Correspondence
Writer, 24
    types of, 24
Writing preparation, 21–24
Written communication, 21–29. *see also* Business writing
    rules for effective, 117–125
Written communication skills, 4
    deficiency in, 22
Written message, 15

Y

"you attitude," 26, 27, 28–29